ON RELIGION

Friedrich Schleiermacher

On Religion: Speeches to Its Cultured Despisers

TRANSLATED BY JOHN OMAN

FOREWORD BY JACK FORSTMAN

Westminster/John Knox Press
Louisville, Kentucky

The text of *On Religion* is translated from the third German edition originally published by Routledge & Kegan Paul Ltd., London.

First Harper Torchbooks edition published 1958

First Westminster/John Knox Press edition published 1994

Foreword by Jack Forstman ©1994 Westminster/John Knox Press, Louisville, Kentucky

Cover design by Frank Peronne
Frontispiece engraving courtesy of Albert L. Blackwell

This book is printed on acid-free paper that meets the American National Standards Institute Z39.48 standard. ∞

PRINTED IN THE UNITED STATES OF AMERICA

00 01 02 03 04 — 10 9 8 7 6 5 4 3

Library of Congress Cataloging-in-Publication Data

Schleiermacher, Friedrich, 1768–1834.
    [Über die Religion. English]
    On religion : speeches to its cultured despisers / Friedrich
Schleiermacher : translated by John Oman : with an introduction by
Jack Forstman. — 1st Westminster/John Knox Press ed.
        p.   cm.
    Translation of: Über die Religion.
    Includes bibliographical references and index.
    ISBN 0-664-25556 (alk. paper)
    1. Religion—Early works to 1800.   I. Oman, John, 1860-1939.
II. Title.
BL 48.S33   1994
200—dc20   94-19997

CONTENTS

FOREWORD

JACK FORSTMAN

IF a book can signal the beginning of an era, then Schleiermacher's *On Religion: Speeches to Its Cultured Despisers*
marks the beginning of the era of Protestant Liberal Theology. By normal reckoning that era lasted about one hundred
twenty years and came to an end with the publication of
Karl Barth's *Romans*.

These statements as indications of the historical importance of the *Speeches* are accurate enough, but they are mis-
leading. Schleiermacher's conception of religion in general
and of Christianity in particular was strikingly "original,"
but he appropriated a good many themes that had been ar-
ticulated before him, especially in the decades most recent to
him. Also, of course, it is a mistake to suppose that all
Protestant Liberal Theology bears the mark of Schleiermacher, and it is false to suppose that Protestant Liberal
Theology came to an end with Barth's *Romans*. The generalization, then, is a convenience of historians that rightly
highlights the historical importance of the *Speeches*.

A better way to indicate the importance of this book is to
say that it properly belongs to an astonishingly small number
of classics in Christian theology. By classic I mean a book that
has not only major historical significance of the sort indicated
in the opening paragraph but that continues also to stimulate
and to form in substantive ways the thinking of some who are
preoccupied with the questions of what religion and Christian
faith are. The *Speeches* are the best door into Schleiermacher's thought, and that thought will likely continue to exercise its power here and there into the distant future. Reading
the *Speeches* is more than an exercise in trying to understand
an important moment in the history of Christian theology. It
rightly evokes reflection and discussion of the author's understanding of religion without respect to time.

For both its historical and its continuing contemporary significance it is good that the book is here reprinted in a relatively accessible form. The translation is the one made by British theologian John Oman in 1893. It is a good translation, and it has the advantage of using an English that is more closely related to the rather ornate German that characterizes Schleiermacher's style in this work. Both Oman's English and Schleiermacher's German are different from their present-day counterparts. In following the flow and rhythm of the sentences, the reader's eye will occasionally stumble over an elaborate construction, a quaint phrase, or an unusual adjective, but the text is penetrable and clear. Most important, it gives us Schleiermacher, and understanding Schleiermacher rewards the effort.

The Schleiermacher it gives us is the young Schleiermacher who, as Reformed (Calvinist) Chaplain at the Charity Hospital in Berlin, a predominately evangelical (Lutheran) city, had sufficient free time to participate actively in the fermenting avant garde culture of that time and place. That avant garde movement was what is called early German Romanticism, and it found its voice in the lively conversations that took place in the salons of wealthy Jewish women. Schleiermacher was introduced to the weekly drawing-room gatherings of Henriette Herz by the young Count Alexander Dohna, with whom Schleiermacher had become friends when not long before he had been tutor to the younger Dohna children at the family estate.

He fit the group. He was brilliant, witty, and articulate; he had a gift for friendship. He also shared the group's reaction against enlightened rationality and detachment and against neo-classical ideals and an emphasis on proper decorum. (Friedrich Schlegel, who became Schleiermacher's close friend, referred to the representatives of the Enlightenment mode as "harmonious dullards.") More important, Schleiermacher shared his new friends' sense of individuality and their appreciation of the infinite diversity of the world. He held their view of the human situation as one that can penetrate and understand neither infinite variety nor infinite unity but that strives to bring both together in a way that destroys neither pole and acknowledges the limitations of human finitude. Schleiermacher expresses this view early in the First Speech ("Defence"). It is foundational for the development of the *Speeches,* and it remained so in everything he wrote and taught throughout his life.

Schleiermacher was eagerly welcomed as a participant in the conversations that took place weekly in Henrietta Herz's home, but he was an enigma to most of the participants. He was a minister of the church, and most of the regulars had intentionally and passionately liberated themselves not only from the church or synagogue but also from religion as such. They were "cultured despisers of religion," and they could not understand how Schleiermacher could so genuinely share and contribute to their new ways of seeing but be, at the same time, a confirmed Christian and minister of the church.

His closest friends within the circle decided to resolve the issue by insisting that he write a book. Friedrich Schlegel contrived the plan. On the morning of Schleiermacher's twenty-ninth birthday (November 21, 1797) he was visited by Alexander Dohna, his brother, Henrietta Herz, Dorothea Viet, the brilliant daughter of the Jewish philosopher Moses Mendelssohn, who was married to a Berlin banker, and Friedrich Schlegel.*

The surprise birthday party was a happy occasion. Schleiermacher made and relished strong friendships, and these people were his best friends. They showered him with gifts and laid out chocolates and pastries they had brought. There was good conversation.

The festivities were interrupted when, on signal from Schlegel, the friends said in unison, "You must write a book." Schlegel refused to drop the subject until he had wrested a firm promise from Schleiermacher. Schleiermacher did not take promises lightly, but it was nine months before he could put pen to paper. Eight months later, on April 15, 1799, he could write Henrietta Herz that he had given the "final stroke to Religion."

The book that this stroke brought to completion is astonishing in at least five respects. First, he presented an utterly fresh understanding of religion. It was, of course, not without

*Friedrich Schlegel and Dorothea Viet fell in love, had an affair, and after Dorothea's divorce, were married. The affair is the poorly disguised subject of Schlegel's "shocking" novel, *Lucinde,* which Schleiermacher defended in a series of letters published by Schlegel.

points of contact in the past, but Schleiermacher's presentation stood in bold contrast with the views that were prevalent in that time (dogmatic orthodoxy, speculative Neology, enlightened "natural religion," and Pietism). Second, he set forth a view of religion that was in principle free from reliance on authority. Third, he described religion as belonging essentially to the human sphere and thus as essentially limited. Truly religious people are never able to claim that they possess the truth as such, and in its entirety. Fourth, his approach to religion was descriptive and analytical. In the fashion of early German Romanticism he tried to "display" what actually constitutes religion. Finally, he tried to show that religion is inevitably social and thus always has a definite form ("positive" religion, as the language of his time put it). In this connection he made a case for Christianity that was at least coherent with the descriptive analysis he set forth in the earlier part of the book.

The person reading this text for the first time may want to look for these astonishing turns of thought in three arguments or descriptions Schleiermacher presents. The first is a foretaste of Schleiermacher's later lectures on "dialectics," or philosophy, and is found in the "First Speech." The situation of the human being in the world is that she or he can grasp neither the whole that is "beyond" and "behind" this world nor the most particular individual elements of this whole. Human life is an oscillation between these two unreachable poles without access either to ultimate unity or ultimate diversity. To move too far toward the one is to lose the other, and vice versa. This situation is the essence of the limitations of human life within the world. Second (the basic view developed in the "Second Speech"), religion is neither a knowing nor a doing but something whose occasion or foundation touches a locus in the human being more fundamental than either knowing or doing. Schleiermacher describes this locus as "feeling" and the occasion as "a sense and taste for the Infinite in the finite." We must understand, however, that this description is a generalization. Religion as such does not occur, only determinate forms of religion. Third, human life in the world is essentially social, and anyone who comes to a determinate sense and taste for the Infinite in the finite will be impelled to communicate it and to identify with a community or to form a new one. The only way religion can show itself is in specific, determinate forms, and in recognition of this condition Schleiermacher, finally, makes a case for Christianity. It is not the Christianity that finds its essence in knowing (orthodoxy, speculative philosophy) or in doing ("natural religion" or Pietism). Schleiermacher was convinced that Christianity is rooted in the inner life of the people and from that base is productive of new ways of speaking (knowing) and a new mode of life (doing). This is the Christianity he commended to the "cultured despisers" of religion, and he thought his friends were closer to it than they thought.

WHEN Schleiermacher wrote Henrietta Herz that he had given "the final stroke to Religion," he meant he had finished the book. A good many of his contemporaries and a good many in the intervening years have understood that phrase in a quite different way! Schlegel himself, although he had become "religious" by the time the book was published, had moved in his religiousness to a preoccupation with esoteric matters. He wrote Schleiermacher that his new orientation was occasioned by the *Speeches* but was different. He himself, he wrote, was moving to the beyond, whereas Schleiermacher, he quite rightly saw, was rooted in the here and now. In a review in his journal, the *Athanaeum,* Schlegel referred to the stimulating power of the *Speeches* but criticized its author for being exoteric and for not grasping how the human situation occurs through the separation and reunion of the divine from and with itself. The Idealist philosophers, and especially Hegel and those influenced by Hegel, who built their speculations on the Orphic myth of separation and return, also opposed the conceptualities of Schleiermacher that were originally expressed in this book. On the other side, the *Speeches* got Schleiermacher in trouble with the church. He was charged with Spinozism, pantheism, and a too-strong challenge to received Christian teaching, and forms of these charges have kept more conservative church theologians at a distance from Schleiermacher in the years since.

It is impossible to say what effect the *Speeches* had on the growing body of "cultured despisers of religion" across Germany, but the book did establish Schleiermacher as a major Protestant theologian. In time it won for him a teaching post on the theological faculty at the University in Halle, and after that university was closed by the Napoleonic occupying forces, his reputation gave him a hand in planning for the new University of Berlin where, after its founding, he was Professor of Theology and Dean of the Faculty until his death in 1834.

Schleiermacher has influenced diverse strands of Protestant theology since his time. In the nineteenth century Samuel Taylor Coleridge in England and Horace Bushnell in the United States reflected aspects of Schleiermacher's thought in their theological work. In the early part of the present century substantive traces of his thought can be found in theologians as different from each other as, for example, Wilhelm Hermann and Rudolf Otto and, in the generation just past, Rudolf Bultmann and Paul Tillich. A major reappropriation of Schleiermacher in our own day, though, of course, using other sources as well, can be seen in the thoroughly impressive constructive theology of Edward Farley. One can predict with confidence that there will be others. Schleiermacher's theological work that began most imposingly with the *Speeches* clearly belongs in that relatively small category of theological classics.

One does not fully understand the whole of Schleiermacher by reading the *Speeches*. The most important text is his comprehensive theological work, *The Christian Faith.* Moreover, it is true of Schleiermacher, as it is true of anyone who produces a corpus of work over an extended period of time, that he changed in various ways the formulation of his thoughts, developed them more fully, and addressed them to different subjects. Twice, as a matter of fact, he revised the *Speeches,* in 1806 and 1821, and the reader will certainly want to give careful attention to the explanatory notes added in the 1821 revision, at the end of each Speech. But the revisions of the *Speeches* do not change its basic conceptions, and although Schleiermacher's full corpus of work goes far beyond this book, it not only is coherently a piece of the whole but is most certainly the door that opens the way into the thought world of this remarkable theologian.

All the more reason, therefore, to welcome the reprinting of the work in English translation in a form that is readily accessible.

PREFACE

In making this translation, I have been deeply impressed
with the truth of Friedrich Schlegel's saying, that the
modern literature, though in several languages, is only one.
Though this work, so far as I know, is now translated for
the first time, it does not now begin to enter into English
thought. Traces of the movement at least, of which it is
the most characteristic product, may be found in our
philosophy, our theology, and our literature. Seeing, then,
that this book claims more than a merely philosophical
interest, it may well be thought that I should have done
something more to give it an English accent. Intuition,
used broadly for immediate knowledge, and the All, the
Whole, the World-Spirit for aspects of the world we feel
and seem to know, can hardly be acknowledged as natural
to our native tongue. But, though unfamiliar, I hope that,
in their connections, they are not incomprehensible. My
excuse for imposing upon the reader the necessity of a
second translation in thought, must be found in Schleiermacher's own opinion. There are two ways, he considered,
of making a good translation : either the author must be
left alone as far as possible and the reader be made to
approach, or the reader be left and the author be manipulated. In the former case, the work is translated as we
believe the author would have done it, had he learned the
language of the translation ; in the latter, as he would have
written, had it been his native tongue. In philosophical

works, he thought the former method alone practicable. If the wisdom and science of the author are not to be transformed and subjected to the wildest caprice, the language of the translation must be bent to the language of the original. As we have not yet any example of a breach of this rule that encourages imitation, I have not been bold enough to make the attempt. Still I would fain believe that, except the first half of the Second Speech, the book is not beyond measure difficult. That section is acknowledged, even by the most patient Germans, to be obscure, and I would direct the reader's attention to the summary in the Appendix of its first form, which is very much simpler. Further, I might suggest that in the first reading the Explanations be omitted, and that it be borne in mind that they are not meant to elucidate the text, but rather to expand or modify it into harmony with later positions. For a more careful study of the book, I have sought to make the Index helpful.

My thanks are due to Professor Calderwood for encouragement in the work, and to my friend, Mr. G. W. Alexander, M.A., for revising the proofs and for many suggestions in the translation.

ALNWICK, 1893   JOHN OMAN

ON RELIGION

ON RELIGION

—•—

FIRST SPEECH

DEFENCE

It may be an unexpected and even a marvellous undertaking, that any one should still venture to demand
from the very class that have raised themselves above
the vulgar, and are saturated with the wisdom of the
centuries, attention for a subject so entirely neglected by
them. And I confess that I am aware of nothing that
promises any easy success, whether it be in winning for my
efforts your approval, or in the more difficult and more
desirable task of instilling into you my thought and in-
spiring you for my subject. From of old faith has not
been every man's affair. At all times but few have discerned
religion itself, while millions, in various ways, have been
satisfied to juggle with its trappings. Now especially the
life of cultivated people is far from anything that might
have even a resemblance to religion. Just as little, I know,
do you worship the Deity in sacred retirement, as you visit
the forsaken temples. In your ornamented dwellings, the
only sacred things to be met with are the sage maxims of
our wise men, and the splendid compositions of our poets.
Suavity and sociability, art and science have so fully taken
possession of your minds, that no room remains for the
eternal and holy Being that lies beyond the world. I

know how well you have succeeded in making your earthly life so rich and varied, that you no longer stand in need of an eternity. Having made a universe for yourselves, you are above the need of thinking of the Universe that made you. You are agreed, I know, that nothing new, nothing convincing can any more be said on this matter, which on every side by sages and seers, and I might add by scoffers and priests, has been abundantly discussed. To priests, least of all, are you inclined to listen. They have long been outcasts for you, and are declared unworthy of your trust, because they like best to lodge in the battered ruins of their sanctuary and cannot, even there, live without disfiguring and destroying it still more. All this I know, and yet, divinely swayed by an irresistible necessity within me, I feel myself compelled to speak, and cannot take back my invitation that you and none else should listen to me.

Might I ask one question ? On every subject, however small and unimportant, you would most willingly be taught by those who have devoted to it their lives and their powers. In your desire for knowledge you do not avoid the cottages of the peasant or the workshops of the humble artizans. How then does it come about that, in matters of religion alone, you hold every thing the more dubious when it comes from those who are experts, not only according to their own profession, but by recognition from the state, and from the people ? Or can you perhaps, strangely enough, show that they are not more experienced, but maintain and cry up anything rather than religion ? Scarcely, my good sirs ! Not setting much store on a judgment so baseless I confess, as is right, that I also am a member of this order. I venture, though I run the risk, if you do not give me an attentive hearing, of being reckoned among the great crowd from which you admit so few exceptions.

This is at least a voluntary confession, for my speech would not readily have betrayed me. Still less have I any expectations of danger from the praise which my brethren will bestow on this undertaking, for my present aim lies almost entirely outside their sphere, and can have but small resemblance to what they would most willingly see and hear.[1] With the cry of distress, in which most of them join, over the downfall of religion I have no sympathy, for I know no age that has given religion a better reception than the present. I have nothing to do with the conservative and barbarian lamentation whereby they seek to rear again the fallen walls and gothic pillars of their Jewish Zion.

Why then, as I am fully conscious that in all I have to say to you I entirely belie my profession, should I not acknowledge it like any other accident? Its prepossessions shall in no way hinder us. Neither in asking nor in answering shall the limits it holds sacred be valid between us. As a man I speak to you of the sacred secrets of mankind according to my views—of what was in me as with youthful enthusiasm I sought the unknown, of what since then I have thought and experienced, of the innermost springs of my being which shall for ever remain for me the highest, however I be moved by the changes of time and mankind. I do not speak from any reasoned resolve, nor from hope, nor from fear. Nor is it done from any caprice or accident. Rather it is the pure necessity of my nature; it is a divine call; it is that which determines my position in the world and makes me what I am. Wherefore, even if it were neither fitting nor prudent to speak of religion, there is something which compels me and represses with its heavenly power all those small considerations.

You know how the Deity, by an immutable law, has compelled Himself to divide His great work even to infinity. Each definite thing can only be made up by melting together two opposite activities. Each of His eternal thoughts can only be actualized in two hostile yet twin forms, one of which cannot exist except by means of the other. The whole corporeal world, insight into which is the highest aim of your researches, appears to the best instructed and most contemplative among you, simply a never-ending play of opposing forces. Each life is merely the uninterrupted manifestation of a perpetually renewed gain and loss, as each thing has its determinate existence by uniting and holding fast in a special way the opposing forces of Nature. Wherefore the spirit also, in so far as it manifests itself in a finite life, must be subject to the same law. The human soul, as is shown both by its passing actions and its inward characteristics, has its existence chiefly in two opposing impulses. Following the one impulse, it strives to establish itself as an individual. For increase, no less than sustenance, it draws what surrounds it to itself, weaving it into its life, and absorbing it into its own being. The other impulse, again, is the dread fear to stand alone over against the Whole, the longing to surrender oneself and be absorbed in a greater, to be taken hold of and determined. All you feel and do that bears on your separate existence, all you are accustomed to call enjoyment or possession works for the first object. The other is wrought for when you are not directed towards the individual life, but seek and retain for yourselves what is the same in all and for all the same existence, that in which, therefore, you acknowledge in your thinking and acting, law and order, necessity and connection, right and fitness. Just as no material thing can exist by only one of the forces of corporeal nature, every soul shares in the two original tendencies of spiritual nature. At the extremes one impulse may preponderate almost to the exclusion of the other, but the perfection of the living world consists in this, that between these opposite ends all combinations are actually present in humanity.

And not only so, but a common band of consciousness embraces them all, so that though the man cannot be other than he is, he knows every other person as clearly as himself, and comprehends perfectly every single manifestation of humanity. Persons, however, at the extremes of this great series, are furthest removed from such a knowledge of the whole. The endeavour to appropriate, too little influenced by the opposite endeavour, takes the form of insatiable sensuality that is mindful only of its individual life, and endeavours only in an earthly way to incorporate into it more and more material and to keep itself active and strong. Swinging eternally between desire and enjoyment, such persons never get beyond consciousness of the individual, and being ever busy with mere self-regarding concerns, they are neither able to feel nor know the common, the whole being and nature of humanity. To persons, on the other hand, too forcibly seized by the opposite impulse, who, from defective power of grasp, are incapable of acquiring any characteristic, definite culture, the true life of the world must just as much remain hidden. It is not granted them to penetrate with plastic mind and to fashion something of their own, but their activity dissipates itself in a futile game with empty notions. They never make a living study of anything, but devote their whole zeal to abstract precepts that degrade everything to means, and leave nothing to be an end. They consume themselves in mistaken hate against everything that comes before them with prosperous force. How are these extremes to be brought together, and the long series be made into a closed ring, the symbol of eternity and completeness ?

Persons in whom both tendencies are toned down to an unattractive equilibrium are not rare, but, in truth, they stand lower than either. For this frequent phenomenon which so many value highly, we are not indebted to a living union of both impulses, but both are distorted and smoothed away to a dull mediocrity in which no excess appears, because all fresh life is wanting. This is the position to which a false discretion seeks to bring the younger generation. But were the extremes avoided in no other way, all men would have departed from the right life and from contemplation of the truth, the higher spirit would have vanished from the world, and the will of the Deity been entirely frustrated. Elements so separated or so reduced to equilibrium would disclose little even to men of deep insight, and, for a common eye that has no power of insight to give life to the scattered bones, a world so peopled would be only a mock mirror that neither reflects their own forms nor allows them to see behind it.

Wherefore the Deity at all times sends some here and there, who in a fruitful manner are imbued with both impulses, either as a direct gift from above, or as the result of a severe and complete self-training. They are equipped with wonderful gifts, their way is made even by an almighty indwelling word. They are interpreters of the Deity and His works, and reconcilers of things that otherwise would be eternally divided. I mean, in particular, those who unite those opposing activities, by imprinting in their lives a characteristic form upon just that common nature of spirit, the shadow of which only appears to most in empty notions, as an image upon mist. They seek order and connection, right and fitness, and they find just because they do not lose themselves. Their impulse is not sighed out in inaudible wishes, but works in them as creative power. For this power they create and acquire, and not for that degraded animal sensuality. They do not devour destructively, but, creatively recasting, they breathe into life and life's tools a higher spirit, ordering and fashioning a world that bears the impress of their mind. Earthly things they wisely control, showing themselves lawgivers and inventors, heroes and compellers of nature, or, in narrower circles, as good fairies they create and diffuse in quiet a nobler happiness. By their very existence they prove themselves ambassadors of God, and mediators between limited man and infinite humanity. To them the captive under the power of empty notions may look, to perceive in their works the right object of his own incomprehensible requirements, and in their persons the material hitherto

despised, with which he ought to deal. They interpret
to him the misunderstood voice of God, and reconcile
him to the earth and to his place thereon. Far more
the earthly and sensual require such mediators from
whom to learn how much of the highest nature of
humanity is wanting to their own works and ways. They
stand in need of such a person to oppose to their base
animal enjoyment another enjoyment, the object of which
is not this thing or that, but the One in All, and All in One,
an object that knows no other bounds but the world, that
the spirit has learned to comprehend. He is needed to
show to their anxious, restless self-love, another self-love
whereby man in this earthly life and along with it loves
the highest and the eternal, and to their restless passionate
greed a quiet and sure possession.

Acknowledge, then, with me, what a priceless gift the
appearance of such a person must be when the higher feeling has risen to inspiration, and can no longer be kept
silent, when every pulse-beat of his spiritual life takes
communicable form in word or figure, so that, despite of his
indifference to the presence of others, he almost unwillingly
becomes for others the master of some divine art. This is
the true priest of the highest, for he brings it nearer those
who are only accustomed to lay hold of the finite and the
trivial. The heavenly and eternal he exhibits as an object of
enjoyment and agreement, as the sole exhaustless source of
the things towards which their whole endeavour is directed.
In this way he strives to awaken the slumbering germ of
a better humanity, to kindle love for higher things, to
change the common life into a nobler, to reconcile the
children of earth with the Heaven that hears them, and
to counterbalance the deep attachment of the age to the
baser side. This is the higher priesthood that announces
the inner meaning of all spiritual secrets, and speaks from
the kingdom of God. It is the source of all visions and
prophecies, of all the sacred works of art and inspired

speeches that are scattered abroad, on the chance of finding some receptive heart where they may bring forth fruit.

Might it sometime arrive that this office of mediator cease, and a fairer destiny await the priesthood of humanity! Might the time come, which an ancient prophecy describes, when no one should need to be taught of man, for they should all be taught of God! If everywhere the sacred fire burned, fervid prayers would not be needed to call it down from heaven, but only the placid quiet of holy virgins to maintain it. Nor would it burst forth in oft-dreaded flames, but would strive only to communicate equally to all its hidden glow. In quiet, then, each one would illumine himself and others. The communication of holy thoughts and feelings would be an easy interchange, the different beams of this light being now combined and again broken up, now scattered, and again here and there concentrated on single objects. A whispered word would then be understood, where now the clearest expression cannot escape misconception. Men could crowd together into the Holy of Holies who now busy themselves with the rudiments in the outer courts. How much pleasanter it is to exchange with friends and sympathizers completed views, than to go into the wide wilderness with outlines barely sketched! But how far from one another now are those persons between whom such intercourse might take place! They are scattered with as wise an economy among mankind, as the hidden points from which the elastic primordial matter expands on every side are in space. The outer boundaries of their sphere of operations just touch so that there is no void, yet one never meets the other. A wise economy indeed! for all their longing for intercourse and friendliness is thus wholly directed towards those who stand most in need, and they labour the more persistently to provide for themselves the comrades they lack.

To this very power I now submit, and of this very nature is my call. Permit me to speak of myself. You know that what is spoken at the instigation of piety cannot be pride, for piety is always full of humility. Piety was the mother's womb, in whose sacred darkness my young life was nourished and was prepared for a world still sealed for it. In it my spirit breathed ere it had yet found its own place in knowledge and experience. It helped me as I began to sift the faith of my fathers and to cleanse thought and feeling from the rubbish of antiquity. When the God and the immortality of my childhood vanished from my doubting eyes it remained to me.[2] Without design of mine it guided me into active life. It showed me how, with my endowments and defects, I should keep myself holy in an undivided existence, and through it alone I have learnt friendship and love. In respect of other human excellences, before your judgment-seat, ye wise and understanding of the people, I know it is small proof of possession to be able to speak of their value. They can be known from description, from observation of others, or, as all virtues are known, from the ancient and general traditions of their nature. But religion is of such a sort and is so rare, that whoever utters anything of it, must necessarily have had it, for nowhere could he have heard it. Of all that I praise, all that I feel to be the true work of religion, you would find little even in the sacred books. To the man who has not himself experienced it, it would only be an annoyance and a folly.

Finally, if I am thus impelled to speak of religion and to deliver my testimony, to whom should I turn if not to the sons of Germany? Where else is an audience for my speech? It is not blind predilection for my native soil or for my fellows in government and language, that makes me speak thus, but the deep conviction that you alone are capable, as well as worthy, of having awakened in you the sense for holy and divine things. Those proud Islanders whom many unduly honour, know no watchword but *gain* and *enjoyment*. Their zeal for knowledge is only a sham

fight, their worldly wisdom a false jewel, skilfully and
deceptively composed, and their sacred freedom itself too
often and too easily serves self-interest. They are never
in earnest with anything that goes beyond palpable utility.[3]
All knowledge they have robbed of life and use only as
dead wood to make masts and helms for their life's voyage
in pursuit of gain. Similarly they know nothing of religion,
save that all preach devotion to ancient usages and defend its
institutions, regarding them as a protection wisely cherished
by the constitution against the natural enemy of the state.

For other reasons I turn from the French. On them,
one who honours religion can hardly endure to look, for
in every act and almost in every word, they tread its
holiest ordinances under foot. The barbarous indifference
of the millions of the people, and the witty frivolity with
which individual brilliant spirits behold the sublimest fact
of history that is not only taking place before their eyes,
but has them all in its grasp, and determines every movement of their lives, witnesses clearly enough how little they
are capable of a holy awe or a true adoration. What does
religion more abhor than the unbridled arrogance with
which the rulers of the people bid defiance to the eternal
laws of the world ? What does it inculcate more strongly
than that discreet and lowly moderation of which aught,
even the slightest feeling, does not seem to be suggested
to them ? What is more sacred to it than that lofty
Nemesis, of whose most terrible dealings in the intoxication
of infatuation they have no understanding ? Where varied
punishments that formerly only needed to light on single
families to fill whole peoples with awe before the heavenly
Being and to dedicate to eternal Fate the works of the poets for
centuries, are a thousandfold renewed in vain, how ludicrously
would a single lonely voice resound unheard and unnoticed.

Only in my native land is that happy clime which
refuses no fruit entirely. There you find, though it be
only scattered, all that adorns humanity. Somewhere,

in individuals at least, all that grows attains its most beautiful form. Neither wise moderation, nor quiet contemplation is wanting ; there, therefore, religion must find a refuge from the coarse barbarism and the cold worldly mind of the age.

Or will you direct me to those whom you look down upon as rude and uncultured, as if the sense for sacred things had passed like an old-fashioned garment to the lower portion of the people, as if it became them alone to be impressed with belief and awe of the unseen ? You are well disposed towards these, our brethren. You would have them addressed also, on other higher subjects, on morals, justice and freedom, that for single moments, at least, their highest endeavours should be turned towards better things, and an impression of the worth of man be awakened in them. Let them be addressed at the same time on religion ; arouse occasionally their whole nature ; let the holiest impulse, asleep or hidden though it be, be brought to life ; enchant them with single flashes, charmed from the depths of their hearts ; open out of their narrow lives a glimpse into infinity ; raise even for a moment their low sensuality to the high consciousness of human will and of human existence, and much cannot fail to be won. But, pray you, do you turn to this class when you wish to unfold the inmost connection and the highest ground of human powers and actions, when idea and feeling, law and fact are to be traced to their common source, when you would exhibit the actual as eternal and necessarily based in the nature of humanity ? Is it not as much as can be looked for if your wise men are understood by the best among you ? Now that is just my present endeavour in regard to religion. I do not seek to arouse single feelings possibly belonging to it, nor to justify and defend single conceptions, but I would conduct you into the profoundest depths whence every feeling and conception receives its form. I would show you from what human tendency religion proceeds and how it belongs to what is for you highest and dearest. To the roof of the temple I would lead you that you might survey the whole sanctuary and discover its inmost secrets.

Do you seriously expect me to believe that those who daily distress themselves most toilsomely about earthly things have pre-eminent fitness for becoming intimate with heavenly things, those who brood anxiously over the next moment and are fast bound to the nearest objects can extend their vision widest over the world, and that those, who, in the monotonous round of a dull industry have not yet found themselves will discover most clearly the living Deity! Surely you will not maintain that to your shame? You alone, therefore, I can invite, you who are called to leave the common standpoint of mankind, who do not shun the toilsome way into the depths of man's spirit to find his inmost emotions and see the living worth and connection of his outward works.

Since this became clear to me, I have long found myself in the hesitating mood of one who has lost a precious jewel, and does not dare to examine the last spot where it could be hidden. There was a time when you held it a mark of special courage to cast off partially the restraints of inherited dogma. You still were ready to discuss particular subjects, though it were only to efface one of those notions. Such a figure as religion moving gracefully, adorned in eloquence, still pleased you, if only that you wished to maintain in the gentler sex a certain feeling for sacred things. But that time is long past. Piety is now no more to be spoken of, and even the Graces, with most unwomanly hardness, destroy the tenderest blossoms of the human heart, and I can link the interest I require from you to nothing but your contempt. I will ask you, therefore, just to be well informed and thorough-going in this contempt.

Let us then, I pray you, examine whence exactly religion has its rise. Is it from some clear intuition, or from some vague thought? Is it from the different kinds and sects

of religion found in history, or from some general idea which
you have perhaps conceived arbitrarily ? Some doubtless
will profess the latter view. But here as in other things the
ready judgment may be without ground, the matter being
superficially considered and no trouble being taken to gain
an accurate knowledge. Your general idea turns on fear of
an eternal being, or, broadly, respect for his influence on the
occurrences of this life called by you providence, on expectation of a future life after this one, called by you immortality. These two conceptions which you have rejected,
are, you consider, in one way or another, the hinges of all
religion. But say, my dear sirs, how you have found this ;
for there are two points of view from which everything
taking place in man or proceeding from him may be
regarded. Considered from the centre outwards, that
is according to its inner quality, it is an expression of
human nature, based in one of its necessary modes of acting
or impulses or whatever else you like to call it, for I will
not now quarrel with your technical language. On the
contrary, regarded from the outside, according to the definite attitude and form it assumes in particular cases, it is
a product of time and history. From what side have you
considered religion that great spiritual phenomenon, that
you have reached the idea that everything called by this
name has a common content ? You can hardly affirm that
it is by regarding it from within. If so, my good sirs, you
would have to admit that these thoughts are at least in
some way based in human nature. And should you say
that as now found they have sprung only from misinterpre-
tations or false references of a necessary human aim, it
would become you to seek in it the true and eternal, and to
unite your efforts to ours to free human nature from the
injustice which it always suffers when aught in it is misunderstood or misdirected.

By all that is sacred, and according to that avowal, something must be sacred to you, I adjure you, do not neglect

this business, that mankind, whom with us you honour, do not most justly scorn you for forsaking them in a grave matter. If you find from what you hear that the business is as good as done, even if it ends otherwise than you expect, I venture to reckon on your thanks and approval.

But you will probably say that your idea of the content of religion is from the other view of this spiritual phenomenon. You start with the outside, with the opinions, dogmas and usages, in which every religion is presented. They always return to providence and immortality. For these externals you have sought an inward and original source in vain. Wherefore religion generally can be nothing but an empty pretence which, like a murky and oppressive atmosphere, has enshrouded part of the truth. Doubtless this is your genuine opinion. But if you really consider these two points the sum of religion in all the forms in which it has appeared in history, permit me to ask whether you have rightly observed all these phenomena and have rightly comprehended their common content? If your idea has had its rise in this way you must justify it by instances. If anyone says it is wrong and beside the mark, and if he point out something else in religion not hollow, but having a kernel of excellent quality and extraction, you must first hear and judge before you venture further to despise. Do not grudge, therefore, to listen to what I shall say to those who, from first to last, have more accurately and laboriously adhered to observation of particulars.

You are doubtless acquainted with the histories of human follies, and have reviewed the various structures of religious doctrine from the senseless fables of wanton peoples to the most refined Deism, from the rude superstition of human sacrifice to the ill-put together fragments of metaphysics and ethics now called purified Christianity, and you have found them all without rhyme or reason. I am far from wishing to contradict you. Rather, if you really mean that the most cultured religious system is no better than the rudest, if you only perceive that the divine cannot lie in a series that ends on both sides in something ordinary and despicable, I will gladly spare you the trouble of estimating further all that lies between. Possibly they may all appear to you transitions and stages towards the final form. Out of the hand of its age each comes better polished and carved, till at length art has grown equal to that perfect plaything with which our century has presented history. But this consummation of doctrines and systems is often anything rather than consummation of religion. Nay, not infrequently, the progress of the one has not the smallest connection with the other. I cannot speak of it without indignation. All who have a regard for what issues from within the mind, and who are in earnest that every side of man be trained and exhibited, must bewail how the high and glorious is often turned from its destination and robbed of its freedom in order to be held in despicable bondage by the scholastic spirit of a barbarian and cold time. What are all these systems, considered in themselves, but the handiwork of the calculating understanding, wherein only by mutual limitation each part holds its place? What else can they be, these systems of theology, these theories of the origin and the end of the world, these analyses of the nature of an incomprehensible Being, wherein everything runs to cold argufying, and the highest can be treated in the tone of a common controversy? And this is certainly—let me appeal to your own feeling—not the character of religion.

If you have only given attention to these dogmas and opinions, therefore, you do not yet know religion itself, and what you despise is not it. Why have you not penetrated deeper to find the kernel of this shell? I am astonished at your voluntary ignorance, ye easy-going inquirers, and at the all too quiet satisfaction with which you linger by the first thing presented to you. Why do you not regard the religious life itself, and first those pious exaltations of the mind in which all other known activities are set aside or almost suppressed, and the whole soul is dissolved in the immediate feeling of the Infinite and Eternal ? In such moments the disposition you pretend to despise reveals itself in primordial and visible form. He only who has studied and truly known man in these emotions can rediscover religion in those outward manifestations. He will assuredly perceive something more in them than you. Bound up in them all something of that spiritual matter lies, without which they could not have arisen. But in the hands of those who do not understand how to unbind it, let them break it up and examine it as they may, nothing but the cold dead mass remains.

This recommendation to seek rather in those scattered and seemingly undeveloped elements your object that you have not yet found in the developed and the complete to which you have hitherto been directed, cannot surprise you who have more or less busied yourselves with philosophy, and are acquainted with its fortunes. With philosophy, indeed, it should be quite otherwise. From its nature it must strive to fashion itself into the closest connection. That special kind of knowledge is only verified and its communication assured by its completeness, and yet even here you must commence with the scattered and incomplete. Recollect how very few of those who, in a way of their own, have penetrated into the secrets of nature and spirit, viewing and exhibiting their mutual relation and inner harmony in a light of their own, have put forth at once a system of their knowledge. In a finer, if more fragile form, they have communicated their discoveries.

On the contrary, if you regard the systems in all schools, how often are they mere habitations and nurseries of the dead letter. With few exceptions, the plastic spirit of high contemplation is too fleeting and too free for those rigid forms whereby those who would willingly grasp and retain what is strange, believe they are best helped. Suppose that any one held the architects of those great edifices of philosophy, without distinction, for true philosophers ! Suppose he would

learn from them the spirit of their research ! Would you not
advise him thus, " See to it, friend, that you have not lighted
upon those who merely follow, and collect, and rest satisfied
with what another has furnished : with them you will never
find the spirit of that art: to the discoverers you must
go, on whom it surely rests." To you who seek religion I
must give the same advice. It is all the more necessary,
as religion is as far removed, by its whole nature, from all
that is systematic as philosophy is naturally disposed to it.

Consider only with whom those ingenious erections
originate, the mutability of which you scorn, the bad proportions of which offend you, and the incongruity of which,
with your contemptuous tendency, almost strikes you as
absurd. Have they come from the heroes of religion?
Name one among those who have brought down any
kind of new revelation to us, who has thought it worth
his while to occupy himself with such a labour of
Sisyphus, beginning with Him who first conceived the idea
of the kingdom of God, from which, if from anything in
the sphere of religion, a system might have been produced
to the new mystics or enthusiasts, as you are accustomed to
call them, in whom, perhaps, an original beam of the inner
light still shines. You will not blame me if I do not reckon
among them the theologians of the letter, who believe the
salvation of the world and the light of wisdom are to be
found in a new vesture of formulas, or a new arrangement
of ingenious proofs. In isolation only the mighty thunder
of their speech, announcing that the Deity is revealing
Himself through them, is accustomed to be heard when the
celestial feelings are unburdened, when the sacred fires
must burst forth from the overcharged spirit. Idea and
word are simply the necessary and inseparable outcome of
the heart, only to be understood by it and along with it.
Doctrine is only united to doctrine occasionally to remove
misunderstanding or expose unreality.

From many such combinations those systems were gradu-

ally compacted. Wherefore, you must not rest satisfied with
the repeated oft-broken echo of that original sound. You
must transport yourselves into the interior of a pious soul and
seek to understand its inspiration. In the very act, you
must understand the production of light and heat in a soul
surrendered to the Universe.[4] Otherwise you learn nothing
of religion, and it goes with you as with one who should too
late bring fuel to the fire which the steel has struck from
the flint, who finds only a cold, insignificant speck of coarse
metal with which he can kindle nothing any more.

I ask, therefore, that you turn from everything usually
reckoned religion, and fix your regard on the inward emotions and dispositions, as all utterances and acts of inspired
men direct. Despite your acquirements, your culture and
your prejudices, I hope for good success. At all events, till
you have looked from this standpoint without discovering anything real, or having any change of opinion, or
enlarging your contemptuous conception, the product of
superficial observation, and are still able to hold in ridicule
this reaching of the heart towards the Eternal, I will not
confess that I have lost. Then, however, I will finally
believe that your contempt for religion is in accordance with
your nature, and I shall have no more to say.

Yet you need not fear that I shall betake myself in the
end to that common device of representing how necessary
religion is for maintaining justice and order in the world.
Nor shall I remind you of an all-seeing eye, nor of the un-
speakable short-sightedness of human management, nor of
the narrow bounds of human power to render help. Nor
shall I say how religion is a faithful friend and useful stay
of morality, how, by its sacred feelings and glorious prospects, it makes the struggle with self and the perfecting of
goodness much easier for weak man. Those who profess
to be the best friends and most zealous defenders do indeed
speak in this way. Which of the two is more degraded in
being thus thought of together, I shall not decide, whether

justice and morality which are represented as needing support, or religion which is to support them, or even whether it be not you to whom such things are said.

Though otherwise this wise counsel might be given you, how could I dare to suppose that you play with your consciences a sort of fast and loose game, and could be impelled by something you have hitherto had no cause to respect and love to something else that without it you already honour, and to which you have already devoted yourselves? Or suppose that these Speeches were merely to suggest what you should do for the sake of the people! How could you, who are called to educate others and make them like yourselves, begin by deceiving them, offering them as holy and vitally necessary what is in the highest degree indifferent to yourselves, and which, in your opinion, they can again reject as soon as they have attained your level? I, at least, cannot invite you to a course of action in which I perceive the most ruinous hypocrisy towards the world and towards yourselves. To recommend religion by such means would only increase the contempt to which it is at present exposed. Granted that our civil organizations are still burdened with a very high degree of imperfection and have shown but small power to prevent or abolish injustice, it would still be a culpable abandonment of a weighty matter, a faint-hearted unbelief in the approach of better things, if religion that in itself is not otherwise desirable must be called in.

Answer me this one question. Could there be a legal constitution resting on piety?[5] Would not the whole idea that you hold so sacred vanish as soon as you took such a point of departure? Deal with the matter directly, therefore, if it seems to be in such an evil plight. Improve the laws, recast the whole constitution, give the state an iron hand, give it a hundred eyes if it has not got them already. At least do not allow those it has to sleep veiled in delusion. If you leave a business like this to an intermediary, you have never managed it. Do not declare to the disgrace of mankind that your loftiest creation is but a parasitic plant that can only nourish itself from strange sap.

Speaking from your standpoint, law must not even require morality to assure for it the most unlimited jurisdiction in its own territory. It must stand quite alone. Statesmen must make it universal. Now quite apart from the question whether what only exists in so far as it proceeds from the heart can be thus arbitrarily combined, if this general jurisdiction is only possible when religion is combined with law, none but persons skilled to infuse the spirit of religion into the human soul should be statesmen. And in what dark barbarousness of evil times would that land us!

Just as little can morality be in need of religion. A weak, tempted heart must take refuge in the thought of a future world. But it is folly to make a distinction between this world and the next. Religious persons at least know only one. If the desire for happiness is foreign to morality, later happiness can be no more valid than earlier; if it should be quite independent of praise, dread of the Eternal cannot be more valid than dread of a wise man. If morality loses in splendour and stability by every addition, how much more must it lose from something that can never hide its foreign extraction.

All this, however, you have heard of sufficiently from those who defend the independence and might of the moral law. Yet let me add, that to wish to transport religion into another sphere that it may serve and labour is to manifest towards it also great contempt. It is not so ambitious of conquest as to seek to reign in a foreign kingdom. The power that is its due, being earned afresh at every moment, satisfies it. Everything is sacred to it, and above all everything holding with it the same rank in human nature.[6] But it must render a special service; it must have an aim; it must show itself useful! What degradation! And its defenders should be eager for it!

At the last remove, morality and justice also must conduce to some further advantage. It were better that such utilitarians should be submerged in this eternal whirlpool of universal utility, in which everything good is allowed to go down, of which no man that would be anything for himself understands a single sensible word, than that they should venture to come forward as defenders of religion, for of all men they are least skilled to conduct its case. High renown it were for the heavenly to conduct so wretchedly the earthly concerns of man! Great honour for the free and unconcerned to make the conscience of man a little sharper and more alert! For such a purpose religion does not descend from heaven. What is loved and honoured only on account of some extraneous advantage may be needful, but it is not in itself necessary, and a sensible person simply values it according to the end for which it is desired. By this standard, religion would be valueless enough. I, at least, would offer little, for I must confess that I do not believe much in the unjust dealings it would hinder, nor the moral dealings it would produce. If that is all it could do to gain respect, I would have no more to do with its case. To recommend it merely as an accessory is too unimportant. An imaginary praise that vanishes on closer contemplation, cannot avail anything going about with higher pretensions. I maintain that in all better souls piety springs necessarily by itself; that a province of its own in the mind belongs to it, in which it has unlimited sway; that it is worthy to animate most profoundly the noblest and best and to be fully accepted and known by them. That is my contention, and it now behoves you to decide whether it is worth your while to hear me, before you still further strengthen yourselves in your contempt.

EXPLANATIONS OF THE FIRST SPEECH

(1) Page 3.—Though I had been several years in the ministry when this was written, I stood very much alone among my professional brethren, and my acquaintance with them was small. What is here rather hinted at than uttered was more a distant presentiment than clear knowledge. Longer experience, however, and friendly relations have only confirmed the judgment, that any deeper insight into the nature of religion generally, or any genuinely historical, real way of regarding the present state of religion is much too rare among the members of our clerical order. We should have fewer complaints of the increase of the sectarian spirit and of factious religious associations, if so many of the clergy were not without understanding of religious wants and emotions. Their stand-point generally is too low. From the same cause we have the miserable views so often expressed respecting the means necessary for remedying this so-called decay of religion. It is an opinion that will probably find little favour, which yet, for the right understanding of this passage I cannot hide, that a deeper speculative discipline would best remove this evil. Most of the clergy, however, and most of those who train them, do not acknowledge this necessity, because they foolishly suppose it would render them more unpractical.

(2) Page 9.—The first conception both of God and immortality, which at a time when the soul lives entirely in images is always highly sensuous, does not, by any means, always vanish. With most it is gradually purified and elevated. The analogy with the human in the conception of the Highest Being and the analogy with the earthly still remains the shell of the hidden kernel. But those who are early absorbed in a pure contemplative endeavour take another way. There is nothing in God, they say to themselves, opposed, divided or isolated. Wherefore nothing human can be said of Him. Nothing earthly is to be transferred from the earthly world that gave it birth in our souls. Both conceptions, therefore, in their first forms are found untenable, they become incapable of living reproduction and disappear. But this does not involve any positive unbelief, not even any positive doubt. The childish form

vanishes with the known sensuous co-efficient, but the unknown greatness remains in the soul, and its reality is apparent in the endeavour to connect it with another co-efficient and so to bring it to a higher actual consciousness. In this endeavour faith is implicit, even when no fully satisfactory solution is reached. The unknown greatness, even though it do not appear in any definite result, is yet present in all operations of the spirit. The author was, therefore, far removed from suggesting that there ever was a time when he was an unbeliever or an atheist. Such a misunderstanding could only arise in those who have never felt the speculative impulse to annihilate anthropomorphism in the conception of the Highest Being, an impulse most clearly expressed in the writings of the profoundest Christian teachers.

(3) Page 10.—It is to be remembered that the severe judgment of the English people was given at a time when it seemed necessary to protest strongly against the prevailing Anglomania. Moreover, the popular interest in missions and the spread of the Bible was not then as apparent as it is now. Yet I would not on that account retract much from my earlier judgment. For one thing the English are well accustomed to organized private companies, whereby they unite their individual resources for important undertakings. The results obtained in this way are so great that persons, caring for nothing but the progress of culture and the gain to be made of it, are not excluded from sharing in enterprises that have taken their rise with a far smaller number of truly pious people, and yet the principle is not weakened. Nor is it to be denied that those undertakings are regarded by a great number more from a political and mercantile point of view. The pure interest of Christian piety does not dominate as appears in this, that the religious needs at home have been attended to much later and with much less brilliant result. These are merely indications whereby I would express my belief that a closer acquaintance with the state of religion in England would rather confirm than disprove the above opinion. The same would apply to what was said about the scientific spirit. As France and England were almost the only countries in which we were interested, and which had much influence in Germany, it seemed superfluous to glance elsewhere. At present it might not be wrong to say a word on the capacity in the Greek Church for such researches. Despite the fine veil cast over it by the fascinating panegyrics of a Stourdza, all depth is lost in the mechanism of antiquated usages and liturgical forms. In all that is most important for a mind aroused to reflection, it still stands far behind the Catholic Church.

(4) Page 18.—A pious spirit, which is here unquestionably the sub-

ject of discourse, is elsewhere always defined as a soul surrendered to God. But here the Universe is put for God and the pantheism of the author is undeniable! This is the interpolation, not interpretation of superficial and suspicious readers who do not consider that the subject here is the production of light and warmth in such a spirit, the springing of such pious emotions as pass immediately into religious ideas and views (light) and into a temperament of surrender to God (warmth). It was therefore desirable to call attention to the way in which such emotions take their rise. They arise when a man surrenders himself to the Universe, and are only habitual in a spirit in which such surrender is habitual. Not only in general, but on each occasion we are conscious of God and of His divine power and godhead by the word of creation, and not by any one thing taken by itself, but by it only in so far as it is embraced in the unity and completeness in which alone God is immediately revealed. The further development of this subject can be seen in my " Glaubenslehre," § 8, 2, and § 36, 1, 2.

(5) Page 19.—That the state would not be a constitution if it rested on piety, does not mean that the state so long as it labours under imperfection can do without piety, the thing that best supplies all deficiency and imperfection. This would only mean, however, that it is politically necessary for the citizens to be pious in proportion as they are not equally and adequately pervaded by the legal principles of the state. Humanly speaking this perfection is not to be looked for, but were it once effected the state, in respect of its own particular sphere of operation, could dispense with the piety of its members. This appears from the fact that in states where constitutionalism has not quite triumphed over arbitrariness, the relation of piety between the governor and the governed is most prominent and religious institutions have most sway. This ceases when the constitution is strengthened, unless indeed an institution have some special historical basis. When afterwards (page 20) it is said that statesmen must be able to produce universally in men the sense of law, it will doubtless appear absurd to those who think of the servants of the state. But the word statesman is here taken in the sense of the ancient πολιτικὸς, and it means less that he accomplishes something definite in the state, a thing entirely accidental, than that he first of all lives in the idea of the state. The dark times referred to are the theocratic times. I make this reference because Novalis, my very dear friend in other respects, wished once more to glorify the theocracy. It is still, however, my strong conviction that it is one of the most essential tendencies of Christianity to separate completely church and state, and I can just as little agree with that

glorification of the theocracy as with the opposite view that the church should ever more and more be absorbed in the state.

(6) Page 20.—I am not using the privileges of the rhetorical method to say to the despisers of religion at the very beginning that piety surpasses morality and law. Also I was not concerned in this place to say which is first, for, in my opinion, piety and scientific speculation share with each other, and the more closely they are conjoined the more both advance. The distinction however will be found in my " Glaubenslehre," but here I had to defend the equal rank of morality, law and piety in human nature. In so far as the two former do not involve an immediate relation of man to the Highest Being, they are inferior to the third, but all alike regulate as essentially what is eminent and characteristic in human nature. They are functions of human nature not to be subordinated to one another, and in so far are equal. Man can just as little be thought of without capacity for morality or endeavour after government as without capacity for religion.

SECOND SPEECH

You know how the aged Simonides, by long and repeated hesitation, put to silence the person who troubled him with the question, What are the gods? Our question, What is religion? is similar and equally extensive, and I would fain begin with a like hesitation. Naturally I would not mean by ultimate silence, as he did, to leave you in perplexity. But you might attempt something for yourselves; you might give steady and continuous attention to the point about which we are inquiring; you might entirely exclude other thoughts. Do not even conjurors of common spirits demand abstinence from earthly things and solemn stillness, as a preparation, and undistracted, close attention to the place where the apparition is to show itself? How much more should I claim? It is a rare spirit that I am to call forth, which can, only when long regarded with fixed attention, be recognized as the object of your desire. You must have that unbiassed sobriety of judgment that seizes clearly and accurately every outline. Without being misled by old memories or hindered by preconceptions, you must endeavour to understand the object presented simply by itself. Even then it may not win your love, and otherwise I cannot hope for any unanimity about the meaning of religion or any recognition of its worth.

I could wish to exhibit religion in some well known form, reminding you, by feature, carriage and deportment, of what here and there at least you have seen in life. Religion, however, as I wish to show it, which is to say, in its own original, characteristic form, is not accustomed to appear openly, but is only seen in secret by those who love it. Not that this applies to religion alone. Nothing that is essentially characteristic and peculiar can be quite the same as that which openly exhibits and represents it. Speech, for example, is not the pure work of science nor morals of intention. Among ourselves at the present time this is specially recognized. It belongs to the opposition of the new time to the old that no longer is one person one thing, but everyone is all things. Just as among civilized peoples, by extensive intercourse their characteristic ways of thought no longer appear unalloyed, so in the human mind there is such a complete sociableness founded, that no special faculty or capacity, however much it may be separated for observation, can ever, in separation, produce its work. Speaking broadly, one is, in operation, influenced and permeated by the ready love and support of the others. The predominating power is all you can distinguish. Wherefore every activity of the spirit is only to be understood, in so far as a man can study it in himself. Seeing you maintain that in this way you do not know religion, it is incumbent upon me to warn you against the errors that naturally issue from the present state of things. We shall, therefore, begin by reviewing the main points in your own position to see whether they are right, or whether we may from them reach the right.

Religion is for you at one time a way of thinking, a faith, a peculiar way of contemplating the world, and of combining what meets us in the world : at another, it is a way of acting, a peculiar desire and love, a special kind of conduct and character. Without this distinction of a theoretical and practical you could hardly think at all, and though both sides belong to religion, you are usually accustomed to give heed chiefly to only one at a time. Wherefore, we shall look closely at religion from both sides.

We commence with religion as a kind of activity.

Activity is twofold, having to do with life and with art. You would ascribe with the poet earnestness to life and cheerfulness to art ; or, in some other way, you would contrast them. Separate them you certainly will. For life, duty is the watchword. The moral law shall order it, and virtue shall show itself the ruling power in it, that the individual may be in harmony with the universal order of the world, and may nowhere encroach in a manner to disturb and confuse. This life, you consider, may appear without any discernible trace of art. Rather is it to be attained by rigid rules that have nothing to do with the free and variable precepts of art. Nay, you look upon it almost as a rule that art should be somewhat in the background, and non-essential for those who are strictest in the ordering of life. On the other hand, imagination shall inspire the artist, and genius shall completely sway him. Now imagination and genius are for you quite different from virtue and morality, being capable of existing in the largest measure along with a much more meagre moral endowment. Nay you are inclined, because the prudent power often comes into danger by reason of the fiery power, to relax for the artist somewhat of the strict demands of life.

How now does it stand with piety, in so far as you regard it as a peculiar kind of activity ? Has it to do with right living ? Is it something good and praiseworthy, yet different from morality, for you will not hold them to be identical ? But in that case morality does not exhaust the sphere which it should govern. Another power works alongside of it, and has both right and might to continue working. Or will you perhaps betake yourselves to the position that piety is a virtue, and religion a duty or section of duties ? Is religion incorporated into morality and subordinated to it, as a part to the whole ? Is it, as some suppose, special duties towards God, and therefore a part of all morality which is the performance of all duties ? But, if I have rightly appreciated or accurately reproduced what you say, you do not think so.

You rather seem to say that the pious person has something entirely peculiar, both in his doing and leaving undone, and that morality can be quite moral without therefore being pious.

And how are religion and art related? They can hardly be quite alien, because, from of old, what is greatest in art has had a religious character. When, therefore, you speak of an artist as pious, do you still grant him that relaxation of the strict demands of virtue? Rather he is then subjected, like every other person. But then to make the cases parallel, you must secure that those who devote themselves to life do not remain quite without art. Perhaps this combination gives its peculiar form to religion. With your view, there seems no other possible issue.

Religion then, as a kind of activity, is a mixture of elements that oppose and neutralize each other. Pray is not this rather the utterance of your dislike than your conviction? Such an accidental shaking together, leaving both elements unaltered, does not, even though the most accurate equality be attained, make something specific. But suppose it is otherwise, suppose piety is something which truly fuses both, then it cannot be formed simply by bringing the two together, but must be an original unity. Take care, however, I warn you, that you do not make such an admission. Were it the case, morality and genius apart would be only fragments of the ruins of religion, or its corpse when it is dead. Religion were then higher than both, the true divine life itself. But, in return for this warning, if you accept it, and discover no other solution, be so good as tell me how your opinion about religion is to be distinguished from nothing? Till then nothing remains for me but to assume that you have not yet, by examination, satisfied yourselves about this side of religion. Perhaps we shall have better fortune with the other side— what is known as the way of thinking, or faith.

You will, I believe, grant that your knowledge, however many-sided it may appear, falls, as a whole, into two contrasted sciences. How you shall subdivide and name belongs to the controversies of your schools, with which at present I am not concerned. Do not, therefore, be too critical about my terminology, even though it come from various quarters. Let us call the one division physics or metaphysics, applying both names indifferently, or indicating sections of the same thing. Let the other be ethics or the doctrine of duties or practical philosophy. At least we are agreed about the distinction meant. The former describes the nature of things, or if that seems too much, how man conceives and must conceive of things and of the world as the sum of things. The latter science, on the contrary, teaches what man should be for the world, and what he should do in it. Now, in so far as religion is a way of thinking of something and a knowledge about something, has it not the same object as these sciences? What does faith know about except the relation of man to God and to the world—God's purpose in making him, and the world's power to help or hinder him? Again it distinguishes in its own fashion a good action from a bad. Is then religion identical with natural science and ethics? You would not agree, you would never grant that our faith is as surely founded, or stands on the same level of certainty as your scientific knowledge! Your accusation against it is just that it does not know how to distinguish between the demonstrable and the probable. Similarly, you do not forget to remark diligently that very marvellous injunctions both to do and leave undone have issued from religion. You may be quite right; only do not forget that it has been the same with that which you call science. In both spheres you believe you have made improvements and are better than your fathers.

What then, are we to say that religion is? As before, that it is a mixture—mingled theoretical and practical knowledge? But this is even less permissible, particularly if, as appears, each of these two branches of knowledge has its own characteristic mode of procedure. Such a mixture of elements that would either counteract or separate, could only be made most arbitrarily. The utmost gain to be looked for would be to furnish us with another method for putting known results into shape for beginners, and for stimulating them to a further study. But if that be so, why do you strive against religion? You might, so long as beginners are to be found, leave it in peace and security. If we presumed to subject you, you might smile at our folly, but, knowing for certain that you have left it far behind, and that it is only prepared for us by you wiser people, you would be wrong in losing a serious word on the matter. But it is not so, I think. Unless I am quite mistaken, you have long been labouring to provide the mass of the people with just such an epitome of your knowledge. The name is of no consequence, whether it be " religion" or "enlightenment" or aught else. But there is something different which must first be expelled, or, at least, excluded. This something it is that you call belief, and it is the object of your hostility, and not an article you would desire to extend.

Wherefore, my friends, belief must be something different from a mixture of opinions about God and the world, and of precepts for one life or for two. Piety cannot be an instinct craving for a mess of metaphysical and ethical crumbs. If it were, you would scarcely oppose it. It would not occur to you to speak of religion as different from your knowledge, however much it might be distant. The strife of the cultured and learned with the pious would simply be the strife of depth and thoroughness with superficiality ; it would be the strife of the master with pupils who are to emancipate themselves in due time.

Were you, after all, to take this view, I should like to plague you with all sorts of Socratic questions, till I compelled many of you to give a direct answer to the question, whether it is at all possible to be wise and pious at the same time. I should also wish to submit whether in other well-known matters you do not acknowledge the principle that things similar are to be placed together and particulars to be subordinated to generals? Is it that you may joke with the world about a serious subject, that in religion only the principle is not applied? But let us suppose you are serious. How does it come, then, that in religious faith, what, in science, you separate into two spheres, is united and so indissolubly bound together that one cannot be thought of without the other? The pious man does not believe that the right course of action can be determined, except in so far as, at the same time, there is knowledge of the relations of man to God; and again right action, he holds, is necessary for right knowledge. Suppose the binding principle lies in the theoretic side. Why then is a practical philosophy set over against a theoretic, and not rather regarded as a section? Or suppose the principle is in the practical side, the same would apply to a theoretic philosophy. Or both may be united, only in a yet higher, an original knowledge. That this highest, long-lost unity of knowledge should be religion you cannot believe, for you have found it most, and have opposed it most, in those who are furthest from science. I will not hold you to any such conclusion, for I would not take up a position that I cannot maintain.[1] This, however, you may well grant, that, concerning this side of religion, you must take time to consider what is its proper significance.

Let us be honest with one another. As we recently agreed, you have no liking for religion. But, in carrying on an honourable war which is not quite without strain, you would not wish to fight against such a shadow as that with which we have so far been battling. It must be something special that could fashion itself so peculiarly in the human heart, something thinkable, the real nature of which can so be presented as to be spoken of and argued about, and I consider it very wrong that out of things so disparate as modes of knowing and modes of acting, you patch together

an untenable something, and call it religion, and then are
so needlessly ceremonious with it. But you would deny
that you have not gone to work with straightforwardness.
Seeing I have rejected systems, commentaries and apo-
logies, you would demand that I unfold all the original
sources of religion from the beautiful fictions of the Greeks
to the sacred scriptures of the Christians. Should I not
find everywhere the nature of the Gods, and the will of
the Gods? Is not that man everywhere accounted holy
and blessed who knows the former, and does the latter?

But that is just what I have already said. Religion
never appears quite pure. Its outward form is ever determined by something else. Our task first is to exhibit its
true nature, and not to assume off-hand, as you seem to do,
that the outward form and the true nature are the same.
Does the material world present you with any element in its
original purity as a spontaneous product of nature? Must
you, therefore, as you have done in the intellectual world,
take very gross things for simple? It is the one ceaseless
aim of all analysis to present something really simple. So
also it is in spiritual things. You can only obtain what is
original by producing it, as it were, by a second, an artificial
creation in yourselves, and even then it is but for the
moment of its production. Pray come to an understanding
on the point, for you shall be ceaselessly reminded of it.

But let us go on to the sources and original writings
of religion. To attach them to your sciences of resistance and of action, of nature and of spirit is an unavoidable necessity, because they are the sources of your
terminology. Furthermore the best preparation for
awaking consciousness for your own higher subject is to
study what has already been more or less scientifically
thought. The deepest and highest in a work is not always
either first or last. Did you but know how to read between
the lines! All sacred writings are like these modest books
which were formerly in use in our modest Fatherland. Under

a paltry heading they treated weighty matters, and, offering but few explanations, aimed at the most profound inquiry. Similarly, the sacred writings include metaphysical and moral conceptions. Except where they are more directly poetic, this seems the beginning and the end. But of you it is expected that, seeing through the appearance, you will recognize the real intent. It is as when nature gives precious metals alloyed with baser substances, and our skill knows how to discover them and restore them to their refulgent splendour. The sacred writings were not for perfect believers alone, but rather for children in belief, for novices, for those who are standing at the entrance and would be invited in, and how could they go to work except as I am now doing with you? They had to accept what was granted. In it they had to find the means for stimulating the new sense they would awake, by giving a severe concentration and lofty temper to the mind. Can you not recognize, even in the way these moral and metaphysical conceptions are treated, in the creative, poetic impulse, though it necessarily works in a poor and thankless speech, an endeavour to break through from a lower region to a higher? As you can easily see, a communication of this sort could be nothing other than poetical or rhetorical. Akin to the rhetorical is the dialectic, and what method has from of old been more brilliantly or more successfully employed in revealing the higher nature, not only of knowledge, but of the deeper feelings? But if the vehicle alone satisfies, this end will not be reached. Wherefore, as it has become so common to seek metaphysics and ethics chiefly, in the sacred writings, and to appraise them accordingly, it seems time to approach the matter from the other end, and to begin with the clear cut distinction between our faith and your ethics and metaphysics, between our piety and what you call morality. This is what I would attain by this digression. I wished to throw some light on the conception that is dominant among you. That being done, I now return.

In order to make quite clear to you what is the original
and characteristic possession of religion, it resigns, at once,
all claims on anything that belongs either to science or
morality. Whether it has been borrowed or bestowed it is
now returned. What then does your science of being, your
natural science, all your theoretical philosophy, in so far
as it has to do with the actual world, have for its aim?
To know things, I suppose, as they really are; to show the
peculiar relations by which each is what it is; to determine
for each its place in the Whole, and to distinguish it rightly
from all else; to present the whole real world in its
mutually conditioned necessity; and to exhibit the oneness
of all phenomena with their eternal laws. This is truly
beautiful and excellent, and I am not disposed to depreciate. Rather, if this description of mine, so slightly
sketched, does not suffice, I will grant the highest and most
exhaustive you are able to give.

And yet, however high you go; though you pass from the
laws to the Universal Lawgiver, in whom is the unity of all
things; though you allege that nature cannot be comprehended without God, I would still maintain that religion has
nothing to do with this knowledge, and that, quite apart from
it, its nature can be known. Quantity of knowledge is not
quantity of piety. Piety can gloriously display itself, both
with originality and individuality, in those to whom this
kind of knowledge is not original. They may only know it
as everybody does, as isolated results known in connection
with other things. The pious man must, in a sense, be a
wise man, but he will readily admit, even though you somewhat proudly look down upon him, that, in so far as he is
pious, he does not hold his knowledge in the same way as you.

Let me interpret in clear words what most pious persons
only guess at and never know how to express. Were
you to set God as the apex of your science as the
foundation of all knowing as well as of all knowledge,
they would accord praise and honour, but it would not be
their way of having and knowing God. From their way,

as they would readily grant, and as is easy enough to see, knowledge and science do not proceed.

It is true that religion is essentially contemplative. You would never call anyone pious who went about in impervious stupidity, whose sense is not open for the life of the world. But this contemplation is not turned, as your knowledge of nature is, to the existence of a finite thing, combined with and opposed to another finite thing. It has not even, like your knowledge of God—if for once I might use an old expression—to do with the nature of the first cause, in itself and in its relation to every other cause and operation. The contemplation of the pious is the immediate conscious- ness of the universal existence of all finite things, in and through the Infinite, and of all temporal things in and through the Eternal. Religion is to seek this and find it in all that lives and moves, in all growth and change, in all doing and suffering. It is to have life and to know life in immediate feeling, only as such an existence in the Infinite and Eternal. Where this is found religion is satisfied, where it hides itself there is for her unrest and anguish, extremity and death. Wherefore it is a life in the infinite nature of the Whole, in the One and in the All, in God, having and possessing all things in God, and God in all. Yet religion is not knowledge and science, either of the world or of God. Without being knowledge, it recognizes knowledge and science. In itself it is an affection, a revelation of the Infinite in the finite, God being seen in it and it in God.

Similarly, what is the object of your ethics, of your science of action ? Does it not seek to distinguish precisely each part of human doing and producing, and at the same time to combine them into a whole, according to actual relations ? But the pious man confesses that, as pious, he knows nothing about it. He does, indeed, contemplate human action, but it is not the kind of contemplation from which an ethical system takes its rise. Only one thing he

seeks out and detects, action from God, God's activity
among men. If your ethics are right, and his piety as
well, he will not, it is true, acknowledge any action as
excellent which is not embraced in your system. But to
know and to construct this system is your business, ye
learned, not his. If you will not believe, regard the case
of women. You ascribe to them religion, not only as an
adornment, but you demand of them the finest feeling for
distinguishing the things that excel : do you equally expect
them to know your ethics as a science?

It is the same, let me say at once, with action itself.
The artist fashions what is given him to fashion, by virtue
of his special talent. These talents are so different that
the one he possesses another lacks ; unless someone,
against heaven's will, would possess all. But when anyone
is praised to you as pious, you are not accustomed to ask
which of these gifts dwell in him by virtue of his piety.
The citizen—taking the word in the sense of the ancients,
not in its present meagre significance—regulates, leads, and
influences in virtue of his morality. But this is something
different from piety. Piety has also a passive side. While
morality always shows itself as manipulating, as self-
controlling, piety appears as a surrender, a submission to
be moved by the Whole that stands over against man.
Morality depends, therefore, entirely on the consciousness
of freedom, within the sphere of which all that it produces
falls. Piety, on the contrary, is not at all bound to this
side of life. In the opposite sphere of necessity, where
there is no properly individual action, it is quite as active.
Wherefore the two are different. Piety does, indeed, linger
with satisfaction on every action that is from God, and
every activity that reveals the Infinite in the finite, and yet
it is not itself this activity. Only by keeping quite outside
the range both of science and of practice can it maintain
its proper sphere and character. Only when piety takes
its place alongside of science and practice, as a necessary,

an indispensable third, as their natural counterpart, not less in worth and splendour than either, will the common field be altogether occupied and human nature on this side complete.

But pray understand me fairly. I do not mean that one could exist without the other, that, for example, a man might have religion and be pious, and at the same time be immoral. That is impossible. But, in my opinion, it is just as impossible to be moral or scientific without being religious. But have I not said that religion can be had without science? Wherefore, I have myself begun the separation. But remember, I only said piety is not the measure of science. Just as one cannot be truly scientific without being pious, the pious man may not know at all, but he cannot know falsely. His proper nature is not of that subordinate kind, which, according to the old adage that like is only known to like, knows nothing except semblance of reality.

His nature is reality which knows reality, and where it encounters nothing it does not suppose it sees something. And what a precious jewel of science, in my view, is ignorance for those who are captive to semblance. If you have not learned it from my Speeches or discovered it for yourselves, go and learn it from your Socrates. Grant me consistency at least. With ignorance your knowledge will ever be mixed, but the true and proper opposite of knowledge is presumption of knowledge. By piety this presumption is most certainly removed, for with it piety cannot exist.

Such a separation of knowledge and piety, and of action and piety, do not accuse me of making. You are only ascribing to me, without my deserving it, your own view and the very confusion, as common as it is unavoidable, which it has been my chief endeavour to show you in the mirror of my Speech. Just because you do not acknowledge religion as the third, knowledge and action are so much apart that you can discover no unity, but believe that right knowing can be had without right acting, and *vice versa.* I hold that is it only in contemplation that there is division. There, where it is necessary, you despise it, and instead transfer it to life, as if in life itself objects could be found independent one of the other. Consequently you have no living insight into any of these activities. Each is for you a part, a fragment. Because you do not deal with life in a living way, your conception bears the stamp of perishableness, and is altogether meagre. True science is complete vision ; true practice is culture and art self-produced ; true religion is sense and taste for the Infinite. To wish to have true science or true practice without religion, or to imagine it is possessed, is obstinate, arrogant delusion, and culpable error. It issues from the unholy sense that would rather have a show of possession by cowardly purloining than have secure possession by demanding and waiting. What can man accomplish that is worth speaking of, either in life or in art, that does not arise in his own self from the influence of this sense for the Infinite ? Without it, how can anyone wish to comprehend the world scientifically, or if, in some distinct talent, the knowledge is thrust upon him, how should he wish to exercise it ? What is all science, if not the existence of things in you, in your reason ? what is all art and culture if not your existence in the things to which you give measure, form and order ? And how can both come to life in you except in so far as there lives immediately in you the eternal unity of Reason and Nature, the universal existence of all finite things in the Infinite ? [2]

Wherefore, you will find every truly learned man devout and pious. Where you see science without religion, be sure it is transferred, learned up from another. It is sickly, if indeed it is not that empty appearance which serves necessity and is no knowledge at all. And what else do you take this deduction and weaving together of ideas to be, which neither live nor correspond to any living thing ? Or in ethics, what else is this wretched uniformity that thinks it can grasp the highest human life in a single dead formula? The former arises because there is no fundamental feeling of that living nature which everywhere presents variety and individuality, and the latter because the sense fails to give infinity to the finite by determining its nature and boundaries only from the Infinite. Hence the dominion of the mere notion; hence the mechanical erections of your systems instead of an organic structure; hence the vain juggling with analytical formulas, in which, whether categorical or hypothetical, life will not be fettered. Science is not your calling, if you despise religion and fear to surrender yourself to reverence and aspiration for the primordial. Either science must become as low as your life, or it must be separated and stand alone, a division that precludes success. If man is not one with the Eternal in the unity of intuition and feeling which is immediate, he remains, in the unity of consciousness which is derived, for ever apart.

What, then, shall become of the highest utterance of the speculation of our days, complete rounded idealism, if it do not again sink itself in this unity, if the humility of religion do not suggest to its pride another realism than that which it so boldly and with such perfect right, subordinates to itself? It annihilates the Universe, while it seems to aim at constructing it. It would degrade it to a mere allegory, to a mere phantom of the one-sided limitation of its own empty consciousness. Offer with me reverently a tribute to the manes of the holy, rejected Spinoza. The high World-Spirit pervaded him; the Infinite was his beginning and his end; the Universe was his only and his everlasting love. In holy innocence and in deep humility he beheld himself mirrored in the eternal world, and perceived how he also was its most worthy mirror. He was full of religion, full of the Holy Spirit. Wherefore, he stands there alone and unequalled; master in his art, yet without disciples and without citizenship, sublime above the profane tribe.

Why should I need to show that the same applies to art? Because, from the same causes, you have here also a thousand phantoms, delusions, and mistakes. In place of all else I would point to another example which should be as well known to you all. I would point in silence—for pain that is new and deep has no words. It is that superb youth, who has too early fallen asleep, with whom everything his spirit touched became art. His whole contemplation of the world was forthwith a great poem. Though he had scarce more than struck the first chords, you must associate him with the most opulent poets, with those select spirits who are as profound as they are clear and vivacious. See in him the power of the enthusiasm and the caution of a pious spirit, and acknowledge that when the philosophers shall become religious and seek God like Spinoza, and the artists be pious and love Christ like Novalis, the great resurrection shall be celebrated for both worlds.[3]

But, in order that you may understand what I mean by this unity and difference of religion, science and art, we shall endeavour to descend into the inmost sanctuary of life. There, perhaps, we may find ourselves agreed. There alone you discover the original relation of intuition and feeling from which alone this identity and difference is to be understood. But I must direct you to your own selves. You must apprehend a living movement. You must know how to listen to yourselves before your own consciousness. At least you must be able to reconstruct from your consciousness your own state. What you are to notice is the rise of your consciousness and not to reflect upon something already there. Your thought can only embrace what is sundered. Wherefore as soon as you have made any given definite activity of your soul an object of communication or of contemplation, you have already begun to separate. It is impossible, therefore, to adduce any definite example, for, as soon as anything is an example, what I wish to indicate is already past. Only the faintest trace of the original unity could then be shown. Such as it is, however, I will not despise it, as a preliminary.

Consider how you delineate an object. Is there not both a stimulation and a determination by the object, at one and the same time, which for one particular moment forms your existence? The more definite your image, the more, in this way, you become the object, and the more you lose yourselves.. But just because you can trace the growing preponderance of one side over the other, both must have been one and equal in the first, the original moment that has escaped you. Or sunk in yourselves, you find all that you formerly regarded as a disconnected manifold compacted now indivisibly into the one peculiar content of your being. Yet when you give heed, can you not see as it disappears, the image of an object, from whose influence, from whose magical contact this definite consciousness has proceeded? The more your own state sways you the paler and more unrecognizable your image becomes. The greater your emotion, the more you are absorbed in it, the more your whole nature is concerned to retain for the memory an imperishable trace of what is necessarily fleeting, to carry over to what you may engage in, its colour and impress, and so unite two moments into a duration, the less you observe the object that caused it. But just because it grows pale and vanishes, it must before have been nearer and clearer. Originally it must have been one and the same with your feeling. But, as was said, these are mere traces. Unless you will go back on the first beginning of this consciousness, you can scarcely understand them.

And suppose you cannot? Then say, weighing it quite generally and originally, what is every act of your life in itself and without distinction from other acts. What is it merely as act, as movement? Is it not the coming into being of something for itself, and at the same time in the Whole? It is an endeavour to return into the Whole, and to exist for oneself at the same time. These are the links from which the whole chain is made. Your whole life is such an existence for self in the Whole. How now are you in the Whole? By your senses. And how are you for yourselves? By the unity of your self-consciousness, which is given chiefly in the possibility of comparing the varying degrees of sensation. How both can only rise together, if both together fashion every act of life, is easy to see. You become sense and the Whole becomes object. Sense and object mingle and unite, then each returns to its place, and the object rent from sense is a perception, and you rent from the object are for yourselves, a feeling. It is this earlier moment I mean, which you always experience yet never experience. The phenomenon of your life is just the result of its constant departure and return. It is scarcely in time at all, so swiftly it passes; it can scarcely be described, so little does it properly exist. Would that I could hold it fast and refer to it your commonest as well as your highest activities.

Did I venture to compare it, seeing I cannot describe it, I would say it is fleeting and transparent as the vapour which the dew breathes on blossom and fruit, it is bashful and tender as a maiden's kiss, it is holy and fruitful as a bridal embrace. Nor is it merely like, it is all this. It is the first contact of the universal life with an individual. It fills no time and fashions nothing palpable. It is the holy wedlock of the Universe with the incarnated Reason for a creative, productive embrace. It is immediate, raised above all error and misunderstanding. You lie directly on the bosom of the infinite world. In that moment, you are its soul. Through one part of your nature you feel, as your own, all its powers and its endless life. In that moment it is your body, you pervade, as your own, its muscles and members and your thinking and forecasting set its inmost nerves in motion. In this way every living, original movement in your life is first received. Among the rest it is the source of every religious emotion. But it is not, as I said, even a moment. The incoming of existence to us, by this immediate union, at once stops as soon as it reaches consciousness. Either the intuition displays itself more vividly and clearly, like the figure of the vanishing mistress to the eyes of her lover ; or feeling issues from your heart and overspreads your whole being, as the blush of shame and love over the face of the maiden. At length your consciousness is finally determined as one or other, as intuition or feeling. Then, even though you have not quite surrendered to this division and lost consciousness of your life as a unity, there remains nothing but the knowledge that they were originally one, that they issued simultaneously from the fundamental relation of your nature. Wherefore, it is in this sense true what an ancient sage has taught you, that all knowledge is recollection. It is recollection of what is outside of all time, and is therefore justly to be placed at the head of all temporal things.

And, as it is with intuition and feeling on the one hand, so it is with knowledge which includes both and with activity on the other. Through the constant play and mutual influence of these opposites, your life expands and has its place in time. Both knowledge and activity are a desire to be identified with the Universe through an object. If the power of the objects preponderates, if, as intuition or feeling, it enters and seeks to draw you into the circle of their existence, it is always a knowledge. If the preponderating power is on your side, so that you give the impress and reflect yourselves in the objects, it is activity in the narrower sense, external working. Yet it is only as you are stimulated and determined that you can communicate yourselves to things. In founding or establishing anything in the world you are only giving back what that original act of fellowship has wrought in you, and similarly everything the world fashions in you must be by the same act. One must mutually stimulate the other. Only in an interchange of knowing and activity can your life consist. A peaceful existence, wherein one side did not stimulate the other, would not be your life. It would be that from which it first developed, and into which it will again disappear.

There then you have the three things about which my Speech has so far turned,—perception, feeling and activity, and you now understand what I mean when I say they are not identical and yet are inseparable. Take what belongs to each class and consider it by itself. You will find that those moments in which you exercise power over things and impress yourselves upon them, form what you call your practical, or, in the narrower sense, your moral life; again the contemplative moments, be they few or many, in which things produce themselves in you as intuition, you will doubtless call your scientific life. Now can either series alone form a human life? Would it not be death? If each activity were not stimulated and renewed by the other, would it not be self-consumed? Yet they are not identical. If you would understand your life and speak comprehensibly of it, they must be distinguished. As it stands with these two in respect of one another, it must stand with the third in respect of both. How then are you to name this third, which is the series of feeling? What life will it form? The religious as I think, and as you will not be able to deny, when you have considered it more closely.

The chief point in my Speech is now uttered. This is the peculiar sphere which I would assign to religion—the whole of it, and nothing more. Unless you grant it, you must either prefer the old confusion to clear analysis, or produce something else, I know not what, new and quite wonderful. Your feeling is piety, in so far as it expresses, in the manner described, the being and life common to you and to the All. Your feeling is piety in so far as it is the result of the operation of God in you by means of the operation of the world upon you. This series is not made up either of perceptions or of objects of perception, either of works or operations or of different spheres of operation, but purely of sensations and the influence of all that lives and moves around, which accompanies them and conditions them. These feelings are exclusively the elements of religion, and none are excluded. There is no sensation that is not pious,⁴ except it indicate some diseased and impaired state of the life, the influence of which will not be confined to religion. Wherefore, it follows that ideas and principles are all foreign to religion. This truth we here come upon for the second time. If ideas and principles are to be anything, they must belong to knowledge which is a different department of life from religion.

Now that we have some ground beneath us, we are in a better position to inquire about the source of this confusion. May there not be some reason for this constant connection of principles and ideas with religion ? In the same way is there not a cause for the connection of action with religion ? Without such an inquiry it would be vain to proceed farther. The misunderstanding would be confirmed, for you would change what I say into ideas and begin seeking for principles in them. Whether you will follow my exposition, who can tell ? What now is to hinder that each of the functions of life just indicated should not be an object for the others ? Or does it not rather manifestly belong to their inner unity and equality that they should in this manner strive to pass over into one another ? So at least it seems to me. Thus, as a feeling person, you can become an object to yourself and you can contemplate your own feeling. Nay, you can, as a feeling person, become an object for yourself to operate upon and more and more to impress your deepest nature upon. Would you now call the general description of the nature of your feelings that is the product of this contemplation a principle, and the description of each feeling, an idea, you are certainly free to do so. And if you call them religious principles and ideas, you are not in error. But do not

forget that this is scientific treatment of religion, knowledge about it, and not religion itself.

Nor can the description be equal to the thing described.
The feeling may dwell in many sound and strong, as for
example in almost all women, without ever having been
specially a matter of contemplation. Nor may you say
religion is lacking, but only knowledge about religion.
Furthermore, do not forget what we have already established, that this contemplation presupposes the original
activity. It depends entirely upon it. If the ideas and
principles are not from reflection on a man's own feeling,
they must be learned by rote and utterly void. Make sure
of this, that no man is pious, however perfectly he understands these principles and conceptions, however much he
believes he possesses them in clearest consciousness, who
cannot show that they have originated in himself and, being
the outcome of his own feeling, are peculiar to himself.
Do not present him to me as pious, for he is not. His soul
is barren in religious matters, and his ideas are merely
supposititious children which he has adopted, in the secret
feeling of his own weakness. As for those who parade
religion and make a boast of it, I always characterize them
as unholy and removed from all divine life. One has conceptions of the ordering of the world and formulas to express
them, the other has prescriptions whereby to order himself
and inner experiences to authenticate them. The one weaves
his formulas into a system of faith, and the other spins out of
his prescriptions a scheme of salvation. It being observed
that neither has any proper standing ground without feeling,
strife ensues as to how many conceptions and declarations,
how many precepts and exercises, how many emotions and
sensations must be accepted in order to conglomerate a
sound religion that shall be neither specially cold nor enthusiastic, dry nor shallow. O fools, and slow of heart ! They
do not know that all this is mere analysis of the religious
sense, which they must have made for themselves, if it is
to have any meaning.

But if they are not conscious of having anything to
analyze, whence have they those ideas and rules? They
have memory and imitation, but that they have religion do
not believe. They have no ideas of their own from which
formulas might be known, so they must learn them by rote,
and the feelings which they would have accompanying
them are copies, and like all copies, are apt to become cari-
catures. And out of this dead, corrupt, second-hand stuff,
a religion is to be concocted! The members and juices of
an organized body can be dissected; but take these elements
now and mix them and treat them in every possible way;
and will you be able to make heart's blood of them?
Once dead, can it ever again move in a living body?
Such restoration of the products of living nature out of its
component parts, once divided, passes all human skill, and,
just as little, would you succeed with religion, however
completely the various kindred elements be given from
without. From within, in their original, characteristic
form, the emotions of piety must issue. They must be in-
dubitably your own feelings, and not mere stale descriptions
of the feelings of others, which could at best issue in a
wretched imitation.

Now the religious ideas which form those systems can and
ought to be nothing else than such a description, for religion
cannot and will not originate in the pure impulse to know.
What we feel and are conscious of in religious emotions is
not the nature of things, but their operation upon us. What
you may know or believe about the nature of things is far
beneath the sphere of religion. The Universe is ceaselessly
active and at every moment is revealing itself to us. Every
form it has produced, everything to which, from the fulness
of its life, it has given a separate existence, every occurrence
scattered from its fertile bosom is an operation of the
Universe upon us. Now religion is to take up into our
lives and to submit to be swayed by them, each of these
influences and their consequent emotions, not by themselves

but as a part of the Whole, not as limited and in opposition
to other things, but as an exhibition of the Infinite in our life.[5]
Anything beyond this, any effort to penetrate into the nature
and substance of things is no longer religion, but seeks to be
a science of some sort.

On the other hand, to take what are meant as descriptions
of our feelings for a science of the object, in some way the
revealed product of religion, or to regard it as science and
religion at the same time, necessarily leads to mysticism
and vain mythology. For example, it was religion when
the Ancients, abolishing the limitations of time and space,
regarded every special form of life throughout the whole
world as the work and as the kingdom of a being who in
this sphere was omnipresent and omnipotent, because one
peculiar way in which the Universe operates was present as
a definite feeling, and they described it after this fashion.
It was religion when they assigned a peculiar name and
built a temple to the god to whom they ascribed any helpful occurrence whereby in an obvious, if accidental, way,
the laws of the world were revealed, because they had comprehended something as a deed of the Universe, and after
their own fashion set forth its connection and peculiar
character. It was religion when they rose above the rude
iron age, full of flaws and inequalities, and sought again the
golden age on Olympus in the joyous life of the gods,
because beyond all change and all apparent evil that results
only from the strife of finite forms, they felt the ever-stir-
ring, living and serene activity of the World and the World-
Spirit. But when they drew up marvellous and complex
genealogies of the gods, or when a later faith produced a
long series of emanations and procreations, it was not religion. Even though these things may have their source in
a religious presentation of the relation of the human and
the divine, of the imperfect and the perfect, they were, in
themselves, vain mythology, and, in respect of science,
ruinous mysticism. The sum total of religion is to feel

that, in its highest unity, all that moves us in feeling is one ;
to feel that aught single and particular is only possible by
means of this unity ; to feel, that is to say, that our being
and living is a being and living in and through God. But
it is not necessary that the Deity should be presented as
also one distinct object. To many this view is necessary,
and to all it is welcome, yet it is always hazardous and
fruitful in difficulties. It is not easy to avoid the appearance of making Him susceptible of suffering like other
objects. It is only one way of characterizing God, and,
from the difficulties of it, common speech will probably
never rid itself. But to treat this objective conception of
God just as if it were a perception, as if apart from His
operation upon us through the world the existence of God
before the world, and outside of the world, though for the
world, were either by or in religion exhibited as science is,
so far as religion is concerned, vain mythology.[6] What is
only a help for presentation is treated as a reality. It is
a misunderstanding very easily made, but it is quite outside
the peculiar territory of religion.

From all this you will at once perceive how the question,
whether religion is a system or not, is to be treated. It
admits of an entire negative, and also of a direct affirmative,
in a way that perhaps you scarce expected. Religion is
certainly a system, if you mean that it is formed according
to an inward and necessary connection. That the religious
sense of one person is moved in one way, and that of another
in another is not pure accident, as if the emotions formed
no whole, as if any emotions might be caused in the same
individual by the same object. Whatever occurs anywhere, whether among many or few as a peculiar and
distinct kind of feeling is in itself complete, and by its
nature necessary. What you find as religious emotions
among Turks or Indians, cannot equally appear among
Christians. The essential oneness of religiousness spreads
itself out in a great variety of provinces, and again, in each

province it contracts itself, and the narrower and smaller the province there is necessarily more excluded as incompatible and more included as characteristic. Christianity, for example, is a whole in itself, but so is any of the divisions that may at any time have appeared in it, down to Protestantism and Catholicism in modern times. Finally, the piety of each individual, whereby he is rooted in the greater unity, is a whole by itself. It is a rounded whole, based on his peculiarity, on what you call his character, of which it forms one side. Religion thus fashions itself with endless variety, down even to the single personality.

Each form again is a whole and capable of an endless number of characteristic manifestations. You would not have individuals issue from the Whole in a finite way, each being at a definite distance from the other, so that one might be determined, construed and numbered from the others, and its characteristics be accurately determined in a conception? Were I to compare religion in this respect with anything it would be with music, which indeed is otherwise closely connected with it. Music is one great whole; it is a special, a self-contained revelation of the world. Yet the music of each people is a whole by itself, which again is divided into different characteristic forms, till we come to the genius and style of the individual. Each actual instance of this inner revelation in the individual contains all these unities. Yet while nothing is possible for a musician, except in and through the unity of the music of his people, and the unity of music generally, he presents it in the charm of sound with all the pleasure and joyousness of boundless caprice, according as his life stirs in him, and the world influences him. In the same way, despite the necessary elements in its structure, religion is, in its individual manifestations whereby it displays itself immediately in life, from nothing farther removed than from all semblance of compulsion or limitation. In life, the necessary element is taken up, taken up into freedom. Each emotion appears as the free self-determination of this very disposition, and mirrors one passing moment of the world.

It would be impious to demand here something held in constraint, something limited and determined from without. If anything of this kind lies in your conception of system then you must set it quite aside. A system of perceptions and feelings you may yourselves see to be somewhat marvellous. Suppose now you feel something. Is there not at the same time an accompanying feeling or thought—make your own choice—that you would have to feel in accordance with this feeling, and not otherwise were but this or that object, which does not now move you, to be present? But for this immediate association your feeling would be at an end, and a cold calculating and refining would take its place. Wherefore it is plainly an error to assert that it belongs to religion, to be conscious of the connection of its separate manifestations, not only to have it within, and to develope it from within, but to see it described and to comprehend it from without, and it is presumption to consider that, without it, piety is poverty-stricken. The truly pious are not disturbed in the simplicity of their way, for they give little heed to all the so-called religious systems that have been erected in consequence of this view.

Poor enough they are too, far inferior to the theories about music, defective though they be. Among those systematizers there is less than anywhere, a devout watching and listening to discover in their own hearts what they are to describe. They would rather reckon with symbols, and complete a designation which is about as accidental as the designation of the stars. It is purely arbitrary and never sufficient, for something new that should be included, is always being discovered, and a system, anything permanent and secure, anything corresponding to nature, and not the result of caprice and tradition, is not to be found in it. The designation, let the forms of religion be ever so inward and self-dependent, must be from without. Thousands might be moved religiously in the same way, and yet each, led, not so much by disposition, as by external circumstances, might designate his feeling by different symbols.[7] Furthermore, those systematizers are less anxious to present the details of religion than to subordinate them one to the other, and to deduce them from a higher. Nothing is of less importance to religion, for it knows nothing of deducing and connecting. There is no single fact in it that can be called original and chief. Its facts are one and all immediate. Without dependence on any other, each exists for itself. True, a special type of religion is constituted by one definite kind and manner of feeling, but it is mere perversion to call it a principle, and to treat it as if the rest could be deduced from it. This distinct form of a religion is found, in the same way, in every single element of religion. Each expression of feeling bears on it immediately this peculiar impress. It cannot show itself without it, nor be comprehended without it. Everything is to be found immediately, and not proved from something else. Generals, which include particulars, combination and connection belong to another sphere, if they rest on reality, or they are merely a work of phantasy and caprice. Every man may have his own regulation and his own rubrics. What is essential can neither gain nor lose thereby. Consequently, the man who truly knows the nature of his religion, will give a very subordinate place to all apparent connection of details, and will not sacrifice the smallest for the sake of it.

By taking the opposite course, the marvellous thought has arisen of a universality of one religion, of one single form which is true, and in respect of which all others are false. Were it not that misunderstanding must be guarded against, I would say that it is only by such deducing and connecting that such a comparison as true and false, which is not peculiarly appropriate to religion, has ever been reached. It only applies where we have to

do with ideas. Elsewhere the negative laws of your logic
are not in place. All is immediately true in religion, for
except immediately how could anything arise ? But that
only is immediate which has not yet passed through the
stage of idea, but has grown up purely in the feeling.
All that is religious is good, for it is only religious
as it expresses a common higher life. But the whole
circumference of religion is infinite, and is not to be comprehended under one form, but only under the sum total
of all forms.[8] It is infinite, not merely because any single
religious organization has a limited horizon, and, not
being able to embrace all, cannot believe that there is
nothing beyond ; but more particularly, because everyone
is a person by himself, and is only to be moved in his own
way, so that for everyone the elements of religion have
most characteristic differences. Religion is infinite, not only
because something new is ever being produced in time,
by the endless relations both active and passive between
different minds and the same limited matter ; not only
because the capacity for religion is never perfected, but is
ever being developed anew, is ever being more beautifully
reproduced, is ever entering deeper into the nature of man ;
but religion is infinite on all sides. As the knowledge of
its eternal truth and infallibility accompanies knowledge,
the consciousness of this infinity accompanies religion. It is
the very feeling of religion, and must therefore accompany
everyone that really has religion. He must be conscious
that his religion is only part of the whole ; that about the
same circumstances there may be views and sentiments
quite different from his, yet just as pious ; and that there
may be perceptions and feelings belonging to other modifications of religion, for which the sense may entirely fail him.

You see how immediately this beautiful modesty, this
friendly, attractive forbearance springs from the nature
of religion. How unjustly, therefore, do you reproach
religion with loving persecution, with being malignant,

with overturning society, and making blood flow like water. Blame those who corrupt religion, who flood it with an army of formulas and definitions, and seek to cast it into the fetters of a so-called system. What is it in religion about which men have quarrelled and made parties and kindled wars? About definitions, the practical some-times, the theoretical always, both of which belong else-where. Philosophy, indeed, seeks to bring those who would know to a common knowledge. Yet even philo-sophy leaves room for variety, and the more readily the better it understands itself. But religion does not, even once, desire to bring those who believe and feel to one belief and one feeling. Its endeavour is to open in those who are not yet capable of religious emotions, the sense for the unity of the original source of life. But just because each seer is a new priest, a new mediator, a new organ, he flees with repugnance the bald uniformity which would again destroy this divine abundance.

This miserable love of system [9] rejects what is strange, often without any patient examination of its claims, because, were it to receive its place, the closed ranks would be de-stroyed, and the beautiful coherence disturbed. There is the seat of the art and love of strife. War must be carried on, and persecution, for by thus relating detail to finite detail, one may destroy the other, while, in its immediate relation to the Infinite, all stand together in their original genuine connection, all is one and all is true. These syste-matizers, therefore, have caused it all. Modern Rome, god-less but consequent, hurls anathemas and ejects heretics. [10] Ancient Rome, truly pious, and, in a high style religious, was hospitable to every god. The adherents of the dead letter which religion casts out, have filled the world with clamour and turmoil.

Seers of the Infinite have ever been quiet souls. They abide alone with themselves and the Infinite, or if they do look around them, grudge to no one who understands the mighty word his own peculiar way. By means of this wide vision, this feeling of the Infinite, they are able to look beyond their own sphere. There is in religion such a capacity for unlimited manysidedness in judgment and in contemplation as is nowhere else to be found. I will not except even morality and philosophy, not at least so much of them as remains after religion is taken away. Let me appeal to your own experience. Does not every other object whereto man's thinking and striving are directed, draw around him a narrow circle, inside of which all that is highest for him is enclosed, and outside of which all appears common and unworthy ? The man who only thinks methodically, and acts from principle and design, and will accomplish this or that in the world, unavoidably circumscribes himself, and makes everything that does not forward him an object of antipathy. Only when the free impulse of seeing, and of living is directed towards the Infinite and goes into the Infinite, is the mind set in unbounded liberty. Religion alone rescues it from the heavy fetters of opinion and desire. For it, all that is is necessary, all that can be is an indispensable image of the Infinite. In this respect, it is all worthy of preservation and contemplation, however much, in other respects, and in itself, it is to be rejected. To a pious mind religion makes everything holy, even unholiness and commonness, whether he comprehends it or does not comprehend it, whether it is embraced in his system of thought, or lies outside, whether it agrees with his peculiar mode of acting or disagrees. Religion is the natural and sworn foe of all narrowmindedness, and of all onesidedness.

These charges, therefore, do not touch religion. They rest upon the confusion between religion and that knowledge which belongs to theology. It is a knowledge, whatever be its value, and is to be always distinguished from religion. Just as inapplicable are the charges you have made in respect of action. Something of this I have already touched upon, but let us take a general glance at

it in order to set it entirely aside, and to show you exactly
what I mean. Two things must be carefully distinguished.
In the first place, you charge religion with causing not
infrequently in the social, civil, and moral life, improper,
horrible, and even unnatural dealings. I will not demand
proof that these actions have proceeded from pious men.
I will grant it provisionally. But in the very utterance of
your accusation, you separate religion and morality. Do
you mean then that religion is immorality, or a branch of
it ? Scarcely, for your war against it would then be of
quite another sort, and you would have to make success in
vanquishing religion a test of morality. With the exception of a few who have shown themselves almost mad in
their mistaken zeal, you have not yet taken up this position. Or do you only mean that piety is different from
morality, indifferent in respect of it, and capable therefore
of accidentally becoming immoral ? Piety and morality can
be considered apart, and so far they are different. As
I have already admitted and asserted, the one is based on
feeling, the other on action. But how, from this opposition do you come to make religion responsible for action ?
Would it not be more correct to say that such men were
not moral enough, and had they been, they might have
been quite as pious without harm ? If you are seeking
progress—as doubtless you are—where two faculties that
should be equal have become unequal, it is not advisable
to call back the one in advance. It would be better to
urge forward the laggard.

Lest you should think I am merely quibbling, consider
that religion by itself does not urge men to activity at all.
If you could imagine it implanted in man quite alone, it
would produce neither these nor any other deeds. The
man, according to what we have said, would not act, he
would only feel. Wherefore, as you rightly complain, there
have been many most religious men in whom the proper impulses to action have been wanting, and morality been too

much in the background, who have retired from the world and have betaken themselves in solitude to idle contemplation. Religion, when isolated and morbid, is capable of such effects, but not of cruel and horrible deeds. In this way, your accusation can be turned into praise.

However different the actions you blame may be, they have this in common, that they all seem to issue immediately from one single impulse. Whether you call this special feeling religious or not, I am far from disagreeing with you when you so constantly blame it. Rather I praise you the more thorough and impartial you are. Blame also, I pray you, not only where the action appears bad, but still more where it has a good appearance. When action follows a single impulse, it falls into an undue dependence and is far too much under the influence of the external objects that work upon this one emotion. Feeling, whatever it be about, if it is not dormant, is naturally violent. It is a commotion, a force to which action should not be subject and from which it should not proceed. Quiet and discretion, the whole impress of our nature should give action birth and character, and this is as much required in common life as in politics and art. But this divergence could only come because the agent did not make his piety sufficiently evident. Wherefore, it would rather appear that, if he had been more pious he would have acted more morally. The whole religious life consists of two elements, that man surrender himself to the Universe and allow himself to be influenced by the side of it that is turned towards him is one part, and that he transplant this contact which is one definite feeling, within, and take it up into the inner unity of his life and being, is the other. The religious life is nothing else than the constant renewal of this proceeding. When, therefore, anyone is stirred, in a definite way, by the World, is it his piety that straightway sets him to such working and acting as bear the traces of commotion and disturb the pure connection of the moral life? Impossible.

On the contrary, his piety invites him to enjoy what he has won, to absorb it, to combine it, to strip it of what is temporal and individual, that it may no more dwell in him as commotion but be quiet, pure and eternal. From this inner unity, action springs of its own accord, as a natural branch of life. As we agreed, activity is a reaction of feeling, but the sum of activity should only be a reaction of the sum of feeling, and single actions should depend on something quite different from momentary feeling. Only when each action is in its own connection and in its proper place, and not when, dependently and slavishly, it corresponds to one emotion, does it exhibit, in a free and characteristic way, the whole inner unity of the spirit.

Consequently your charge does not touch religion. And, if you are speaking of a morbid state of it, you are speaking of what is quite general and is not in any way original to religion nor specially seated in it, and from which consequently nothing is to be concluded against religion in particular. Religion is of course finite, and therefore subject to imperfections, but it must be apparent to you that, in a healthy state, man cannot be represented as acting from religion or being driven to action by religion, but piety and morality form each a series by itself and are two different functions of one and the same life. But while man does nothing from religion, he should do everything with religion. Uninterruptedly, like a sacred music, the religious feelings should accompany his active life.

That by this representation of religion I am neither deceiving you nor myself, you can easily see, if you observe that each feeling in proportion as it bears the character of piety, is disposed to withdraw itself into the heart and not break forth into deeds. Would not a pious person who was right deeply moved find himself in great perplexity, or even quite fail to understand you, if you asked him by what particular action he proposed to give expression and vent to his feeling ? They are bad spirits and not good that

take possession of man, and drive him. The legions of
angels with which the Father provided His Son, exercised
no power over Him. They had no call to help Him in
any doing or forbearing, but they poured serenity and
calm into a soul exhausted with doing and thinking. For
a little, in that moment when His whole power was roused
for action, these friendly spirits were lost to His view, but
again they hovered round Him in joyous throng and
served Him. But why do I direct you to instances and
speak in images ? Because by starting from the separation which you make between religion and morality, and
following it closely, we have come back to their essential
unity in real life. This separation means corruption in the
one and weakness in the other ; and if one is not what it
should be, neither can be perfect.

There are, however, other actions you often speak of.
The distinct purpose of them is to produce religion.
Being of no importance for morality, they are not moral, and
being of no importance for sense, they are not immoral, but
they are nevertheless disastrous, because they accustom man
to attach himself to what is void and to value what is worthless. Let them be ever so inane and meaningless, they, far
too often, take the place of moral action or hide its absence.

I know what you mean. Spare me the long catalogue
of outward disciplines, spiritual exercises, privations, mortifications and the rest. All these things you accuse religion
of producing, and yet you cannot overlook the fact that the
greatest heroes of religion, the founders and reformers of
the church, have regarded them with great indifference.
There is a difference, I admit, but I believe that, in this
regard also, the subject I defend will justify itself.

First of all, let us understand what we are dealing
with. It is with action as an exercise of feeling, not with
any symbolical or significant action meant to represent
feeling. We have already seen how those dogmas and
opinions that would join themselves more closely to

religion than is fitting, are only designations and descriptions of feeling. In short, they are a knowledge
about feeling, and in no way an immediate knowledge
about the operations of the Universe, that gave rise to the
feeling. We saw also, how it necessarily resulted in evil,
when they were put in place of the feeling, of the proper
and original perception. Similarly this conducting and
exercising of feeling which often turns out so vain and
meaningless, is an acting at second-hand. Just as that
knowledge made feeling an object to be contemplated and
understood, this acting makes it an object to be operated
upon and cultivated. What value this kind of activity may
have, and whether it may not be as unreal as that kind of
knowing, I shall not here decide. In what sense man can
act upon himself and particularly upon his feeling is
difficult to determine, and needs to be well weighed. Can
it be the result of a personal resolve, or does it not rather
appear to be the business of the Whole, and therefore a
given product of life? But as I said, this does not belong
here, and I would rather discuss it with the friends of
religion than with you. So much, however, is certain, and
I grant it fully, that few errors are so disastrous as the
substitution of these disciplinary exercises of feeling for
the original feeling itself. Only, it is plainly an error into
which religious men could not fall.

If you would recall that something quite similar is to be
found in morality, you would perhaps at once agree with me.
Men, as they say, lay down for themselves just such acting
upon their own acting, just such exercisings of morals, to
the end of self-improvement. It happens that these are
sometimes put in place of direct moral action, of goodness
and righteousness themselves, but you would not admit that
it is through moral men. Men do all kinds of things,
accepting them from one and transmitting them to another,
though they have no meaning or value for themselves.

These actions are always, however, to be understood as

being done to rouse, sustain and direct religious feeling. Where the activity is self-produced and really has this meaning, it manifestly rests on the man's own feeling. A special state of feeling of which the man is conscious, is presupposed, a knowledge of his own inner life with its weaknesses and inequalities. It presupposes an interest, a higher self-love directed to himself, as a morally feeling person, as an essential part of the spiritual world. When this love ceases, the action also must cease. By supplanting feeling, it abolishes itself, and such an error could only arise among those who are in their hearts hostile to piety.

For them such exercisings of feeling have a special worth, as if they also had some of the hidden virtue, seeing they can outwardly imitate what, in others, has a deep significance. Consciously or unconsciously, they deceive themselves and others with the appearance of a higher life which they do not really have. Either it is base hypocrisy or wretched superstition, and I willingly expose it to your condemnation. No exercise of this kind is of any value, and we shall reject not only what, regarded by itself, is manifestly void, unnatural and perverted, but all that in this way arises, however specious. Severe mortifications, dull renunciation of the beautiful, empty phrases and usages and charities shall all be reckoned at the same value. Every superstition shall be alike unholy.

But we must never confuse it with the well-meant endeavours of pious souls. The difference is easy to discern. Each religious person fashions his own asceticism according to his need, and looks for no rule outside of himself, while the superstitious person and the hypocrite adhere strictly to the accepted and traditional, and are zealous for it, as for something universal and holy. This zeal is natural, for if they were expected to think out for themselves, their own outward discipline and exercise, their own training of the feelings, having regard to their own personal state, they would be in an evil case, and their inward poverty could be no longer hidden.

The most general, almost preliminary truths have long delayed us. They should have been understood of themselves, but neither you, nor many who would at least wish to be counted among you, understood the relation of religion to the other branches of life. Wherefore, it was necessary to drain off at once the sources of the commonest misconceptions, that they might not afterwards retard us. This having been done to the utmost of my ability, we have now, I hope, firm ground beneath us. We have attached ourselves to that moment, which is never directly observed, but in which all the different phenomena of life fashion themselves together, as in the buds of some plants blossom and fruit are both enclosed. When, therefore, we have asked where now among all it produces is religion chiefly to be sought, we have found only one right and consistent answer. Chiefly where the living contact of man with the world fashions itself as feeling. These feelings are the beautiful and sweet scented flowers of religion, which, after the hidden activity opens, soon fall, but which the divine growth ever anew produces from the fulness of life. A climate of paradise is thus created in which no penuriousness disturbs the development, and no rude surrounding injures the tender lights and fine texture of its flowers. To this I would now conduct you, your vision having been purified and prepared.

First of all, then, follow me to outward nature, which is to many the first and only temple of the Godhead. In virtue of its peculiar way of stirring the heart, it is held to be the inmost sanctuary of religion. At present, however, this outward nature, although it should be more, is little else than the outer court, for the view with which you next oppose me is utterly to be repudiated. The fear of the powers which rule in nature, which spare nothing, which threaten the life and works of man, is said to give the first feeling of the Infinite, or even to be the sole basis of religion. Surely in that case you must admit that if piety came with fear it must go with fear.

Let us then consider the matter. Manifestly the great aim of all industry spent in cultivating the earth is to destroy the dominion of the powers of nature over man, and to bring all fear of them to an end. Already a marvellous amount has been done. The lightnings of Zeus terrify no more since Hephaistus has prepared for us a shield against them; and Hestia protects what she has won from Poseidon, even against the angriest blows of his trident; the sons of Ares unite with those of Æsculapius to ward off the deadly arrows of Apollo. Man is ever learning to resist and to destroy one of these gods by means of the others, and is preparing soon, as conqueror and lord, to be but a smiling spectator at this play. Were fear then the ground of reverence for the powers of nature, by thus mutually destroying one another, they would gradually appear ordinary and common; for what man has controlled or attempted to control, he can measure, and what is measurable cannot stand in awful opposition to him as the Infinite. The objects of religion would thus be ever more and more unfaithful to it. But, are they? Would not these gods, conducting themselves towards one another as brethren and kinsfolk, and caring for man as the youngest son of the same Father, be just as zealously worshipped? If you are still capable of being filled with reverence for the great powers of nature, does it depend on your security or insecurity? When you stand under your lightning conductors, have you, perhaps, a laugh ready wherewith to mock the thunder? Is not nature protecting and sustaining quite as much an object of adoration? Or, consider it in this way. Does the great and infinite alone threaten man's existence and oppose his working? Does he not also suffer from much that is small and paltry, which, because it cannot be definitely comprehended or fashioned into something great, you call accident and the accidental? Has this ever been made an object of religion and been

worshipped? If you have such a small conception of the
Fate of the Ancients, you must have understood little of
their poetic piety. Under this dread Fate the sustaining
powers were as much embraced as the destructive. Very
different from that slavish fear, to banish which was a credit
and a virtue, was the holy reverence for Fate, the rejection
of which, in the best and most cultured times of Antiquity,
was accounted, among better disposed persons, absolute
recklessness.[11] Such a sacred reverence I will readily acknowledge as the first element of religion, but the fear you
mean is not only not religion itself, it is not even preparatory or introductory. If it should be praised, it must be
for urging men, by the desire to be rid of it, into earthly
fellowship in the state. But piety first begins when it is
put aside, for the aim of all religion is to love the World-
Spirit [12] and joyfully to regard his working, and fear is not
in love.

But that joy in Nature, which so many extol, is just as
little truly religious. I almost hate to speak of their
doings when they dart off into the great, glorious world to
get for themselves little impressions : how they inspect the
delicate markings and tints of flowers, or gaze at the magic
play of colours in the glowing evening sky, and how they
admire the songs of the birds on a beautiful country-side.
They are quite full of admiration and transport, and will
have it that no instrument could conjure forth these sounds
and no brush attain this gloss and marking. But suppose
we take their course and subtilize after their fashion!
What is it that they do admire ? Rear the plant in a dark
cellar, and, if you are successful, you can rob it of all these
beauties, without in the least degree altering its nature.
Suppose the vapour above us somewhat differently disposed ;
instead of that splendour, you would have before your eyes
one unpleasant grayness, and yet what you are contemplating
would be essentially the same. Once more, try to imagine
how the midday sun, the glare of which you cannot endure,

already appears to the inhabitants of the East the glimmering twilight. Is it not manifest, then, when they have not the same sensation, that they have gone after a mere void appearance? But they do not believe in it merely as an appearance; it is for them really true. They are in perplexity between appearance and reality, and what is so doubtful cannot be a religious stimulus, and can call forth no genuine feeling. Were they children who, without further thinking and willing, without comparison and reflection, received the light and splendour, their hearts being opened for the world by the soul of the world, so that they are stirred to pious feeling by every object; or were they sages in whose clear intuition all strife between appearance and reality is resolved, and who, therefore, undisturbed by these refinements, can again be stirred like children, their joy would be a real and pure feeling, a living impulse, a gladly communicative contact between them and the world. If you understand this better way, then you can say that this also is a necessary and indispensable element of religion. But do not present me that empty affected thing that sits so loose and is but a wretched mask for their cold, hard refinement, as an emotion of piety. In opposing religion, do not ascribe to it what does not belong to it. Do not scoff, as if man entered most easily into this sanctuary by being debased to fear of the irrational, and by vain trifling with transitory show, as if piety were easiest, and most becoming to timid, weak, sensitive souls.

The next thing to meet us in corporeal nature is its material boundlessness, the enormous masses which are scattered over illimitable space and which circulate in measureless orbits. Many hold that the exhaustion of the imagination, when we try to expand our diminished pictures of them to their natural size, is the feeling of the greatness and majesty of the Universe. This arithmetical amazement which, just on account of their ignorance, is easiest to awake in infants and ignoramuses, you are quite right in finding somewhat childish and worthless. But would those who are accustomed to take this view grant us that, when these great orbits had not yet been calculated, when half of those worlds were not discovered, nay, when it was not yet known that these shining points were worlds, piety, lacking one essential element, was necessarily poorer? Just as little can they deny that, in so far as it can be conceived—and without that it means nothing for us—the infinity of mass and number is only finite and the mind can comprehend every infinity of this kind into short formulæ, and reckon with them, as daily happens. But they would certainly not grant that anything of their reverence for the greatness and majesty of the Universe is lost through advancing education and skill. As soon, however, as we are in a position to compare these units, which are our measure of size and motion, with those great world units, this spell of number and mass must disappear. As long as this feeling rests on difference of mass, it is merely a feeling of personal incapacity, which is doubtless a religious feeling, but is not that glorious reverence, as exalting as it is humbling, which is the feeling of our relation to the Whole. Neither a world operation too great for an organization, nor anything beyond it from smallness, can constitute this feeling, but it must be just as strong when the operation is equal and conformable to our powers.

What moves us so wondrously is not the contrast between small and great, but the essence of greatness, the external law in virtue of which size and number in general first arose. Life alone can work on us in a characteristic way, and not what is captive to weight and in so far dead. The religious sense corresponds not to the masses in the outer world, but to their eternal laws. Rise to the height of seeing how these laws equally embrace all things, the greatest and the smallest, the world systems and the mote which floats in the air, and then say whether you are not conscious of the divine unity and the eternal immutability of the world.

By the most constant repetition, some elements in these laws cannot escape even common perception. There is the order in which all movements return in the heavens and on the earth, the recognized coming and going of all organized forces, the perpetual trustworthiness of the rules of mechanics, and the eternal uniformity in the striving of plastic Nature. But, if it is allowable to make a comparison, this regularity gives a less great and lively religious feeling than the sense of law in all difference. Nor should this appear strange to you.

Suppose you are looking at a fragment of a great work of art. In the separate parts of this fragment you perceive beautiful outlines and situations, complete and fully to be understood without anything besides. Would not the fragment then rather appear a work by itself than a part of a greater work, and would you not judge that, if the whole was wrought throughout in this style, it must lack breadth and boldness and all that suggests a great spirit? If a loftier unity is to be suspected, along with the general tendency to order and harmony, there must be here and there situations not fully explicable. Now the world is a work of which you only see a part. Were this part perfectly ordered and complete in itself, we could be conscious of the greatness of the whole only in a limited way.

You see that the irregularity of the world, so often employed against religion, has really a greater value for religion than the order which is first presented to us in our study of the world and which is visible in a smaller part. The perturbations in the course of the stars point to a higher unity and a bolder combination than those we have already discovered in the regularity of their orbits. The anomalies, the idle sports of plastic Nature, compel us to see that she handles her most definite forms with free, nay capricious arbitrariness, with a phantasy the laws of which only a higher standpoint can show.

Wherefore, in the religion of the Ancients, only inferior

divinities and ministering virgins had the oversight of all that recurred uniformly and had an already discovered order, but the exceptions which were not understood, the revolutions for which there was no law, were the work of the father of the gods. We also have strange, dread, mysterious emotions, when the imagination reminds us that there is more in nature than we know. They are easy to distinguish from the quiet and settled consciousness that everything is involved in the most distant combinations of the Whole, that every individual thing is determined by the yet unexplored general life. This consciousness is produced by what we understand in Nature, but I mean those dim presentiments which are the same in all, even though, as is right, only the educated seek to elucidate them and change them into a more lively activity of perception. In others, being comprehended in ignorance and misunderstanding, they grow to a delusion which we call pure superstition, under which, however, there manifestly lies a pious shudder of which we shall not be ashamed.

Furthermore, consider how you are impressed by the universal opposition of life and death. The sustained, conquering power, whereby every living thing nourishes itself, forcefully awakes the dead and enters it on a new course by drawing it into its own life. On every side we find provision prepared for all living, not lying dead, but itself alive and everywhere being reproduced. With all this multitude of forms of life, and the enormous mass of material which each uses in turn, there is enough for all. Thus each completes his course and succumbs to an inward fate and not to outward want. What a feeling of endless fulness and superabundant riches! How are we impressed by a universal paternal care and a childlike confidence that without anxiety plays away sweet life in a full and abundant world! Consider the lilies of the field, they sow not, neither do they reap, yet your Heavenly Father feedeth them, wherefore be not anxious. This happy view, this serene, easy mind was for one of the greatest heroes of religion, the fair profit of a very limited and meagre communion with nature. How much more should we win who have been permitted by a richer age to go deeper !

Already we know something more of the universally distributed forces, the eternal laws, whereby individual things, that is things which have their souls in themselves apart, in a more definite boundary, in what we call bodies, are fashioned and destroyed. See how attraction and repulsion, everywhere and always active, determine everything ; and how all difference and opposition are again resolved into a higher unity. Only in appearance, can anything finite boast itself of a separate existence. See how all likeness is concealed by being distributed in a thousand different shapes. Nothing simple is to be found, but all is skilfully connected and interwoven. We would see and exhort all who share in the culture of the age to observe, how, in this sense, the Spirit of the World reveals itself as visibly, as completely, in small as in great, and we would not stop with such a consciousness of it as might be had anywhere and from anything. Even without all the knowledge which has made our century glorious, the World-Spirit showed itself to the most ancient sages. Not only did they have, by intuition, the first pure speaking image of the world, but there was kindled in their hearts a love for nature and a joy in her, that is for us still lovely and pleasing. Had this but penetrated to the people, who knows what strong and lofty way religion might have taken from the beginning ? At present it has penetrated to all who would be considered cultured. Through the gradual operation of the fellowship between knowledge and feeling, they have arrived at the immediate feeling that there is nothing even in their own nature that is not a work of this Spirit, an exhibition and application of these laws. In virtue of this feeling, all that touches their life becomes truly a world, a unity permeated by the Divinity that fashions it. It is natural, therefore,

that there should be in them all, that love and joy, that
deep reverence for nature which made sacred the art and
life of Antiquity, which was the source of that wisdom, which
we have returned to and are at length beginning to commend
and glorify by fruits long delayed. Such a feeling of being
one with nature, of being quite rooted in it, so that in all
the changing phenomena of life, even in the change between life and death itself, we might await all that should
befall us with approbation and peace, as merely the working
out of those eternal laws, would indeed be the germ of all
the religious feelings furnished by this side of existence.

But is it so easy to find original in nature the love and
resistance, the unity and peculiarity, whereby it is a Whole
for us ? Just because our sense tends in quite another direction, is there so little truly religious enjoyment of nature. The
sense of the Whole must be first found, chiefly within our
own minds, and from thence transferred to corporeal nature.
Wherefore the spirit is for us not only the seat of religion
but its nearest world.[13] The Universe portrays itself in the
inner life, and then the corporeal is comprehensible from
the spiritual. If the mind is to produce and sustain religion it must operate upon us as a world and as in a world.

Let me reveal a secret to you that lies almost hidden in
one of the oldest sources of poetry and religion. As long
as the first man was alone with himself and nature, the Deity
ruled over him and addressed him in various ways, but he did
not understand and answered nothing. His paradise was
beautiful, the stars shone down on him from a beautiful
heaven, but there awoke in him no sense for the world.
Even from within, this sense was not developed. Still his
mind was stirred with longing for a world, and he collected
the animal creation before him, if perhaps out of them a
world might be formed. Then the Deity recognized that
the world would be nothing, as long as man was alone.
He created a helpmate for him. At length the deep-toned
harmonies awoke in him, and the world fashioned itself

before his eyes. In flesh of his flesh, and bone of his bone, he discovered humanity. In this first love he had a foretaste of all love's forms and tendencies—in humanity he found the world. From this moment he was capable of seeing and hearing the voice of the Deity, and even the most insolent transgression of His laws did not any more shut him out from intercourse with the Eternal Being.[14]

The history of us all is related in this sacred legend. All is present in vain for those who set themselves alone. In order to receive the life of the World-Spirit, and have religion, man must first, in love, and through love, have found humanity. Wherefore, humanity and religion are closely and indissolubly united. A longing for love, ever satisfied and ever again renewed, forthwith becomes religion. Each man embraces most warmly the person in whom the world mirrors itself for him most clearly and purely ; he loves most tenderly the person whom he believes combines all he lacks of a complete manhood. Similarly the pious feelings are most holy that express for him existence in the whole of humanity, whether as blessedness in attaining or of need in coming short.

Wherefore, to find the most glorious elements of religion, let us enter upon the territory where you are in your peculiar, your most loved home. Here your inner life had its birth, here you see the goal of all your striving and doing before your eyes, and here you feel the growth of your powers whereby you are evermore conducted towards it. Humanity itself is for you the true universe, and the rest is only added in so far as it is related to it or forms its surroundings. Even for me, this point of view suffices. Yet it has often pained me that, with all your interest in humanity, and with all your zeal for it, you are always in difficulties with it, and divided from it, and pure love cannot become right prominent in you. Each of you in his own way harasses himself to improve it, and to educate it, and what will not come to an issue you finally cast aside in dejection.

I make bold to say, that this also comes from your lack of religion. You wish to work on humanity, and you select men, individuals for contemplation. They displease you vastly. Among the thousand possible causes, unquestionably that which is finest in itself, and which belongs to the best of you, is that you are, in your own way, far too ethical. You take men singly, and you have an ideal of the individual to which no one corresponds. If you would begin with religion, you would have far more success. If you would only attempt to exchange the objects of your working and the objects of your contemplation! Work on individuals, but rise in contemplation, on the wings of religion, to endless, undivided humanity. Seek this humanity in each individual; regard the nature of every person as one revelation of it, and of all that now oppresses you no trace would remain. I at least boast myself of a moral disposition, I know how to value human excellence, and commonness could almost overwhelm me with the unpleasant feeling of contempt, were it not that religion gives me a great and glorious view of all.

Just consider what a consummate artist the Genius of humanity is. It can make nothing that has not a nature of its own. As soon as it assays its brush, or sharpens its pencil, there appear living and significant features. It imagines and fashions countless forms. Millions wear the costume of the time, and are faithful pictures of its necessities and its tastes. In others there are memories of the past, or presentiments of a distant future. Some are most lofty and striking types of the fairest and divinest, others resemble grotesques produced in the most original and fleeting mood of a master. The common view, based on a misunderstanding of the sacred words that there are vessels of honour and vessels of dishonour, is not pious. Only by comparing details could such an opposition appear to you. You must not contemplate anything alone, you must rather rejoice in everything in its own place. All that we can be

conscious of at once, all, as it were, that stands on one
sheet, presents one movement of the complete working of
the Whole, and belongs, as it were, to one great historical
picture. Would you make light of the chief groups that
give life and affluence to the Whole? Should not each
heavenly form be glorified in having a thousand others
that regard it and are related to it, bowing before it?
Indeed, there is more in this presentation than a mere
simile. Eternal humanity is unweariedly active, seeking to
step forth from its inward, mysterious existence into the
light, and to present itself in the most varied way, in the
fleeting manifestation of the endless life. That is the
harmony of the Universe, the wondrous and unparalleled
unity of that eternal work of art.

Being occupied in the outer court of morality, and there
only with elements, caring for details and satisfied with
them, and despising high religion, you slander its magnificence by your demands for a lamentable dismemberment.
This is sufficient to indicate your need, may you now recognize it and satisfy it! Make search among all the circumstances in which the heavenly order portrays itself, and
perhaps some favourite passage of history may be a divine
sign to you, whereby you may more easily recognize how
real the insignificant is, and how important for the Whole.
Then what you regard with coldness or contempt may draw
you with love. Or, allow yourselves to be pleased with an
old, rejected conception ; seek out among the holy men, in
whom humanity is pre-eminently revealed, someone to be
a mediator between your limited way of thinking, and the
eternal laws of the world. And when you have found one
who, in a way you understand, by imparting himself,
strengthens the weak, and gives life to the dead, traverse
humanity, and let all that has hitherto seemed useless and
wretched be illuminated by the reflection of this new light.

What would the uniform repetition of even a highest ideal
be? Mankind, time and circumstances excepted, would be

identical. They would be the same formula with a different
co-efficient. What would it be in comparison with the endless variety which humanity does manifest? Take any
element of humanity, and you will find it in almost every
possible condition. You will not find it quite by itself, nor
quite combined with all other elements, but you will find all
possible mixtures between, in every odd and unusual combination. And if you could think of unions you do not see,
this gap would be a negative revelation of the Universe, an
indication that, in the present temperature of the world, this
mixture is not possible, in the requisite degree. Your
imagination thus gives you a glimpse beyond the present
boundaries of humanity, and whether it be only a ray from
a vanished past, or an involuntary and unconscious prophecy
of the future, it is a real higher inspiration. And just as
this, that seems to come short of the requisite infinite
variety is not really too little, so what, from your standpoint appears superfluous, is not really too much.

This oft-bewailed superfluity of the commonest forms of
humanity, ever returning unchanged in a thousand copies,
does not disturb the pious mind. The Eternal Mind commands that the forms in which individuality is most difficult
to discern, should stand closest together, and even the finite
mind can see the reason why. And each has something of
its own, and no two are identical. In every life there is some
moment, like the coruscation of baser metals, when, by the
approach of something higher, or by some electric shock, it
surpasses itself and stands on the highest pinnacle of its possibilities. For this moment it was created, in this moment it
fulfilled its purpose, and, after this moment its exhausted
vitality again subsides. To call forth this moment in ordinary souls and to contemplate them during it is a pleasure
to be envied, and to those who have not known it, the whole
existence of them must appear superfluous and despicable.

Yet the existence of such an ordinary soul has a double
meaning in respect of the Whole. If I arrest in thought

the course of that unresting machinery whereby all that is human is woven together and made interdependent, I see that each individual in his inner nature is a necessary complement of a complete intuition of humanity. One shows me how any fragment, if only the plastic impulse of the Whole still quickens it, can calmly progress, fashioning itself in graceful, regular forms; another how, from want of a vivifying and combining warmth, the hardness of the earthly material cannot be overcome; while, in a third, I see how, in an atmosphere too violently agitated, the spirit within is disturbed in its working, so that nothing comes clearly and recognizably to light. One appears as the rude and animal portion of mankind, stirred only by the first ungainly motions of humanity; another is the pure dematerialized spirit that, having been separated from all that is base and unworthy, hovers with noiseless foot over the earth. But everything between also has a purpose. It shows how, in the minute detached phenomena of individual lives, the different elements of human nature all appear at every stage and in every manner. It is not enough that among this countless multitude there are always a few at least who are the distinguished representatives of humanity, who strike different melodious chords that require no further accompaniment, and no subsequent explication, but who, in the one note, charm and satisfy by their harmony the whole soul. But even the noblest only presents mankind in one way and in one of its movements, and in some sense everyone is a peculiar exhibition of humanity and does the same thing, and were a single figure to fail in the great picture, it would be impossible to comprehend it completely and perfectly. If now every one is so essentially connected with that which is the inner kernel of our own life, how can we avoid feeling this connection, and embracing all, without distinction of disposition or mental capacity, with heartfelt liking and affection? That is one meaning that every individual has in respect of the Whole.

Do I, on the other hand, observe the eternal wheels of humanity in motion, this vast interaction, nothing moved by itself, nothing moving only itself, I am greatly quieted about the other side of your complaint, that reason and soul, sensuality and morality, understanding and blind force appear in such separate masses. Why do you see things singly that are not single and do not work by themselves? The reason of one and the disposition of another have as strong a mutual influence as if they were in one and the same subject. The morality that belongs to this sensuality is set apart from it, and do you suppose its dominion is, on that account, limited? Would the sensuality be better ruled if the morality, without being specially concentrated anywhere, were divided out in small, scarce noticeable portions to each individual? The blind power which is allotted to the great mass, is not, in its operation on the Whole, abandoned to a rude peradventure, but the understanding, concentrated at other points, leads it, without being aware of the fact, and it follows, in invisible bands, quite as unconsciously. The outlines of personality which appear to you so definite, from my standpoint, dissolve. The magic circle of prevailing opinions and infectious feelings surrounds all and plays around all like an atmosphere filled with dissolving and magnetic forces. By the most vital diffusion it smelts all things, even the most distant, into a single activity, the issue of which is to impel those who are really in possession of light and truth to activity, so that some are deeply influenced, and others have at least a superficial illumination, brilliant and deceptive.

In this connection of everything with the sphere to which it belongs and in which it has significance all is good and divine, and a fulness of joy and peace is the feeling of those who allow all things to work upon them in this great connection. But they will also feel how contemplation isolates single things in single moments. The common impulse of men, who know nothing of this dependence, is to seize and retain this and that, to hedge in their Ego and to

surround it with manifold outworks. They seek to conduct
their own existence according to their own self-will and not
be disturbed by the eternal current of the world. And
when we who have an entirely opposite impulse perceive
how fate necessarily sweeps all this away and how they
wound and torture themselves in a thousand ways, what is
more natural than the most heartfelt compassion with all
the bitter suffering that must arise from this unequal strife,
and with all the stripes which awful Nemesis deals out on
every side ?

From these wanderings through the whole territory of
humanity, pious feeling returns, quickened and educated,
into its own Ego, and there finds all the influences that had
streamed upon it from the most distant regions. If, on
returning with the consecration of intercourse with the
world still fresh upon us, we give heed how it is with us in
this feeling, we become conscious that our Ego vanishes,
not only into smallness and insignificance, but into one-
sidedness, insufficiency and nothingness. What lies nearer
to mortal man than unaffected humility ? And when gradually our feeling becomes quick and alert to what there is in
the path of humanity that sustains and forwards, and what,
on the contrary, must sooner or later be conquered and
destroyed, if it is not recast and transformed, and when
from this law we regard all doings in the world, what is
more natural than deep contrition for all in us that is hostile
to human nature, the submissive desire to conciliate the
Deity, and the most earnest longing to put ourselves and all
that belongs to us in safety in that sacred region where
alone there is security against death and destruction ?
Advancing further, we perceive how the Whole only
becomes clear to us, how we only reach intuition of it and
unity with it in fellowship with others, by the influence
of those who have long been freed from dependence on
their own fleeting being, and from the endeavour to expand
and isolate it. How, then, can we avoid a feeling of special

affinity to those whose actions have defended our existence, and happily guided it through threatening dangers? Though by us they become conscious of their life in the Whole, we honour them as those who, before us, have reached this union.

Not by examples which are rare, but by passing through these and similar feelings you discover in yourselves the outlines of the fairest and the basest, the noblest and the most despicable. You not only find at times all the manifold degrees of human powers within you, but when self-love is quite submerged in sympathy, all the count-less mixture of human tendencies that you have ever seen in the characters of others appears simply arrested impulses of your own life. There are moments when, de-spite all distinction of sex, culture, or environment, you think, feel, and act as if you were really this or that person. In your own order, you have actually passed through all those different forms. You are a compendium of humanity. In a certain sense your single nature embraces all human nature. Your Ego, being multiplied and more clearly out-lined, is in all its smallest and swiftest changes immortalized in the manifestations of human nature. As soon as this is seen, you can love yourselves with a pure and blameless love. Humility, that never forsakes you, has its counter-part in the feeling that the whole of humanity lives and works in you. Even contrition is sweetened to joyful self-sufficiency. This is the completion of religion on this side. It works its way back to the heart, and there finds the Infinite. The man in whom this is accomplished, is no more in need of a mediator for any sort of intuition of humanity. Rather he is himself a mediator for many.

But there is not merely the swinging of feeling between the world and the individual, in the present moment. Except as something going on, we cannot comprehend what affects us, and we cannot comprehend ourselves, except as thus progressively affected. Wherefore, as feeling persons, we are ever driven back into the past. The spirit furnishes the chief nourishment for our piety, and history immediately and especially is for religion the richest source. History is not of value for religion, because it hastens or controls in any way the progress of humanity in its development, but because it is the greatest and most general revelation of the deepest and holiest. In this sense, however, religion begins and ends with history. Prophecy and history are for religion the same and indistinguishable, and all true history has at first had a religious purpose, and has taken its departure from religious ideas.

What is finest and tenderest in history, moreover, cannot be communicated scientifically, but can only be comprehended in the feeling of a religious disposition. The religious mind recognizes the transmigration of spirits and souls, which to others is but graceful fiction, as, in more than one sense, a wonderful arrangement of the Universe for comparing the different periods of humanity according to a sure standard. After a long period, during which nature could produce nothing similar, some distinguished individual almost entirely the same returns. But only the seers recognize him, and it is they who should judge by his works the signs of different times. A movement of humanity returns exactly like something of which some distant foretime has left you an image, and you are to recognize from the various causes which have now produced it, the course of development and the formula of its law. The genius of some human endowment awakes as from slumber. Here and there rising and falling, it has already finished its course. Now it appears in a new life in another place and under different circumstances. Its quicker increase, its deeper working, its fairer stronger form, indicate how much the climate of humanity has improved, and how much fitter the soil has grown to nourish nobler plants. Peoples and generations of mortals appear as all alike necessary for the completeness of history, though, like individuals, of different worth. Some are estimable and spirited, and work strongly without ceasing, permeating space and defying time. Others are common and insignificant, fitted only to show some peculiar shade of some single form of life. For one moment only they are really living and noticeable. One thought they exhibit, one conception they produce, and then they hasten towards destruction that the power that produced them may be given to something else. As vegetable nature, from the destruction of whole species, and from the ruins of whole generations of plants, produces and nourishes a new race, so spiritual nature rears from the ruins of a glorious and beautiful world of men, a new world that draws its first vital strength from elements decomposed and wondrously transformed. Being deeply impressed with this sense of a universal connection, your glance perhaps passes so often directly from least to greatest and greatest to least, going backwards and forwards, till through dizziness it can neither distinguish great nor small, cause nor effect, preservation nor destruction. This state continues, and then that well-known figure of an eternal fate appears. Its features bear the impress of this state, being a marvellous mixture of obstinate self-will and deep wisdom, of rude unfeeling force and heartfelt love, of which first one seizes you and then another, now inviting you to impotent defiance and now to childlike submission.

Penetrate further and compare this partial striving of the individual, the fruit of opposing views, with the quiet uniform course of the Whole. You will see how the high World-Spirit smilingly marches past all that furiously opposes him. You will see how dread Nemesis, never wearied, follows his steps, meting out punishment to the haughty who resist the gods. Even the stoutest and choicest who have with steadfastness, worthy perhaps of praise and wonder, refused to bow before the gentle breath of the great Spirit, it mows down with iron hand. Would you comprehend the proper character of all changes and of all human progress, a feeling resting on history must show you more surely than aught else, that living gods rule who hate nothing so much as death, and that nothing is to be persecuted and destroyed like this first and last foe of the spirit. The rude, the barbarian, the formless are to be absorbed and recast. Nothing is to be a dead mass that moves only by impact and resists only by unconscious collision ; all is to be individual, connected, complex, exalted life. Blind instinct, unthinking custom, dull obedience, everything lazy and passive, all those sad symptoms of the death slumber of freedom and humanity are to be abolished. To this the work of the minutes and the centuries is directed, it is the great ever advancing work of redemptive love.

Some prominent emotions of religion connected with nature and humanity, I have now sketched in vague outline. I have brought you to the limits of your horizon. Here is the end and summit of religion for all to whom humanity is the whole world. But consider that in your feeling there is something that despises these bounds, something in virtue of which you cannot stay where you are. Beyond this point only infinity is to be looked into. I will not speak of the presentiments which define themselves and become thoughts which might by subtilty be established, that humanity, being capable of motion and cultivation, being not only differently manifested in the individual, but here and there really being different, cannot possibly be the highest, the sole manifestation of the unity of spirit and matter. As the individual is only one form of humanity, so humanity may be only one form of this unity. Beside it many other similar forms may exist, bounding it and standing over against it. But in our own feeling we all find something similar. The dependence of our earth, and therefore of the highest unity it has produced, upon other worlds, has been impressed upon us both by nature and by education. Hence this ever active but seldom understood presentiment of some other marriage of spirit and matter, visible and finite, but above humanity, higher and closer and productive of more beautiful forms. But any sketch that could be drawn would be too definite. Any echo of the feeling could only be fleeting and vague. Hence it is exposed to misconception and is so often taken for folly and superstition.

This is sufficient reference to a thing so immeasurably far from you. More would be incomprehensible. Had you only the religion that you could have! Were you but conscious of what you already have! Were you to consider the few religious opinions and feelings that I have so slightly sketched, you would be very far from finding them all strange to you. Something of the same kind you must have had in your thoughts before. But I do not know whether to lack religion quite, or not to understand it, is the greater misfortune. In the latter case also it fails of its purpose, and you impose upon yourselves in addition.

Two things I would specially blame in you. Some things you select and stamp as exclusively religious, other things you withdraw from religion as exclusively moral. Both you apparently do on the same ground. Religion with you is the retribution which alights on all who resist the Spirit of the Whole, it is the hatred everywhere active against haughtiness and audacity, the steady advance of all human things to one goal. You are conscious of the feeling that points to this unfailing progress. After it has been purified from all abuses, you would willingly see it sustained and extended. But you will then have it that this is exclusively religion, and you would exclude other feelings that take their rise from the same operation of the mind in exactly the same way.

How have you come to this torn off fragment? I will tell you. You do not regard it as religion but as an echo of moral action, and you simply wish to foist the name upon it, in order to give religion the last blow. What we have agreed to acknowledge as religion does not arise exclusively in the moral sphere, not at least in the narrow sense in which you understand the word. Feeling knows nothing of such a limited predilection. If I direct you specially to the sphere of the spirit and to history, it does not follow that the moral world is religion's Universe. In your narrow sense of it the moral world would produce very few religious emotions. The pious man can detect the operation of the World-Spirit in all that belongs to human activity, in play and earnest, in smallest things and in greatest. Everywhere he perceives enough to move him by the presence of this Spirit and without this influence nothing is his own. Therein he finds a divine Nemesis that those who, being predominantly ethical or rather legal, would, by selecting from religion only the elements suited to this purpose, make of it an insignificant appendage to morals, do yet, purify religion as they may, irrecoverably corrupt their moral doctrine itself and sow in it the seed of new errors. When anyone succumbs in moral action, it sounds well to say it is the will of the Eternal, and that what does not succeed through us, will sometime, by others, come to pass. But if this high assurance belonged to moral action, moral action would be dependent on the degree of receptivity for this assurance in each person at any moment. Morality cannot include immediately aught of feeling without at once having its original power and purity disturbed.

With all those feelings, love, humility, joy, and the others that I pictured as the undulation of the mind between the two points of which the world is one, and your Ego the other, you deal in another way. The ancients knew what was right. They called them all piety. For them those feelings were an essential part of religion, the noblest part. You also recognize them, but you try to persuade yourselves that they are an essential section of your moral action. You would justify these sentiments on moral principles, and assign them their place in your moral system. But in vain, for, if you remain true to yourselves, they will there neither be desired nor endured. If action proceed directly from the emotions of love or affection, it will be insecure and thoughtless. Moral action should not proceed from such a momentary influence of an outward object. Wherefore your doctrine of morals, when it is strict and pure, acknowledges no reverence except for its own law. Everything done from pity or gratitude it condemns as impure, almost as selfish. It makes light of, almost despises, humility. If you talk of contrition it speaks of lost time being needlessly increased. Your own feeling must assure you that the immediate object of all these sentiments is not action. They are spontaneous functions of your deepest and highest life, coming by themselves and ending by themselves.[15] Why do you make such an ado, and begging for grace for them, where they have no right to be? Be content to consider them religion, and then you will not need to demand anything for them except their own sure rights, and you will not deceive yourselves with the baseless claims which you are disposed to make in their name. Return them to religion : the treasure belongs to it alone. As the possessor of it, religion is for morality and all else that is an object of human doing, not the handmaid, but an indispensable friend and sufficient advocate with humanity. This is the rank of religion, as the sum of all higher feelings.

That it alone removes man from one-sidedness and narrowness I have already indicated. Now I am in a position to be more definite. In all activity and working, be it moral or artistic, man must strive for mastery. But when man becomes quite absorbed, all mastery limits and chills, and makes one-sided and hard. The mind is directed chiefly to one point, and this one point cannot satisfy it. Can man, by advancing from one narrow work to another, really use his whole power? Will not the larger part be unused, and turn, in consequence, against himself and devour him? How many of you go to ruin because you are too great for yourselves? A superfluity of power and impulse that never issues in any work, because there is no work adequate, drives you aimlessly about, and is your destruction.

To resist this evil would you have those who are too great for one object of human endeavour, unite them all—art, science, life, and any others you may know of? This would simply be your old desire to have humanity complete everywhere, your ever recurring love of uniformity. But is it possible? Those objects, as soon as they are attended to separately, all alike strive to rouse and dominate the mind. Each tendency is directed to a work that should be completed, it has an ideal to be copied, a totality to be embraced. This rivalry of several objects of endeavour can only end by one expelling the others. Nay, even within this one sphere, the more eminent a mastery a man would attain, the more he must restrict himself. But if this pre-eminence entirely occupy him, and if he lives only to attain it, how shall he duly participate in the world, and how shall his life become a whole? Hence most virtuosos are one-sided and defective, or at least, outside of their own sphere, they sink into an inferior kind of life.

The only remedy is for each man, while he is definitely active in some one department, to allow himself, without definite activity, to be affected by the Infinite. In every species of religious feeling he will then become conscious of all that lies beyond the department which he directly cultivates. The Infinite is near to everyone, for whatever be the object you have chosen for your deliberate technical working, it does not demand much thought to advance from it to find the Universe. In it you discover the rest as precept, or inspiration or revelation. The only way of acquiring what lies outside the direction of the mind we have selected, is to enjoy and comprehend it thus as a whole, not by will as art, but by instinct for the Universe as religion.

Even in the religious form these objects again fall into rivalry. This result of human imperfection causes religion to appear dismembered. Religion takes the form of some peculiar receptivity and taste for art, philosophy or morality, and is consequently often mistaken. Oftener, I say, it appears thus than freed from all participation in one-sidedness, than completed, all-embracing. Yet this complete form of religion remains the highest, and it is only by it, that, with satisfactory result, man sets alongside of the finite that he specially concentrates on, an Infinite ; alongside of the contracting endeavour for something definite and complete, expansive soaring in the Whole and the Inexhaustible. In this way he restores the balance and harmony of his nature, which would be lost for ever, if, without at the same time having religion, he abandon himself to one object, were it the most beautiful, most splendid. A man's special calling is the melody of his life, and it remains a simple, meagre series of notes unless religion, with its endlessly rich variety, accompany it with all notes, and raise the simple song to a full-voiced, glorious harmony.

If then this, that I trust I have indicated clearly enough for you all, is really the nature of religion, I have already answered the questions, Whence do those dogmas and doctrines come that many consider the essence of religion ? Where do they properly belong ? And how do they stand related to what is essential in religion ? They are all the result of that contemplation of feeling, of that reflection and comparison, of which we have already spoken. The conceptions that underlie these propositions are, like your conceptions from experience, nothing but general expressions for definite feelings. They are not necessary for religion itself, scarcely even for communicating religion, but reflection requires and creates them. Miracle, inspiration, revelation, supernatural intimations, much piety can be had without the need of any one of these conceptions. But when feeling is made the subject of reflection and comparison they are absolutely unavoidable. In this sense all these conceptions do certainly belong to the sphere of religion, and indeed belong without condition or the smallest limit to their application. The strife about what event is properly a miracle, and wherein its character properly consists, how much revelation there may be and how far and for what reasons man may properly believe in it, and the manifest endeavour to deny and set aside as much as can be done with decency and consideration, in the foolish notion that philosophy and reason are served thereby, is one of the childish operations of the metaphysicians and moralists in religion. They confuse all points of view and bring religion into discredit, as if it trespassed on the universal validity of scientific and physical conclusions. Pray do not be misled, to the detriment of religion, by their sophistical disputations, nor even by their hypocritical mystery about what they would only too willingly publish. Religion, however loudly it may demand back all those well abused conceptions, leaves your physics untouched, and please God, also your psychology.

What is a miracle? What we call miracle is everywhere else called sign, indication. Our name, which means a wonder, refers purely to the mental condition of the observer. It is only in so far appropriate that a sign, especially when it is nothing besides, must be fitted to call attention to itself and to the power in it that gives it significance. Every finite thing, however, is a sign of the Infinite, and so these various expressions declare the immediate relation of a phenomenon to the Infinite and the Whole. But does that involve that every event should not have quite as immediate a relation to the finite and to nature? Miracle is simply the religious name for event. Every event, even the most natural and usual, becomes a miracle, as soon as the religious view of it can be the dominant. To me all is miracle. In your sense the inexplicable and strange alone is miracle, in mine it is no miracle. The more religious you are, the more miracle would you see everywhere. All dis-

puting about single events, as to whether or not they are to
be called miraculous, gives me a painful impression of the
poverty and wretchedness of the religious sense of the
combatants. One party show it by protesting everywhere
against miracle, whereby they manifest their wish not to
see anything of immediate relationship to the Infinite and
to the Deity. The other party display the same poverty
by laying stress on this and that. A phenomenon for them
must be marvellous before they will regard it as a miracle,
whereby they simply announce that they are bad observers.[16]

What is revelation ? Every original and new communication of the Universe to man is a revelation, as, for example,
every such moment of conscious insight as I have just
referred to. Every intuition and every original feeling
proceeds from revelation. As revelation lies beyond consciousness, demonstration is not possible, yet we are not
merely to assume it generally, but each one knows best
himself what is repeated and learned elsewhere, and what
is original and new. If nothing original has yet been
generated in you, when it does come it will be a revelation
for you also, and I counsel you to weigh it well.

What is inspiration ? It is simply the general expression
for the feeling of true morality and freedom. But do not
mistake me. It is not that marvellous and much-praised
morality and freedom that accompany and embellish actions
with deliberations. It is that action which springs from
the heart of man, despite of, or at least, regardless of,
all external occasion. In the same measure in which this
action is freed from all earthly entanglement, it is felt as
divine and referred to God.

What is prophecy ? Every religious anticipation of the
other half of a religious event, one half being given, is
prophecy. It was very religious of the ancient Hebrews to
measure the divineness of a prophet, neither by the difficulty
of predicting, nor by the greatness of the subject, but,
quite simply, by the issue, for we cannot know from one

thing how complete the feeling is in everything, till we see whether the religious aspect of this one special circumstance has been rightly comprehended.

What is operation of grace? [17] Nothing else manifestly than the common expression for revelation and inspiration, for interchange between the entrance of the world into man, through intuition and feeling, and the outgoing of man into the world, through action and culture. It includes both, in their originality and in their divine character, so that the whole life of the pious simply forms a series of operations of divine grace.

You see that all these ideas, in so far as religion requires, or can adopt ideas, are the first and the most essential. They indicate in the most characteristic manner a man's consciousness of his religion, because they indicate just what necessarily and universally must be in it. The man who does not see miracles of his own from the standpoint from which he contemplates the world, the man in whose heart no revelation of his own arises, when his soul longs to draw in the beauty of the world, and to be permeated by its spirit; the man who does not, in supreme moments, feel, with the most lively assurance, that a divine spirit urges him, and that he speaks and acts from holy inspiration, has no religion. The religious man must, at least, be conscious of his feelings as the immediate product of the Universe; for less would mean nothing. He must recognize something individual in them, something that cannot be imitated, something that guarantees the purity of their origin from his own heart. To be assured of this possession is the true belief.

Belief, on the contrary, usually so called, which is to accept what another has said or done, or to wish to think and feel as another has thought and felt, is a hard and base service. So far is it from being the highest in religion, as is asserted, that it must be rejected by all who would force their way into the sanctuary of religion. To wish to have and hold a faith that is an echo, proves that a man is incapable of religion ; to demand it of others, shows that there is no understanding of religion. You wish always to stand on your own feet and go your own way, and this worthy intent should not scare you from religion. Religion is no slavery, no captivity, least of all for your reason. You must belong to yourselves. Indeed, this is an indispensable condition of having any part in religion.

Every man, a few choice souls excepted, does, to be sure, require a guide to lead and stimulate, to wake his religious sense from its first slumber, and to give it its first direction. But this you accord to all powers and functions of the human soul, and why not to this one ? For your satisfaction, be it said, that here, if anywhere, this tutelage is only a passing state. Hereafter, shall each man see with his own eyes, and shall produce some contribution to the treasures of religion ; otherwise, he deserves no place in its kingdom, and receives none. You are right in despising the wretched echoes who derive their religion entirely from another, or depend on a dead writing, swearing by it and proving out of it.

Every sacred writing is in itself a glorious production, a speaking monument from the heroic time of religion, but, through servile reverence, it would become merely a mausoleum, a monument that a great spirit once was there, but is now no more. Did this spirit still live and work, he would look with love, and with a feeling of equality upon his work which yet could only be a weaker impress of himself. Not every person has religion who believes in a sacred writing, but only the man who has a lively and immediate understanding of it, and who, therefore, so far as he himself is concerned, could most easily do without it.

Your very contempt for the poverty stricken and powerless venerators of religion, in whom, from lack of nourishment, religion died before ever it came to the birth, convinces me that you have a talent for religion. The same

thing appears from your regard for the persons of all true
heroes of religion. That you should treat them with
shallow scoffing or not acknowledge what is great or
powerful in them, I would hardly ascribe to you. This
regard for the persons confirms me in the thought that
your contempt for the thing rests merely on a misunderstanding, and has for its object only the miserable figure
which religion takes in the great incapable mass, and the
abuses which presumptuous leaders carry on.

I have tried, as best I could, therefore, to show you
what religion really is. Have you found anything therein
unworthy of you, nay, of the highest human culture?
Must you not rather long all the more for that universal
union with the world which is only possible through feeling,
the more you are separated and isolated by definite culture
and individuality? Have you not often felt this holy
longing, as something unknown? Become conscious of the
call of your deepest nature and follow it, I conjure you.
Banish the false shame of a century which should not
determine you but should be made and determined by you.
Return to what lies so near to you, yes, even to you, the
violent separation from which cannot fail to destroy the
most beautiful part of your nature.

It appears to me, however, that many among you do not
believe that I can here mean to end my present business.
How can I have spoken thoroughly of the nature of
religion, seeing I have not treated at all of immortality, and
of God only a little in passing? Is it not incumbent upon
me, most of all, to speak of these two things and to represent to you how unhappy you would be without belief in
them? For are not these two things, for most pious
people, the very poles and first articles of religion?

But I am not of your opinion. First of all, I do not
believe I have said nothing about immortality and so little
about God. Both, I believe, are in all and in everything
that I have adduced as an element of religion. Had I not

presupposed God and immortality I could not have said what I have said, for, only what is divine and immortal has room in which to speak of religion.

In the second place, just as little do I consider that I have the right to hold the conceptions and doctrines of God and of immortality, as they are usually understood, to be the principal things in religion. Only what in either is feeling and immediate consciousness, can belong to religion. God and immortality, however, as they are found in such doctrines, are ideas. How many among you—possibly most of you—are firmly convinced of one or other or both of those doctrines, without being on that account pious or having religion. As ideas they can have no greater value in religion than ideas generally.

But that you may not think I am afraid to speak a straightforward word on this subject, because it would be dangerous to speak, till some definition of *God* and *existence* that has stood its trial, has been brought to light and has been accepted in the German Empire as good and valid ; or lest you should, on the other hand, perhaps, believe that I am playing on you a pious fraud and wish, in order to be all things to all men, with seeming indifference to make light of what must be of far greater importance to me than I will confess—lest you should think these things, I shall gladly be questioned and will endeavour to make clear to you that, according to my best conviction, it really is, as I have just now maintained.

Remember in the first place that any feeling is not an emotion of piety because in it a single object as such affects us, but only in so far as in it and along with it, it affects us as revelation of God. It is, therefore, not an individual or finite thing, but God, in whom alone the particular thing is one and all, that enters our life. Nor do we stand over against the World and in it at the same time by any one faculty, but by our whole being. The divine in us, therefore, is immediately affected and

called forth by the feeling.[18]　Seeing then that I have presented nothing but just this immediate and original
existence of God in us through feeling, how can anyone say
that I have depicted a religion without God?　Is not God
the highest, the only unity?　Is it not God alone before
whom and in whom all particular things disappear?　And
if you see the world as a Whole, a Universe, can you do it
otherwise than in God?　If not, how could you distinguish the highest existence, the original and eternal
Being from a temporal and derived individual?　Otherwise than by the emotions produced in us by the world
we do not claim to have God in our feeling, and consequently I have not said more of Him.

If you will not admit that this is to have God, and to
be conscious of Him, I can neither teach nor direct you
farther.　How much you may know I do not judge, for it
does not at present concern me, but in respect of feeling and
sentiment, you would be for me godless.　Science, it is true,
is extolled as giving an immediate knowledge about God,
that is the source of all other knowledge; only we are not
now speaking of science, but of religion.　This way of
knowing about God which most praise and which I also
am to laud, is neither the idea of God as the undivided
unity and source of all, that is placed by you at the head of
all knowledge ; nor is it the feeling of God in the heart, of
which we boast ourselves.　It lags far behind the demands
of science, and is for piety something quite subordinate.
It is an idea compounded from characteristics, from what
are called attributes of God.　These attributes correspond
to the different ways in which the unity of the individual
and the Whole, expresses itself in feeling.　Hence I can
only say of this idea, what I have said of ideas generally,
in reference to religion, that there can be much piety without it, and that it is first formed when piety is made an
object of contemplation.

Yet this idea of God, as it is usually conceived, is dif-

ferent from the other ideas before adduced, for though it
seeks to be the highest and to stand above all, God, being
thought of as too like us, as a thinking and willing Person,
is drawn down into the region of opposition. It therefore
appears natural that the more like man God is conceived,
the more easily another mode of presentation is set over
against it. Hence, we have an idea of the Highest Being,
not as personally thinking and willing, but exalted above
all personality, as the universal, productive, connecting
necessity of all thought and existence.

Nothing seems to me less fitting than for the adherents
of the former view to charge with godlessness those who,
in dread of this anthropomorphism, take refuge in the other,
or for the adherents of this latter view to make the humanness of the idea of God a ground for charging the adherents
of the former with idolatry, or for declaring their piety void.

It matters not what conceptions a man adheres to, he can
still be pious. His piety, the divine in his feeling, may be
better than his conception, and his desire to place the
essence of piety in conception, only makes him misunderstand himself. Consider how narrow is the presentation of
God in the one conception, and how dead and rigid in the
other. Neither corresponds to its object, and thus cannot be
a proof of piety, except in so far as it rests on something in the
mind, of which it has come far short. Rightly understood,
both present, at least, one element of feeling, but, without
feeling, neither is of any value. Many believe in and
accept a God presented in conception, and yet are nothing
less than pious,[19] and in no case is this conception the germ
from which their piety could ever spring, for it has no life
in itself. Neither conception is any sign of a perfect or of
an imperfect religion, but perfection and imperfection
depend upon the degree of cultivation of the religious
sense. As I know of nothing more that could bring us to
an understanding on this subject of conceptions, let us now
go on to consider the development of the religious sense.

As long as man's whole relation to the world has not arrived at clearness, this feeling is but a vague instinct, the world can appear to him nothing but a confused unity. Nothing of its complexity is definitely distinguishable. It is to him a chaos, uniform in its confusion, without division, order, or law. Apart from what most immediately concerns the subsistence of man, he distinguishes nothing as individual except by arbitrarily cutting it off in time and space. Here you will find but few traces of any conceptions, and you will scarcely discern to which side they incline. You will not set much value on the difference, whether a blind fate, only to be indicated by magic rites, exhibits the character of the Whole, or a being, alive indeed, but without definite characteristics, an idol, a fetich, one, or, if many, only distinguishable by the arbitrarily appointed limits of their sphere.

As we advance, the feeling becomes more conscious. Circumstances display themselves in their complexity and definiteness. The multiplicity of the heterogeneous elements and powers, by whose constant and determined strife, phenomena are determined, becomes more prominent in man's consciousness of the world. In the same degree the result of the contemplation of this feeling changes. The opposite forms of the idea stand more distinctly apart. Blind fate changes into a higher necessity, in which, though unattainable and unsearchable, reason and connection rest. Similarly, the idea of a personal God becomes higher, but at the same time divides and multiplies, each power and element becomes animate, and gods arise in endless number. They are now distinguishable by means of the different objects of their activity, and different inclinations and dispositions. A stronger, fairer life of the Universe in feeling you must acknowledge is here exhibited. It is most beautiful when this new won complexity and this innate highest unity are most intimately bound together in feeling, as for example, among the Greeks, whom you so justly revere. Both forms then unite in reflection, one being of more value for thought, the other for art, one showing more of the complexity, the other of the unity. But this stage, even without such a union is more perfect than the former, especially if the idea of the Highest Being is placed rather in the eternal unattainable necessity, than in single gods.

Let us now mount higher where opposing elements are again united, where existence, by exhibiting itself as totality, as unity in variety, as system, first deserves its name. Is not the man who perceives existence both as one and as all, who stands over against the Whole, and yet is one with it in feeling, to be accounted happier in his religion, let his feeling mirror itself in idea as it may ? There as elsewhere then, the manner in which the Deity is present to man in feeling, is decisive of the worth of his religion, not the manner, always inadequate, in which it is copied in idea. Suppose there is someone arrived at this stage, who rejects the idea of a personal God. I will not decide on the justice of the names you are accustomed to apply to him, whether Pantheist or Spinozist. This rejection of the idea of a personal Deity does not decide against the presence of the Deity in his feeling. The ground of such a rejection might be a humble consciousness of the limitation of personal existence, and particularly of personality joined to consciousness. He might stand as high above a worshipper of the twelve gods whom you would rightly name after Lucretius, as a pious person at that stage would be above an idolater.

But we have here the old confusion, the unmistakable sign of defective culture. Those who are at the same stage, only not at the same point, are most strongly repudiated. The proper standard of religiousness, that which announces the stage to which a man has attained, is his sense for the Deity. But to which idea he will attach himself depends purely on what he requires it for, and whether his imagination chiefly inclines towards existence and nature or consciousness and thought.

You will not, I trust, consider it blasphemy or incongruity that such a matter should depend on the direction of the imagination. By imagination I do not mean anything subordinate or confused, but the highest and most original faculty in man. All else in the human mind is simply reflection upon it, and is therefore dependent on it. Imagination in this sense is the free generation of thoughts, whereby you come to a conception of the world ; such a conception you cannot receive from without, nor compound from inferences. From this conception you are then impressed with the feeling of omnipotence. The subsequent translation into thought depends on whether one is willing in the consciousness of his own weakness to be lost in the mysterious obscurity, or whether, first of all, seeking definiteness of thought, he cannot think of anything except under the one form given to us, that of consciousness or self-consciousness. Recoil from the obscurity of indefinite thought is the one tendency of the imagination, recoil from the appearance of contradiction in transferring the forms of the finite to the Infinite is the other.

Now cannot the same inwardness of religion be combined with both ? Would not a closer consideration show that the two ways of conceiving are not very wide apart ? But the pantheistic idea is not to be thought of as death, and no effort is to be spared to surpass in thought the limits of the personal idea.

So much I have thought it necessary to say, not so much in explanation of my own position, as to prevent you from thinking that all are despisers of religion who will not accept the personality of the Highest Being as it is usually set forth. And I am quite convinced that what has been said will not make the idea of the personality of God more uncertain for anyone who truly has it ; nor will anyone more easily rid himself of the almost absolute necessity to acquire it, for knowing whence this necessity comes. Among truly religious men there have never been zealots, enthusiasts, or fanatics for this idea. Even when timidity and hesitation about it is called atheism, truly pious persons will leave it alone with great tranquillity. Not to have the Deity immediately present in one's feeling has always seemed to them more irreligious. They would most unwillingly believe that anyone could in point of fact be quite without religion. They believe that only those who are quite without feeling, and whose nature has become brutish, can have no consciousness of the God that is in us and in the world, and of the divine life and operation whereby all things consist. But whosoever insists, it matters not how many excellent men he excludes, that the highest piety consists in confessing that the Highest Being thinks as a person and wills outside the world, cannot be far travelled in the region of piety. Nay, the profoundest words of the most zealous defenders of his own faith must still be strange to him.

The number who would have something from this God, that is alien to piety, is only too great. He is to give an outward guarantee of their blessedness and incite them to morality. They want to have it before their eyes. They would not have God working on man by freedom, but in the only way in which one free being can work on another, by necessity, by making himself known either by pain or by pleasure. But this cannot incite us to morality. Every external incitement is alien to morality, whether it be hope or fear. To follow it where it concerns morality is unfree, therefore unmoral. But the Highest Being, particularly when he is thought of as free, cannot wish to make freedom itself not free, and morality not moral.[20]

This now brings me to the second point, to immortality. I cannot conceal that in the usual manner of treating this subject there is still more that seems to me inconsistent with the nature of piety. I believe I have just shown you in what way each one bears in himself an unchangeable and eternal nature. If our feeling nowhere attaches itself to the individual, but if its content is our relation to God wherein all that is individual and fleeting disappears, there can be nothing fleeting in it, but all must be eternal. In the religious life then we may well say we have already offered up and disposed of all that is mortal, and that we actually are enjoying immortality. But the immortality that most men imagine and their longing for it, seem to me irreligious, nay quite opposed to the spirit of piety. Dislike to the very aim of religion is the ground of their wish to be immortal. Recall how religion earnestly strives to expand the sharply cut outlines of personality. Gradually they are to be lost in the Infinite that we, becoming conscious of the Universe, may as much as possible be one with it. But men struggle against this aim. They are anxious about their personality, and do not wish to overstep the accustomed limit or to be anything else but a manifestation of it. The one opportunity that death gives them of transcending it, they are very far from wishing to embrace. On the contrary, they are concerned as to how they are to carry it with them beyond this life, and their utmost endeavour is for longer sight and better limbs. But God speaks to them as it stands written, " Whosoever loses his life for my sake, the same shall keep it, and whosoever keeps it, the same shall lose it." The life that they would keep is one that cannot be kept. If their concern is with the eternity of their single person, why are they not as anxious about what it has been as about what it is to be ? What does forwards avail when they cannot go backwards ? They desire an immortality that is no immortality. They are not even capable of comprehending it, for who can endure the effort to conceive an endless temporal existence ? Thereby they lose the immortality they could always have, and their mortal life in addition, by thoughts that distress and torture them in vain. Would they but attempt to surrender their lives from love to God ! Would they but strive to annihilate their person-

ality and to live in the One and in the All ! Whosoever has
learned to be more than himself, knows that he loses little
when he loses himself. Only the man who denying himself
sinks himself in as much of the whole Universe as he can
attain, and in whose soul a greater and holier longing has
arisen, has a right to the hopes that death gives. With him
alone it is really possible to hold further converse about the
endlessness to which, through death, we infallibly soar.[21]

This then is my view of these subjects. The usual conception of God as one single being outside of the world
and behind the world is not the beginning and the end of
religion. It is only one manner of expressing God, seldom
entirely pure and always inadequate. Such an idea may be
formed from mixed motives, from the need for such a being
to console and help, and such a God may be believed in
without piety, at least in my sense, and I think in the true
and right sense. If, however, this idea is formed, not
arbitrarily, but somehow by the necessity of a man's way
of thinking, if he needs it for the security of his piety, the
imperfections of his idea will not cumber him nor contami-
nate his piety. Yet the true nature of religion is neither this
idea nor any other, but immediate consciousness of the Deity
as He is found in ourselves and in the world. Similarly
the goal and the character of the religious life is not the
immortality desired and believed in by many—or what their
craving to be too wise about it would suggest—pretended
to be believed in by many. It is not the immortality that
is outside of time, behind it, or rather after it, and which still
is in time. It is the immortality which we can now have
in this temporal life ; it is the problem in the solution of
which we are for ever to be engaged. In the midst of
finitude to be one with the Infinite and in every moment
to be eternal is the immortality of religion.

EXPLANATIONS OF THE SECOND SPEECH

(1) Page 32.—The rhetorical character of this book and the impossibility of continuing the subject, had my opinion really been
that religion is this restored unity of knowledge, would have allowed
me to say so by a very slight suggestion of irony. My meaning
would then have been that I would not now press this truth upon
my opponents, but that elsewhere and in another form I would
carry it to a victorious issue. Wherefore it seems necessary to guard
myself against this interpretation, especially as so many theologians
seem to maintain at present that religion, and not religion generally,
but the Christian religion, is the highest knowledge. Not only in
dignity but in form is it identified with metaphysical speculations.
It is the most successful and pre-eminent, and all speculations that
do not reach the same results, as for example, if they cannot deduce
the Trinity, have failed. The assertion of others that the more imperfect, especially the Polytheistic religions have no kinship with
Christianity is similar. I reject both, and in respect of the latter I
have sought, in the further progress of this book, and in the Introduction to my " Glaubenslehre," to show how all forms of religion,
even the most imperfect, are the same in kind. In respect of the
former position, if a philosopher as such will attempt to prove a
Trinity in the Highest Being, he does it at his risk, and I would
maintain that this is not a Christian Trinity because, being a
speculative idea, it has its origin in another part of the soul.
Were religion really the highest knowledge, the scientific method
alone would be suitable for its extension, and religion could be
acquired by study, a thing not hitherto asserted. Philosophy would
be the first round in the ladder, the religion of the Christian laity
would as πίστις be an imperfect way of having the highest knowledge, and theology as γνῶσις would be the perfect way and stand
at the top, and no one of the three stages would be consistent with
the other two. This I cannot at all accept ; therefore I cannot hold
religion the highest knowledge, or indeed knowledge at all. Wherefore, what the Christian layman has in less perfection than the

theologian and which manifestly is a knowledge is not religion itself, but something appended to it.

(2) Page 39.—In rhetorical exposition generally, strict definitions are dispensed with, and descriptions are substituted. This whole speech is simply an extended description, mixed with criticism of other conceptions, which in my opinion are false. The chief points being scattered are of necessity repeated in different places, under different expressions. This change of expression presents different sides of the matter, and I find it useful even in more scientific treatment for avoiding the scrupulosity of too rigid a terminology. In this kind of writing it seemed specially appropriate. Wherefore three different expressions follow in rapid succession. It is said here of religion that *through it, the universal existence of all finite things in the Infinite lives immediately in us.* On page 39 it stands *religion is sense and taste for the Infinite.* Sense may be capacity of perception or capacity of sensibility. There it is the latter. In the former editions, *sensibility and taste* stood not quite correctly for *sense and taste* for the Infinite. What I am conscious of or feel, must be imagined, and that is what I call the life of the object in me. But the Infinite, meaning not something unconditioned, but the infinity of existence generally, we cannot be conscious of immediately and through itself. It can only be through a finite object, by means of which our tendency to postulate and seek a world, leads us from detail and part to the All and the Whole. Hence sense for the Infinite and the immediate life of the finite in us as it is in the Infinite, are one and the same. If then, in the first expression, taste be now added to sense, and in the latter expression, the universal existence of all finite things in the Infinite be made explicit, both become essentially identical. Taste includes liking as well as mere faculty, and it is by this liking, this desire to find not merely the finite thing, but to be conscious through it of the Infinite, that the pious person finds that the existence of the finite in the Infinite is universal. There is a similar passage on page 36. The connection shows that the expression *contemplation* is to be taken in the widest sense, not as speculation proper, but as all movement of the spirit withdrawn from outward activity. What, however, has struck most readers is that the Infinite Existence does not appear to be the Highest Being as cause of the World but the World itself. I do not think that God can be placed in such a relation as cause, and I leave you to say whether the World can be conceived as a true All and Whole without God. Therefore I remained satisfied with that expression, that I might not decide on the various ways of conceiving

God and the World as together or as outside of one another, which did not fall to be considered here, and could only have limited the horizon in a hurtful manner.

(3) Page 41.—This passage on the departed Novalis was first inserted in the second edition. Many I believe will wonder at this juxtaposition, not seeing that he is like Spinoza, or that he holds the same conspicuous position in art as Spinoza in science. Without destroying the balance of the Speech, I could only suggest my reason. There is now another reason why I should say no more. During these fifteen years the attention to Spinoza, awakened by Jacobi's writings and continued by many later influences, which was then somewhat marked, has relaxed. Novalis also has again become unknown to many. At that time, however, these examples seemed significant and important. Many coquetted in insipid poetry with religion, believing they were akin to the profound Novalis, just as there were advocates enough of the All in the One taken for followers of Spinoza who were equally distant from their original. Novalis was cried down as an enthusiastic mystic by the prosaic, and Spinoza as godless by the literalists. It was incumbent upon me to protest against this view of Spinoza, seeing I would review the whole sphere of piety. Something essential would have been wanting in the exposition of my views if I had not in some way said that the mind and heart of this great man seemed deeply influenced by piety, even though it were not Christian piety. The result might have been different, had not the Christianity of that time been so distorted and obscured by dry formulas and vain subtilties that the divine form could not be expected to win the regard of a stranger. This I said in the first edition, somewhat youthfully indeed, yet so that I have found nothing now needing to be altered, for there was no reason to believe that I ascribed the Holy Spirit to Spinoza in the special Christian sense of the word. As interpolation instead of interpretation was not then so common or so honourable as at present, I believed that a part of my work was well done. How was I to expect that, because I ascribed piety to Spinoza, I would myself be taken for a Spinozist? Yet I had never defended his system, and anything philosophic that was in my book was manifestly inconsistent with the characteristics of his views and had quite a different basis than the unity of substance. Even Jacobi has in his criticism by no means hit upon what is most characteristic. When I recovered my astonishment, in revising the second edition, this parallel occurred to me. As it was known that Novalis in some points had a tendency to Catholicism, I felt sure that, in praising his art, I should have his

religious aberrations ascribed me as Spinozism had been because I praised Spinoza's piety. Whether my expectation has deceived me I do not yet very well know.

(4) Page 46.—Even among the few who admit that religion originally is feeling stirred in the highest direction, there will be many to whom it will appear that I assert too much when I say that all healthy feelings are pious, or at least that, in order not to be diseased, they should be pious. Even were this granted of all social feelings, it must be shown how piety is to be found in all those feelings that unite men for a higher or even a more sensuous enjoyment of life. Yet I can retract nothing from the universality of the statement and in no way admit that it was a rhetorical hyperbole. To take one example, Protestantism can only completely and consistently defend the domestic and paternal relations of the clergy against the melancholy folly of the peculiar holiness of the celibate life, by showing that wedded love and all foregoing natural attraction of the sexes are not, in the nature of the case, absolutely inconsistent with a pious state. This only happens when the feeling is diseased, when there is a tendency in it to the rage of Bacchus or the folly of Narcissus. In accordance with this analogy I believe that the same could be shown of each department of feeling not inconsistent with morality. But, if it be inferred from this passage that, as all true human feelings belong to the religious sphere, all ideas and principles of every sort are foreign to it, the connection seems to show my meaning. Religion itself is to be rigidly distinguished from what merely belongs to it. Yet, even those feelings which are usually separated from the religious sphere, require ideas for their communication and representation, and principles to exhibit their due measure. But these principles and ideas do not belong to the feelings themselves, and it is similar with the dogmatic and ascetic in respect of religion, as is shown more fully further on.

(5) Page 49.—For understanding my whole view I could desire nothing better than that my readers should compare these Speeches with my "Christliche Glaubenslehre." In form they are very different and their points of departure lie far apart, yet in matter they are quite parallel. But to provide the Speeches for this purpose with a complete commentary was impossible, and I must content myself with single references to such passages as seem to me capable of appearing contrary or at least of lacking agreement. Thus every one perhaps might not find the description here given of an action of things upon us underlying all religious emotions, in agreement with the declaration which goes through the whole

" Glaubenslehre," that the essence of the religious emotions consists in the feeling of an absolute dependence. The matter stands thus. Even there it is admitted that we cannot really have this feeling except it is occasioned by the action of single things. But if the single things are in their action only single, the sole result is definiteness of the sensuous self-consciousness. In the " Glaubenslehre," likewise this is postulated as the substratum of religious emotion. Yet, let the single thing be great or small, our single life reacts against it, and there can be no feeling of dependence except fortuitously in so far as the reaction is not equal to the action. If, however, the single thing does not work upon us as a single thing, but as part of the Whole, it will be, in acting upon us, an opening for the Whole. This result will depend entirely on the mood and attitude of the mind. But then our reaction will appear to us determined by the same cause and in the same way as the action, and being over against the Universe, our state must be the feeling of entire dependence. And this also shows that however we exhibit the World and God they cannot be divided. We do not feel ourselves dependent on the Whole in so far as it is an aggregate of mutually conditioned parts of which we ourselves are one, but only in so far as underneath this coherence there is a unity conditioning all things and conditioning our relations to the other parts of the Whole. Only on this condition can the single thing be, as it is here put, an exhibition of the Infinite, being so comprehended that its opposition to all else entirely vanishes.

(6) Page 50.—By *mythology* I understand in general a purely ideal subject enunciated in historical form. Exactly in accordance with the analogy of Polytheistic Mythology, it seems to me that we have a Monotheistic and a Christian. For this a dialogue of divine persons, such as is found in Klopstock's poems and elsewhere, is not necessary. It is found in more rigid didactic form when something is represented as happening in the Divine Being, as divine resolves made in respect of something that has happened in the world, or again to modify former resolves, not to speak of the special divine resolves that give reality to the idea that prayer is heard. The representations of many divine attributes also have this historical form and are therefore mythological. The divine pity for example, as the idea is mostly understood, is only something when the divine will that lightens the evil is separated from the will that ordained it. Are both regarded as one, then one cannot limit the other, but the divine will that decrees the evil, decrees it only in a definite measure, and the idea of pity is out of place. Similarly, in the idea

of the veracity of God, promise and fulfilment are separated, and both together exhibit a historical transaction. But when the activity that promises, is regarded as the same that accomplishes the fulfil-ment, the conception of divine veracity is something only in so far as many divine activities are linked or not to one expression of them. In this distinction also a history is told, but if the activity that brings to pass and its expression are regarded in general as one, there is hardly place for a special idea of the divine veracity. The same may be shown in other things. By applying this name to them I in nowise blame these representations. Rather I acknow-ledge them as indispensable, for otherwise the subject could not be spoken of in such a way that any distinction could be drawn between the more correct and less correct. Even in more scientific presenta-tions of religion, the use of such mythology has no danger, for there it is always incumbent to think away the historical and the time form generally. In the sphere of religious poetry and oratory also it is indispensable. There we have only to do with the like-minded, and for them the chief worth of those presentations is that by them they communicate and realize their own religious moods. They naturally at once adjust the defective expression. But I blame it as vain mythology when this, that is only a help in need, is regarded as exact knowledge, and treated as the essence of religion.

(7) Page 53.—If here the system of marks or attributes which in its completest form composes the theological outline is represented rather as being determined by outward circumstances than as coming forth of itself from the religious capacity, the oft-repeated assertion, so contemptuous of all historical sense, that the religious movements which in Christianity have determined a great body of the most important ideas, were merely accidental and the fruit of entirely alien interests, is not to be made. I only wished to recall what is also expounded in my " Kurze Darstellung " and in the Introduction to the " Glaubenslehre," that the formation of the idea depends here, as elsewhere, on the dominating language, the degree, manner, and quality of its scientific development embracing of course the manner and quality of the philosophizing. But in respect of religion in and for itself, these are only external circumstances. Apart from the universal, divine connection of all things, we can say, for example, that if Christianity had had a great and preponderating Eastern extension, the Hellenic and Western being, on the contrary, kept back, without being essentially different, it might have been con-tained in another type of doctrines.

(8) Page 54.—This passage also might occasion various miscon-

ceptions. First, in respect of the opposition between true and false religion, I refer to my " Glaubenslehre," §§ 7 and 8 (2nd edit.). It is there treated fully, and I would simply add that, in religion, error only exists by truth and not merely so, but it can be said that every man's religion is his highest truth. Error therein would not only be error, it would be hypocrisy. In religion then everything is immediately true, as nothing is expressed at any moment of it, except the state of mind of the religious person. Similarly, all types of religious association are good, for the best in the existence of each man must be stored up in them. But how little this prejudices the superiority of one type of faith to another is in part plainly stated and in part easy to infer. One may be the utterance of a superior state of mind, or there may be in the religious communion a higher spiritual power and love. Furthermore, the rejection here of the thought of the universality of any one religion and the assertion that only in the sum of all religions is the whole extent of this bias of the mind comprehended, in no way expresses a doubt that Christianity will be able to extend itself over the whole human race, though perhaps among many races, this greatest of all religions may suffer important changes. Just as little did this passage express a wish that other religions should always continue alongside of Christianity. The influence of Judaism and Hellenic Heathenism on Christianity was through a long period visible in hostile, raging commotions. Thus both still appear in Christianity, and therefore in the history of Christianity have a place. The same thing would happen if Christianity should annex the territory of all existing great religions. Consequently the religious sphere would not be enclosed in narrower borders, but all religions would in a historical way be visible in Christianity. From the connection again it is clear that I only deny that a religion is universally true in the sense that everything that exists or has existed outside of it, is not to be called religion at all. Similarly, what follows is to be understood, about every truly pious person willingly acknowledging that to other types of religion much belongs for which the sense fails him. Even if Christianity had supplanted all other religions, he would not have a sense for all that would thereby be historically mirrored in Christianity, for just as little then as now would the Christianity of all Christian people be quite the same. And if no one has an adequate sense for all that is Christian, there can be none with the sense for all there is in other religions that may be the germ of some future Christian peculiarity.

(9) Page 55.—There are still Christian divines who reject the whole

purpose of Christian dogmatics, and there was a far greater number when this passage was first written. They believe that Christianity would have been a healthier development and would have shown a freer, fairer form if no one had ever thought of presenting the Christian conceptions in a finished connection. Hence they labour to prune it, to abolish it, as much as possible, and to have it acknowledged as merely a collection of monographs, as an accidental aggregate of single theses of very unequal value. Their good intentions I do not question, but even then, I was far removed from agreeing with them. It would be a grave misunderstanding to believe that this invective against the mania for system makes light of the endeavour to present the Christian faith in the closest possible connection. The mania for system is merely a morbid degeneration of this praiseworthy and wholesome endeavour. That systematic treatment of religious conceptions is the best which, on the one side, does not take the conception and the idea for original and constitutive, and on the other, that the living mobility of the letter be secured, that it may not die and the spirit be drawn to death with it. Within the great conformity characteristic difference is not only to be endured, it is to be assigned its place. If this were to be taken for the chief aim in my presentation of the Christian faith, I would fain believe that I am in perfect agreement with myself.

(10) Page 55.—I feel that this passage gives a two-fold, grave offence. First I prefer Heathen Rome, on account of its boundless mixture of religions, to Christian Rome which, in comparison, I call godless, and that I condemn the expulsion of heretics, while I myself declare certain views to be heretical, and even seek to systematize heresy. I begin with the latter as the deeper and more important. It does not appear to me possible that there can be a sound dogmatic procedure without a formula of the character of what is Christian, by the application of which it would be possible, from any point of the line of cleavage, to cut off the ordinates, and so to describe the extent of Christian conceptions by approximation. It naturally follows that what lies outside of this extent, and would yet be considered Christian, is what has long been called in the Christian Church heretical. In my dogmatics I could not avoid offering such a formula, and I can only wish to attain my object as fully as possible. But this definition of the subject has nothing to do with the treatment of persons. That many, while contending for the defence of their own opinion, may use a heretical expression without meaning anything heretical, is apparent, and I have declared myself fully on it in the " Glaubenslehre," § 22, 3 and note, and § 25, note.

On many sides the wish has been expressed in the Evangelical Church to renew church discipline in a judicious manner that a Christian congregation may be in a position to withdraw a measure of fellowship from persons disproving by their lives their Christian disposition. This makes it specially necessary to obviate the confusion between this proceeding and the right to pronounce the bann on all we may choose to consider heretics. If heretics are not also without a Christian disposition, the Evangelical Church will rather acknowledge that its sole duty towards them is to maintain fellowship with them that, by mutual understanding, they may the sooner be led into the right way. If individuals or small societies employ a contrary method and, regardless of disposition, exclude from their fellowship all who do not agree with them in the same letter of doctrine, they do not act in an Evangelical spirit, but assume an authority our church grants to none. And now passing to the second point, my preference of Heathen to Christian Rome, and my statement that through tolerance the former was full of gods, and that through persecution of heretics, the latter was godless. First, the character of the expressions used shows that this passage bears specially the rhetorical cast of the book. What, however, is to be taken literally is that the dogmatizing love of system which scorns to assign its place to difference, but rather excludes all difference, plainly suppresses, as much as it can, the living knowledge of God, and changes doctrine into a dead letter. A rule so rigid that it condemns everything of another shade, crushes out productiveness. As this alone contains living knowledge of God, the system itself must become dead. This is the history of the Roman Catholic system in contrast to the Protestant. From this point of view the rise of the Evangelical Church was simply to rescue its own productiveness from fellowship with such a rule. My praise of the receptivity of ancient Rome for strange worships is also to be taken seriously. It involved an acknowledgment of the narrowness and one-sidedness of each individualized Polytheism, and the desire to free the religious need from the limits of political forms. Now these two things were not only praiseworthy in themselves, but were much more favourable to the spread of Christianity than heresy hunting, however well meant, could ever be for its establishment and preservation.

(11) Page 65.—In the " Glaubenslehre," also § 8, note 1, I have declared myself against the opinion that idolatry, embracing, according to the somewhat perspective usage of the Holy Scriptures, all kinds of Polytheism, has arisen from fear. There, however, I wished to

show that, in essence, the lower and the higher stages of religion were alike, which could not be if the former arose from fear and the latter did not. There I am dealing with the conception that piety generally has had its source in fear. Despite the somewhat variable use of δεισιδαιμονία, the proof here given in general would apply to the particular instance, for it could not be said of the Greek and Roman Polytheists that their faith in the gods would have been extinct if, in the courageous use of life, they had shaken off all fear. Similarly, what is said there may here be applied generally, for if fear is not in some way a perversion of love, it can only regard its object as malevolent. Where then higher beings are not worshipped or rather entreated as bad, the motive cannot be fear entirely separated from love. Hence it remains true that in all religions from the beginning love is operative, and all growth towards perfection is simply a progressive purification of love.

(12) Page 65.—It should hardly be necessary to justify the use of the expression *World-Spirit* where I wish to indicate the object of pious adoration in a way that would include all different forms and stages of religion. In particular, I do not believe it can be said with justice that, by this choice of expression, I have sacrificed the interests of the most perfect form of religion to the inferior. On the contrary, I believe, not only that it is a perfectly Christian name for the Highest Being, but that the expression could only have arisen on Monotheistic soil, and is as free from Jewish Particularism as from the incompleteness of the Mohammedan Monotheism which I have attempted to specify in the " Glaubenslehre," § 8, 4. No one will confuse it with *World-Soul.* It neither expresses reciprocal action between the World and the Highest Being, nor any kind of independence of the World from Him. I believe therefore that Christian authors are justified in using the term, even though it has not directly proceeded from the special standpoint of Christianity.

(13) Page 71.—In my " Glaubenslehre," the Introduction of which contains the outlines of what I take to be the philosophy of religion, and therefore has many points of contact with this book, my chief division was into what I have called the æsthetic and the teleological form. Here another ground of classification seems to be assumed. The peculiar world of religion seems to be the mind, regarded as an individual thing having one or more things standing over against it —the mind in our sphere and at our stage of culture. In the same way on the other side, as there indicated, the world of religion may be external nature. Two things there rigidly distinguished seem here to be both ascribed to the religion of the mind, for whether the

active state be referred to the passive, or the passive to the active, all religious emotions are states of mind. Hence the distinction that is here regarded as the higher, is there quite overlooked. By a natural religion, however, I do not mean that religious emotions can come to man through contemplation of the external world. This contemplation is exalted by speculative natural science, which, however, always remains science, and only gives rise to religious emotions in proportion as the soul is conscious of itself in the contemplation, and therefore again by the mental state. In the same way they arise from the immediate relation of nature to our life and existence, only in proportion to its effect upon our mood at any moment, and therefore, again from the mental state. The classification given in the " Glaubenslehre " therefore remains. The religious emotions, whether from nature or the historical life, have all this two-fold form. If the influence of the contemplation of nature is referred to the soul and its activities and its laws, it has a teleological or ethical character ; if it is referred to nature, it has an æsthetic character.

(14) Page 72.—This is only to be taken as an application of the narrative, not as the author's own opinion. I believe it can be shown that the narrative necessarily implies that neither can man come to a consciousness of God, nor can he form general ideas, until he has gained a consciousness of the species, of his subordination as an individual in it and his difference from it. And, it appears as clearly, that neither the consciousness of the Highest Being, nor the endeavour to order the world for itself can be quite lost to the soul till the consciousness of the species has quite vanished.

I will here also explain two passages not specially marked in the text. On page 79 *humility*, formerly given as a natural form of religious emotion, is spoken of as if it were opposed to an exalted feeling of personal existence, and *contrition*, similarly depicted as natural and essential to piety, as if it must be changed to joyful self-sufficiency. Now, I do not consider that a contradiction, for I think that all pious emotions both exalt and debase. Even in Christianity that spreads itself only by awaking the emotions that debase, penitence is quenched in the consciousness of the divine forgiveness. The words " satisfy thyself with my mercy," express just that very joyful self-sufficiency here meant. The opposite feeling to humility, the feeling that in each one the whole of humanity lives and works is just the consciousness to which the Christian of all men should rise. He should feel that all believers form a living organic whole, wherein not only is each member, as Paul puts it, indispensable to all the others. But each one presupposes the characteristic activity of all the others. Further, when it is said that a man who has thus combined both forms of emotion needs no mediator any more, but can himself be a mediator for many, this statement is only to be taken in the limited meaning indicated by earlier expositions, namely, each man has not in himself the right key for understanding all men. To almost everyone much is so alien that he can only acknowledge it when he finds it in a form more akin to himself or linked to something else that has a special value for him. In this sense, therefore, those who unite the most alien elements with those most acknowledged, mediate an understanding. Chiefly in that feeling which is in contrast to humility, the self-consciousness advances to such transparency and accuracy that the most distant ceases to appear strange and ceases to repel. But this feeling will be purest when all human limits are seen in Him from whom all limitation was banished. Hence there is here no derogation from the higher mediatorship of the Redeemer.

(15) Page 85.—Without wishing to retract anything from the leading position in this Speech, which is that all higher feelings belong to religion, or to deny that single actions should not proceed directly from stimulus of single feelings, I would say that this passage is specially applicable only to the ethics of that time, to Kant and Fichte, and particularly Kant. So long as ethics adhered to the imperative method so rigidly followed in those systems, feelings could find no place in morals, for there could not be a command, thou shalt have this or that feeling. Such a system should logically say of them all only what has been said of friendship, that man must have no time to begin it or to cherish it. But ethics should not be restricted to the narrow imperative form. It should assign to these feelings their place in the human soul. It should also acknowledge their ethical worth, not as something that can or ought to be made for some purpose and for which guidance is given in morals, but as a free, natural function of the higher life in close connection with the higher maxims and modes of acting. Ethics would then so far embrace religion, just as a presentation of religion would embrace ethics, yet both would not be on that account one and the same.

(16) Page 89.—The expression here employed that *miracle* is only the religious name for *event*, and that all that happens is miracle might easily be suspected of being a practical denial of the miraculous, for if everything is a miracle then nothing is. This stands in close connection with the explanations given in the "Glaubenslehre," § 14 note, § 34, 2, 3 and § 47. If the reference of an event to the Divine

omnipotence and the contemplation of it in its natural connection
do not exclude one another but may be parallel, which view is first
taken depends upon the direction of the attention.   Where the bearing of an event on our aims most interests us, and the examination
of the connection goes too much into details, the divine provision
will be least observed and the course of nature best.   But which of
the two views will most satisfy us depends on the one side, on how
certain we are that we have grasped the full meaning of the event, so
that we can say with some assurance that this is willed of God, and
on the other how deeply we can penetrate into the natural connection.   All this is mere subjective difference.   Hence it is plainly true
that all the events that most awake religious attention, and in which
at the same time the natural connection is most hidden, are most
regarded as miracle.   Yet it is equally true that in themselves and
in respect of the divine causality all events alike are miracle.   As in
the expositions of the " Glaubenslehre," though absolute miracle is
rejected, the religious interest in the miraculous is acknowledged and
guarded, so here I merely seek to exhibit miracle in its purity and to
remove all foreign ingredients which are more akin to stupid amazement than to the joyful anticipation of a higher meaning.

(17) Page 90.—It is difficult to treat an idea like the *effects of grace*,
which is scarcely at all current except in a peculiarly Christian form,
in such a general way as to embrace everything analogous to be
found in other religious forms.   To it belongs all that distinguishes
a human being as a special favourite of the gods.   *Revelation* is
more receptivity, *inspiration* more productivity.   Now both are
combined in the idea of grace, and pious persons are always
characterized by both.   In what follows, however, the expression
entrance of the world into man is substituted for revelation, and the
original outgoing of man into the world for inspiration.   The latter
will admit of little doubt, for every inspiration must go forth and
accomplish something in the world, and everything original must be
at least occasioned from without, and for the most part is regarded
as inspiration.   The former also is in agreement with the preceding
explanation of revelation, and because here it was necessary to make
it general it could not otherwise be conceived.   Yet it may easily be
charged to it that, for the sake of the less perfect forms of religion,
it puts the Christian in the background.   But it is not to be overlooked that the idea of the Deity does not enter our consciousness except along with the idea of the World, and that this entrance is looked
upon religiously, not speculatively, is shown sufficiently further on.

(18) Page 94.—By what is said in my " Glaubenslehre," § 3-5, I

trust that what is here said, and especially the statement that *all pious emotions exhibit through feeling the immediate presence of God in us,* may be set in a clearer light. It is hardly necessary to remind you that the existence of God generally can only be active, and as there can be no passive existence of God, the divine activity upon any object is the divine existence in respect of that object. It may, however, require to be explained why I represent the unity of our being in contrast to the multiplicity of function, as the divine in us. And you may ask why I say of this unity that it appears in the emotions of piety, seeing it can be shown from other manifestations also that self-consciousness is but a single function. In respect of the former the divine in us must be that in which the capacity to be conscious of God has its seat. Even were the criticisms just, it might still be the divine that is awakened in us in the pious emotions, and that is here the main point. For the rest, the unity of our being cannot, certainly, appear by itself, for it is absolutely inward. Most immediately it appears in the self-consciousness, in so far as single references are in the background. On the other hand, when references to single things are most prominent, the self-consciousness then most appears as a single function.

(19) Page 95.—This exposition also, it is hoped, will be made clearer and at the same time be completed by what is said in the " Glaubenslehre," especially in § 8, note 2. As everyone can compare them, it is not necessary for me to enter on a defence of myself against the supposition—I would not willingly call it accusation— which men whom I greatly honour, and some of whom have already gone hence, have drawn from this Speech. For myself I am supposed to prefer the impersonal form of thinking of the Highest Being, and this has been called now my atheism and again my Spinozism. I, however, thought that it is truly Christian to seek for piety every- where, and to acknowledge it under every form. I find, at least, that Christ enjoined this upon his disciples, and that Paul obeyed not only among the Jews and the Proselytes, but among the Heathen at Athens. When I had said in all simplicity, that it is still not indifferent whether one does not acquire or quite rejects a definite form of representing the Highest Being, and thereby obstructs generally the growth of his piety, I did not think it necessary to protest further against all consequences. I did not remember how often a person going straightforward seems to be going to the left to a person going to the right. But none who reflect on the little that is said about pantheism will suspect me of any materialistic pantheism. And if any one look at it rightly, he will find that, on

the one side, every one must recognize it as an almost absolute
necessity for the highest stage of piety to acquire the conception of a
personal God, and on the other he will recognize the essential imperfection in the conception of a personality of the Highest Being,
nay, how hazardous it is, if it is not most carefully kept pure. The
conception is necessary whenever one would interpret to himself or
to others immediate religious emotions, or whenever the heart has
immediate intercourse with the Highest Being. Yet the profoundest
of the church fathers have ever sought to purify the idea. Were the
definite expressions they have used to clear away what is human
and limited in the form of personality put together, it would be as
easy to say that they denied personality to God as that they ascribed
it to Him. As it is so difficult to think of a personality as truly
infinite and incapable of suffering, a great distinction should be
drawn between a personal God and a living God. The latter idea
alone distinguishes from materialistic pantheism and atheistic blind
necessity. Within that limit any further wavering in respect of
personality must be left to the representative imagination and the
dialectic conscience, and where the pious sense exists, they will guard
each other. Does the former fashion a too human personality, the
latter restrains by exhibiting the doubtful consequences; does the
latter limit the representation too much by negative formulas, the
former knows how to suit it to its need. I was specially concerned
to show that, if one form of the conception does not in itself exclude
all piety, the other as little necessarily includes it. How many men
are there in whose lives piety has little weight and influence, for
whom this conception of personality is indispensable as a general
supplement to their chain of causality which on both sides is broken
off ; and how many, on the other hand, show the deepest piety who, in
what they say of the Highest Being, have never rightly developed the
idea of personality !

(20) Page 99.—This passage is different from the former edition.
Partly the statement that morality generally cannot be manipulated,
though right in the connection, seemed to require closer definition
if there was not to be misunderstanding; partly the whole view
seemed to me only rightly completed by the addition that freedom
and morality would be endangered by the prospect of divine recompense. In the strife on this point, especially as it is carried on
between the Kantians and the Eudaimonists, the great difference
between presenting divine recompense as an inducement and using
it theoretically to explain the order of the world has very often been
overlooked. The former is an immoral and therefore specially an

unchristian procedure, and is never employed by true heralds of Christianity and has no place in the Scriptures ; the other is natural and necessary, for it alone shows how the divine law extends over the whole nature of man, and so far from causing a rift in human nature, it most fully guards its unity. But this explanation will be very different in proportion as love of truth and desire of knowledge are free from all foreign ingredients. It is hardly to be denied that the demands of self-love will most claim arbitrariness for the divine recompense, and as arbitrariness can only have its seat in personality, it will be accompanied by the narrowest conceptions of the divine personality.

(21) Page 101.—This passage has met very much the same fate as the passage which treated of the personality of God. It was also directed against narrow and impure conceptions and it has raised the same misunderstandings. I am supposed to disparage the hope of immortality in the usual sense of the word, representing it as a weakness and contending against it. But this was not the place to declare myself in respect of the truth of the matter, or to offer the view of it which I, as a Christian, hold. This will be found in the second part of my " Glaubenslehre," and both passages should supplement each other. There I had only to answer the question whether this hope was so essential to a pious direction of the mind that the two stood or fell together. What could I do but answer in the negative, seeing it is now usually accepted that the people of the old Covenant did not, in earlier times, have this hope, and seeing also that it is easy to show that, in the state of pious emotion, the soul is rather absorbed in the present moment than directed towards the future ? Only it appears hard that this Speech should deduce not doubtfully the hope so widely diffused among the noblest men of a restoration of the individual life not again to be interrupted, from the lowest stage of self-love, seeing it might as well have been ascribed to the interest of love in the beloved objects. All the forms under which the hope of immortality can present itself as the highest self-consciousness of the spirit being before me, just in contrast to the opponents of the faith it seemed to me natural and necessary to utter the warning that any particular way of conceiving immortality and especially that which has unmistak-able traces of a lower interest hidden behind it, is not to be confused with the reality. I thus sought to prepare for grasping the question, not as it is entirely limited to personality or to a self-consciousness chained to single affinities, but as it is natural in one in whom personal interest is purified by subordination to a self-consciousness

that is ennobled by the consciousness of the human race and of human nature. On the other side, in order to avoid endless and wide-spreading explanations, it was necessary to make the opponents of religion observe that there could be no religious discussion of this matter except among those who have already cultivated in themselves the higher life, given by true piety, which is worthy to conquer death. If I am somewhat severe on the self-deception of a mean way of thinking and feeling, which is proud that it can comprehend immortality and that it is guided by the accompanying hope and fear, I can only say in self-defence that there is nothing of mere rhetoric in it, but that it has always been with me a very strong feeling. I desire no more than that each man, if he would test his piety, should see, not merely, as Plato says, that souls appear before the judges of the Underworld stripped of all alien ornament conferred by the external relations of life, but, laying aside these claims to endless existence and considering himself just as he is, that he then decide whether these claims are anything more than the titles of lands, never possessed and never to be possessed, wherewith the great ones of the earth often think they must adorn themselves. If, thus stripped, he still find that that eternal life is with him to which the end of this Speech points, he will readily understand what I am aiming at in my presentation of the Christian faith. Furthermore, the parallel between the two ideas of God and immortality in respect of the different ways of conception here indicated, is not to be over-looked. The most anthropomorphic view of God usually presupposes a morally corrupt consciousness, and the same holds of such a conception of immortality as pictures the Elysian fields as just a more beautiful and wider earth. As there is a great difference between inability to think of God as in this way personal and the inability to think of a living God at all, so there is between one who does not hold such a sensuous conception of immortality and one who does not hope for any immortality. As we call everyone pious who believes in a living God, so without excluding any kind or manner we would hold the same of those who believe in an eternal life of the spirit.

THIRD SPEECH

As I myself have willingly confessed, the endeavour to
make proselytes from unbelievers is deep rooted in the
character of religion. Yet that is not what now urges
me to speak to you of the cultivation of man for this
noble capacity. For this cultivation we believers know of
only one means—the free expression and communication
of religion. When religion moves in a man with all its
native force, when it carries every faculty of his spirit
imperiously along in the stream of its impulse, we expect
it to penetrate into the hearts of all who live and
breathe within its influence. Every corresponding element
being stirred by this life-giving power, they should attain
a consciousness of their existence, and the attentive ear
should be gladdened by an answering note of kindred
sound. Where the pious person fails to awake a life
like his by the natural expression of his own life, he will
despise nobly every strange charm, every exercise of force,
in the calm conviction that the time has not yet come
for anything congenial to appear.

The unsuccessful issue is not new to any of us. How
often have I struck up the music of my religion, seeking
to move the bystanders! Beginning with single soft
notes, I have soon been swept on by youthful impetuosity
to the fullest harmony of the religious feelings. But
nothing stirred, nothing answered in the hearers. I have
entrusted these words to a larger and more versatile

circle, yet from how many, despite of those advantages, will they return in sadness without having been understood, yea, without having awaked the vaguest suspicion of their purpose! And how often, for all who proclaim religion, and for me along with them, will this fate which has been appointed us from the beginning, be renewed! Yet this shall never distress us. The difficulty we know may not otherwise be met, and we shall never be moved from our quiet equanimity to attempt in any other fashion to force our way of thinking either upon this or the future generation.

Everyone of us misses in himself not a little that belongs to a complete humanity, and many lack much. What wonder, then, if the number in whom religion refuses to develope should be great! Necessarily it must be great, else how could we come to see it in—if I might so say—its incarnate, historical existence, or discern the bounds it sets on all sides to the other capacities of man, or how by them again it is in manifold ways bounded. Or how should we know how far man can anywhere succeed without it, and where it sustains him and forwards him; or guess that, without his knowledge, it is busy in him.

But especially in these times of universal confusion and upheaval, it is natural that its slumbering spark should not glow up in many, however lovingly or patiently we tend it, and that, even in persons in whom under happier circumstances it would have broken through all obstacles, it is not brought to life. In all human things nothing remains unshaken. Every man must continually face the possibility of having to abandon the very belief that determines his place in the world and binds him to the earthly order of things. And he may find no other, but may sink in the general whirlpool. One class shun no concentration of their own powers and shout also towards every side for help, that they may hold fast what they take

to be the poles of the world and of society, of art and of
science, which by an indescribable destiny, as it were of
their own accord, suddenly leap from their sockets and
allow all that has so long revolved around them to fall ;
the other class, with a like restless zeal, are busy clearing
away the ruins of fallen centuries, seeking to be the first to
settle on the fruitful ground that is being formed beneath
from the quickly cooling lava of the dread volcano.

Even without leaving his place, every man is so mightily
affected by the vehement shaking of all things that, in the
universal giddiness, he must be glad to fix his eye steadily
enough on any one object, to be able to keep to it and con-
vince himself gradually that something still stands. In
such a state of things it would be foolish to expect that
many could be fit to cultivate and retain religious feelings
which prosper best in quiet. In the midst of this ferment,
indeed, the aspect of the moral world is more majestic and
noble than ever, and at moments there are hints of more
significant traits than ever before in the centuries. Yet
who can rescue himself from the universal turmoil ? Who
can escape the power of narrower interests ? Who has
calm enough to stand still and steadfastness enough for
undisturbed contemplation ?

But suppose the happiest times and suppose the best
will not only to arouse by communication the capacity for
religion where it does exist, but, by every possible way,
to ingraft and to impart it. Where, then, is there such a
way ? All that the activity and art of one man can do for
another is to communicate conceptions to be the basis of
thoughts, and so far to associate them with his own ideas
that they may be remembered at fitting times. But no
one can arrive at the point of making others think what
thoughts he will. There is a contrariety that cannot be
eliminated from words, and much less can you get beyond
this means and freely produce what inner activity you
will. In short, on the mechanism of the spirit everyone

can, in some measure, work, but into its organization, into
the sacred workshop of the Universe, no one can enter at
pleasure. No one can change or disarrange, take from
or add to. At the most he may, by means of this mechanism,
retard the development of the spirit. Part of the growth
may thus be violently mutilated, but nothing can be
moulded. From this sanctuary of his organization which
force cannot enter, all that pertains to the true life of man,
all that should be an ever alert, operative impulse in him,
proceeds.

And such is religion. In the spirit it inhabits it is uninterruptedly active and strong, making everything an
object for itself and turning every thought and action into
a theme for its heavenly phantasy. Like everything
else, then, that should be ever present, ever active in the
human soul, it lies far beyond the domain of teaching and
imparting. Instruction in religion, meaning that piety
itself is teachable, is absurd and unmeaning. Our opinions
and doctrines we can indeed communicate, if we have
words and our hearers have the comprehending, imagining
power of the understanding. But we know very well that
those things are only the shadows of our religious emotions,
and if our pupils do not share our emotions, even though
they do understand the thought, they have no possession
that can truly repay their toil. This retreat into oneself,
there to perceive oneself, cannot be taught. Even the
most inspired person who can see, it matters not before
what object he finds himself, the original light of the
Universe, cannot by the word of instruction transfer this
power and dexterity to another.

There is, indeed, an imitative talent which in some
perhaps we can so far arouse as to make it easy for them,
when sacred feelings are represented in powerful tones, to
produce in themselves somewhat similar emotions. But
does that touch their deepest nature? Is it, in the true
sense of the word, religion? If you would compare the

sense for the Universe with the sense for art, you must not compare the possessors of a passive religiousness—if you care so to name it—with those who, without producing works of art themselves, are responsive to everything that has to do with viewing them. The works of art of religion are always and everywhere exposed. The whole world is a gallery of religious scenes, and every man finds himself in the midst of them. Wherefore, you must liken them to persons who cannot be made to feel till commentaries and imaginings on works of art are brought as medicinal charms for the deadened sense, and who even then only lisp, in an ill-understood terminology, some inappropriate words that are not their own. So much and no more you can accomplish by mere teaching. This is the goal of all conscious educating and exercising in such things. Show me one man to whom you have imparted power of judgment, the spirit of observation, feeling for art or morality, then will I pledge myself to teach religion also.

Of course there is in religion a mastership and a discipleship. But this attachment is no blind imitation. It is not the master that makes disciples, but he is their master because of their choice.[1] And if, by the utterance of our own religion, religion is awakened in others, we cannot retain it in our power or attach it to ourselves. As soon as it lives, their religion also is free and goes its own way. On blazing up in the soul, the sacred spark spreads to a free and living flame, fed by its own atmosphere. More or less it illumines for the soul the whole circuit of the world, so that, following his own impulse, he may settle far away from the place where first the new life was lit. Compelled simply by the feeling of weakness and finitude, by an original, inward determination to settle in some definite quarter, without being ungrateful to his first guide, he makes choice of that climate which suits him best. There he seeks for himself a centre, and moving self-limited in his new course, of his own choice and spontaneous liking, he calls himself the disciple of him who first settled in this dear spot and showed its splendour.[2]

I do not, therefore, aim at training either you or others to religion. Nor would I teach you by resolve or rule to train yourselves. I would not leave the sphere of religion —as by doing so I would—but a little longer I would tarry with you within. The Universe itself trains its own observers and admirers, and how that comes to pass we shall now see, as far as it can be seen.

You know how each element of humanity discloses itself by the place it maintains against the others. By this universal strife everything in every man attains a determinate form and size. Now this strife is only sustained by the fellowship of the single elements, by the movement of the Whole. Hence every man and every thing in every man is a work of the Whole. This is the only way in which the pious sense can conceive man. Now I wish to return to the religious limitation of our contemporaries which you praise and I bewail. I wish to regard it in this aspect and to make it clear why we are thus and not otherwise, and what must happen if our limits are to be widened. Would that I could at the same time make you conscious that you also by your being and doing are tools of the Universe, and that your deed, towards quite other things directed, has an influence upon the present state of religion.

Man is born with the religious capacity as with every other. If only his sense for the profoundest depths of his own nature is not crushed out, if only all fellowship between himself and the Primal Source is not quite shut off, religion would, after its own fashion, infallibly be developed. But in our time, alas! that is exactly what, in very large measure, does happen. With pain I see daily how the rage for calculating and explaining suppresses the sense. I see how all things unite to bind man to the finite, and to a very small portion of the finite, that the infinite may as far as possible vanish from his eyes.

Who hinders the prosperity of religion? Not you, not the doubters and scoffers. Even though you were all of one mind to have no religion, you would not disturb Nature in her purpose of producing piety from the depths of the soul, for your influence could only later find prepared soil. Nor, as is supposed, do the immoral most hinder the prosperity of religion, for it is quite a different power to which their endeavours are opposed. But the discreet and practical men of to-day are, in the present state of the world, the foes of religion, and their great preponderance is the cause why it plays such a poor and insignificant *rôle*, for from tender childhood they maltreat man, crushing out his higher aspirations.

With great reverence I regard the longing of young minds for the marvellous and supernatural. Joyfully taking in the motley show of things, they seek at the same time something else to set over against it. They search everywhere for something surpassing the accustomed phenomena and the light play of life. However many earthly objects are presented for their knowing, there seems still another sense unnourished. That is the first stirrings of religion. A secret, inexplicable presentiment urges them past the riches of this world. Every trace of another is welcome to them, and they delight themselves in fictions of unearthly beings. All that it is most evident to them cannot be here, they embrace with that strong and jealous love devoted to objects, the right to which is strongly felt, but cannot be established. True, it is a delusion to seek the Infinite immediately outside of the finite, but is it not natural in those who know but the surface of even the finite and sensuous? Is it not the delusion of whole peoples and whole schools of wisdom?

Were there but guardians of religion among those who care for the young, how easily could this natural error be

corrected! And, in clearer times, how greedily would
young souls then abandon themselves to the impressions
of the Infinite in its omnipresence!

It were even better if life were left quietly to take its
own course. Let it be supposed that the taste for grotesque figures is as natural to the young imagination in
religion as in art, and let it be richly satisfied. Have no
anxiety when the earnest and sacred mythology, that is
considered the very essence of religion, is immediately
united with the careless games of childhood. Suppose that
the Heavenly Father, the Saviour, the angels are but
another kind of fairies and sylphs. In many, perhaps, the
foundation may be laid for an insufficient and dead letter.
While the images grow pale, the word, as the empty frame
in which they have been fixed, may remain hanging. But
man, thus treated, would be more left to himself, and a
right-thinking, uncorrupted soul that knew how to keep
himself free from the titillation of scraping and scheming,
would more easily find, in due time, the natural issue from
this labyrinth.

Now, on the contrary, that tendency is, from the beginning, forcibly suppressed. Everything mysterious and
marvellous is proscribed. Imagination is not to be filled
with airy images! It is just as easy to store the memory
with real objects and to be preparing for life! Poor young
souls, desiring quite other fare, are wearied with moral tales
and have to learn how beautiful and necessary it is to be
genteel and discreet. The current conceptions of things
that they would of themselves have encountered soon
enough, are impressed upon them, as if it were an urgent
business that could never be too soon accomplished.
Without regard to their real want, there is given them that
of which far too soon there will be too much.

In proportion as man must busy himself in a narrow way
with a single object, to rescue the universality of the sense
an impulse awakes in everyone to allow the dominating

activity and all its kindred to rest, and to open all organs to the influence of all impressions. By a secret and most helpful sympathy this impulse is strongest when the general life reveals itself most clearly in our own breasts and in the surrounding world. But to yield to this impulse in comfortable inactivity cannot be permitted, for, from the middle-class standpoint, it would be laziness and idling. In everything there must be design and aim ; somewhat has always to be performed, and if the spirit can no more serve, the body must be exercised. Work and play, but no quiet, submissive contemplation !

But most of all, men are to be taught to analyze and explain. By this explaining they are completely cheated of their sense, for, as it is conducted, it is absolutely opposed to any perceptive sense. *Sense* of its own accord seeks objects for itself, it advances to meet them and it offers to embrace them. It communicates something to them which distinguishes them as its possession, its work.

It will find and be found. But this *explaining* knows nothing of this living acquisition, of this illuminating truth, of the true spirit of discovery in childlike intuition. But from first to last, objects are to be transcribed accurately in thought as something simply given. They are, God be thanked, for all men ever the same, and who knows how long already they have been docketed in good order with all their qualities defined. Take them, then, only as life brings them, and understand that and nothing more. But to seek for yourselves and to wish to have living intercourse with things is eccentric and high-flown. It is a vain endeavour, availing nothing in human life, where things are only to be seen and handled as they have already presented themselves.

Fruitful in human life this endeavour is not, except that, without it, an active life, resting on true inward culture, is not to be found. The sense strives to comprehend the undivided impress of something whole ; it will perceive what each thing is and how it is ; it will know everything in its peculiar character. But that is not what they mean by understanding. What and how are too remote for them, around whence and to what end, they eternally circle. They seek to grasp nothing in and for itself, but only in special aspects, and therefore, not as a whole, but only piecemeal. To inquire or thoroughly examine whether the object they would understand is a whole, would lead them too far. Were this their desire, they could hardly escape so utterly without religion.

But all must be used for some excellent purpose, wherefore they dissever and anatomize. This is how they deal with what exists chiefly for the highest satisfaction of the sense, with what, in their despite, is a whole in itself, I mean with all that is art in nature and in the works of man. Before it can operate they annihilate it by explaining it in detail. Having first by decomposition robbed it of its character as art, they would teach and impress this or that lesson from the fragments.

You must grant that this is the practice of our people of understanding, and you must confess that a superabundance of sense is necessary if anything is to escape this hostile treatment. On that account alone the number must be small who are capable of such a contemplation of any object as might awake in them religion.

But this development is still more checked. The utmost is done to divert the remaining sense from the Universe. Truth and all that in it is, must be confined in the limits of the civil life. All actions must bear upon this life, while, again, it is believed that the boasted inner harmony of man means that everything bears upon his actions and they never think that, if it is to be a true and free life, the existence of an individual in the state, even as of the state itself, must have arisen from the Whole. But they are sunk in blind idolatry of the existing civil life, they are convinced that it affords material enough for the sense and

displays rich enough pictures. Hence they have a right
to guard against discontented seeking for something else
and departure from the natural centre and axis. All
emotions and endeavours not so directed, are but useless
and exhausting exercises, from which, by purposeful
activity, the soul must as much as possible be restrained.
Pure love to art, or even to nature itself, is for them an
extravagance, only to be endured because it is not quite
so bad as other tendencies, and because many find in it consolation and compensation in various ills. Knowledge is
sought with a wise and sober moderation and never without regard to practical life. The smallest thing that has
influence in this sphere is not to be neglected, and the
greatest, just because it goes further, is decried, as if it
were mean and perverted.

That, nevertheless, there are things which, to some little
depth must be explored, is for them a necessary evil, and
that a few are ever to be found who, from unconquerable
liking, undertake it, they thank the gods, and with sacred
pity regard them as willing sacrifices. They most sincerely
lament that there are feelings which cannot be tamed by
the external sway of their formulas and precepts, and that
in this way many men are rendered socially unhappy or
immoral. People for whom the moral side of civil life is
everything, and whom, though they may step a little
beyond their trade, I reckon also among this class, consider this one of the profoundest evils of human nature, to be
got rid of with all possible speed. The good people believe
that their own activity is everything and exhausts the task
of humanity, and that, if all would do what they do, they
would require no sense for anything except for action.
Wherefore they dock everything with their shears, and
they will not suffer a single characteristic phenomenon that
might awake a religious interest to grow. What can be
seen and understood from their standpoint is all they allow,
and it is merely a small, barren circle, without science, with-

out morals, without art, without love, without spirit, I might almost say without letter.[3] In short, it is without anything whereby the world might disclose itself, and yet it has many lofty pretensions to the same. They think, indeed, that they have the true and real world, and that they are the people who grasp and treat all things in their true connection.

Would that they could but once see that, for anything to be known as an element of the Whole, it must necessarily be contemplated in its characteristic nature and in its fullest completeness! In the Universe it can be nothing except by the totality of its effects and relations. That is the sum and substance, and, to perceive it, every matter must be considered, not from some outside point, but from its own proper centre, which is to say, in its separate existence, its own proper nature. This is to have all points of view for everything, and the opposite is to have one point of view for all, which is the most direct way to leave the Universe behind, to sink in lamentable narrowness and become a serf bound to the spot of earth on which we happen to stand.

In the relations of man to this world there are certain openings into the Infinite, prospects past which all are led that their sense may find its way to the Whole. Immediate feelings of definite content may not be produced by this glimpse, but there may be a general susceptibility to all religious feelings. Those prospects therefore, are wisely blocked up, and in the opening some philosophical caricature is placed as an ill-favoured place is at times covered by some sorry picture.

And if, as happens at times, the omnipotence of the Universe makes itself manifest in those people of understanding themselves, if some ray penetrating falls upon their eyes and their soul cannot be shielded from some stirring of those emotions, the Infinite is never a goal to which they fly for rest. It is as a post at the end of a course, simply a point to be rounded, without touching, at the greatest speed, and the sooner they can return to their old place the better.

Birth and death are such points. Before them it is impossible to forget that our own self is completely surrounded by the Infinite. Despite of their frequency, so soon as they touch us more nearly, they always stir a quiet longing and a holy reverence. The measurelessness of sense perception is also a hint at least of a still higher infinity. But nothing would please better those persons of understanding than to be able to use the greatest radius of the system of the worlds, as men now use the meridian of the earth, for measuring and reckoning in common life. And, if the images of life and death do approach them, believe me, however much they may speak of religion, it does not lie so near their hearts as to use the occasion to win some few young people for caution and economy in the use of their powers and for the noble art of lengthening life.

Punished they certainly are. They reach no standpoint from which they might themselves rear, from the foundation, this worldly wisdom in which they trust, but move slavishly and reverently in ancient forms or divert themselves with little improvements. This is the extreme of utilitarianism to which the age with rapid strides is being hurried by worthless scholastic word-wisdom. This new barbarism is a fit counterpart of the old. It is the beautiful fruit of the paternal eudaimonistic politics which has supplanted rude despotism and permeates all departments of life. We have all been affected, and the capacity for religion, not being able to keep pace in its development with other things, has suffered in the early bud.

These men, the crazy buttresses of a crumbling time, I distinguish from you, even as you would not have yourselves made equal with them, for they do not despise religion, and they are not to be called cultured. But they destroy religion as much as they can, and they train the age and enlighten men, even to transparency, if they had their will.   They are still the dominating party, and you and we are but a very few.   Whole towns and countries are educated on their principles.   Those again who have come through this education, are found in society, in science, and in philosophy.   Nay, philosophy is their peculiar place of abode.   And now it is not merely ancient philosophy— using the present highly historical classification into ancient new and newest—but the new also they have annexed. By their vast influence on every worldly interest and the semblance of philanthropy which dazzles the social inclination, this way of thinking ever holds religion in subjection, and resists every movement whereby its life might anywhere reveal itself with full power.

Religion at present can only be advanced by the strongest resistance to this general tendency, and it cannot begin except by radical opposition.   As everything follows the law of affinity, sense can only triumph by taking possession of an object on which this kind of understanding so hostile to it, hangs but loosely.   This it will acquire most easily and with superfluity of free power.   Now this object is the inner, not the outer world.   The enlightening psychology, the masterpiece of this kind of understanding, has at length exhausted itself by extravagance and lost almost all good name.   The calculating understanding has here first vacated the field and left it open once more for pure obser- vation.   A religious man must be reflective, his sense must be occupied in the contemplation of himself.   Being occu- pied with the profoundest depths, he abandons meanwhile all external things, intellectual as well as physical, leaving them to be the great aim of the researches of the people of understanding.   In accordance with this law, the feeling for the Infinite is most readily developed in persons whose nature keeps them far from that which is the central point of all the opponents of the universal complete life.   Hence it comes that, from of old, all truly religious characters have had a mystical trait, and that all imaginative natures, which are too airy to occupy themselves with solid and rigid worldly affairs, have at least some stirrings of piety. This is the character of all the religious appearances of our time ; from those two colours, imagination and mysticism, though in various proportions, they are all composed. Appearances I say, because, in this state of things, more is scarcely to be expected.

Imaginative natures fail in penetrative spirit, in capacity for mastering the essential. A light changing play of beautiful, often charming, but merely fortuitous and entirely subjective combinations, satisfies them and is the highest they can conceive, and a deeper and inner connection presents itself in vain. They are really only seeking the infinity and universality of charming appearances. According as it is viewed this may be less or very much more than their sense can attain, but to appearance they have accommodated themselves, and instead of a healthy and powerful life, they have only disconnected and fleeting emotions. The mind is easily kindled, but it is with a flame as unsteady as it is ready. They have emotions of religion just as they have of art, philosophy and all things great and beautiful —they are attracted by the surface.

To the very nature of the other class, again, religion pre-eminently belongs. But their sense always remains turned towards themselves, for, in the present condition of the world, they do not know how to attain anything beyond, and they soon fail in material for cultivating their feeling to an independent piety. There is a great and powerful mysticism, not to be considered by the most frivolous man without reverence and devotion, which, by its heroic simplicity and proud scorn of the world, wrings admiration from the most judicious. It does not arise from being sated and overladen by external influences, but, on every occasion, some secret power ever drives the man back upon himself, and he finds himself to be the plan and key of the

Whole. Convinced by a great analogy and a daring faith that it is not necessary to forsake himself, but that the spirit has enough in itself to be conscious of all that could be given from without, by a free resolve, he shuts his eyes for ever against all that is not himself. Yet this contempt is no ignorance, this closing of the sense no incapacity.

Thus, alas! it stands with our party at the present day. They have not learned to open their souls to Nature. Their living relation to it suffers from the clumsy way in which objects are rather indicated than shown, and they have neither sense nor light remaining from their self-contemplation sufficient to penetrate this ancient darkness. Wherefore, in scorn of this evil age, they would fain have nothing to do with its work in them. Their higher feeling is thus untrained and needy, and their true inward fellowship with the world is both confined and sickly. Alone with their sense, they are compelled to circulate eternally in an all too narrow sphere, and, after a sickly life, their religious sense dies, from want of attraction, of indirect weakness.

Another end awaits those whose sense for the highest turns boldly outwards, seeking there expansion and renovation for its life. Their disharmony with the age only too clearly appears, for they suffer a violent death, happy if you will, yet fearful, the suicide of the spirit. Not knowing how to comprehend the world, the essence and larger sense of which remains strange to them among the paltry views to which an outward constraint limits them, they are deceived by confused phenomena, abandoned to unbridled fancies, and seek the Universe and its traces where they never were. Finally they unwillingly rend asunder utterly the connection of the inner and the outer, chase the impotent understanding and end in a holy madness, the source of which almost no man knows. They are loud screaming but not understood victims of the general contempt and maltreatment of the heart of man. Only victims, however, not heroes, for whosoever succumbs, though it be in the final test, cannot be reckoned among the recipients of the inmost mysteries.

This complaint that there are no permanent, openly recognized representatives of religion among us, is not to recall my earlier assertions that our age is not less favourable to religion than any other. The amount of religion in the world is not diminished, but it is broken up and driven apart by an oppressive force. It reveals itself in small and fleeting though frequent manifestations that rather exalt the variety of the Universe and delight the eye of the observer, than produce for itself a great and sublime impression. I abide by the conviction that there are many who breathe out the sweetest fragrance of the young life in sacred longing and love to the Eternal and the Changeless, and who late at least, and perhaps never, are overcome by the world; that there are none to whom once, at least, the high World-Spirit has not appeared, casting on them, while they were ashamed for themselves and blushed at their unworthy limitation, one of those piercing glances that the downcast eye feels without seeing. By this I abide, and the conscience of everyone can judge of it. But heroes of religion, holy souls, as they have been seen, who are entirely permeated by religion which is all in all to them, are wanting and must be wanting to this generation. And as often as I reflect on what must happen and what direction our culture must take, if religious men of a higher type are again to appear as a natural if rare product of their age, I think that your whole endeavour—whether consciously, you may yourselves decide—is not a little helpful for a palingenesis of religion. Partly your general working, partly the endeavours of a narrower circle, partly the sublime ideas of a few spirits notable among mankind, shall serve this purpose.[4]

The strength and compass, as well as the purity and clearness of every perception, depend upon the keenness and vigour of the sense. Suppose the wisest man without opened senses. He would not be nearer religion than the most thoughtless and wanton who only had an open and true sense. Here then we must begin. An end must be made to the slavery in which the sense of man is held, for the benefit of exercisings of the understanding whereby nothing is exercised, of those enlightenments that make nothing clear, of those dissectings whereby nothing is resolved. This is an end for which you will all labour with united powers. It has happened to the improvements in education as to all revolutions that have not been begun on the highest principles : things have gradually glided back into the old course, and only a few changes in externals preserve the memory of what was at first considered a marvellously great occurrence. Hence our judicious and practical education of to-day is but little distinguished from the ancient mechanical article, and that little is neither in spirit nor in working. This has not escaped you. It begins to be as detestable to all truly cultured people as it is to me. A juster idea of the sacredness of childhood and the eternity of inviolable liberty is spreading. Even in the first stages of development, it is seen that the manifestations of liberty must be expected and inquired for. Soon those barriers shall be broken down; the intuitive power will take possession of its whole domain, every organ will be opened, and it will be possible for objects, in all ways, to affect man.

With this regained liberty of sense, however, a limitation and firm direction of the activity may very well consist. This is the great demand from contemporaries and posterity, with which the best among you are coming forward. You are tired of seeing barren, encyclopædic versatility. Only by this way of self-limitation have you become what you are, and you know there is no other way to culture. You insist, therefore, that everyone should seek to become something definite, and follow something with steadfastness and concentration. No one can perceive the justice of this counsel better than the man who has ripened to a certain universality of sense, for he must know that, except by separation and limitation, perception would have no objects. I rejoice, therefore, at these efforts, and would they had had more success. Religion would thereby receive excellent help, for this very limitation of effort, if only the sense itself is not limited, all the more surely prepares for the sense the way to the Infinite and opens again the long interrupted intercourse. Whosoever has seen and known much and can then resolve, with his whole might, to do and forward something for its own sake, must recognize, if he is not to contradict himself, that other things have been made and have a right to existence for their own sakes. And when he has succeeded to the utmost in the object of his choice, it will least of all escape him at the summit of perfection that, without all the rest, this is nothing. This recognition of the strange and annihilation of the personal that urge themselves everywhere upon a thoughtful man, this seasonably changing love and contempt for all that is finite and limited are not possible without a dim presentiment of the World and God, and they must call forth a more definite longing for the One in the All.

Every man knows from his own consciousness three spheres of the sense in which its different manifestations are divided. First there is the interior of the Ego itself; second, the outer world, in so far as it is indefinite and incomplete—call it mass, matter, element, or what you will; the third seems to unite both, the sense turning, in constant change, within and without, and only finding peace in perceiving the absolute unity of both sides, which is the sphere of the individual, of what is complete in itself, of all that is art in nature, and in the works of man. Everyone is not equally at home in all those spheres, but from each there is a way to pious exaltations of the soul which take characteristic form simply according to the variety of the ways in which they have been found.

Study yourselves with unswerving attention, put aside all that is not self, proceed with the sense ever more closely directed to the purely inward. The more you pass by all foreign elements, making your personality appear diminished almost to the vanishing point, the clearer the Universe stands before you, and the more gloriously the terror of annihilating the fleeting is rewarded by the feeling of the eternal.

Look outside again on one of the widely distributed elements of the world. Seek to understand it in itself, and seek it in particular objects, in yourself and everywhere. Traverse again and again your way from centre to circumference, going ever farther afield. You will rediscover everything everywhere, and you will only be able to recognize it in relation to its opposite. Soon everything individual and distinct will have been lost and the Universe be found.

What way now leads from the third sphere, from the sense for art? Its immediate object is by no means the Universe itself. It is an individual thing complete in itself and rounded off. There is satisfaction in each enjoyment, and the mind, peacefully sunk in it, is not driven to such a progress as would make the single thing gradually disappear and be replaced by the Universe. Is there nowhere any way, but must this sphere for ever remain apart, and artists be condemned to be irreligious? Or is there perhaps some other relation between art and religion? I could wish to leave the question for your own solution, for to me the inquiry is too difficult and too strange. But you have used your sense and love for art to good purpose, and I would willingly leave you to yourselves on your native soil. One of my thoughts on the matter, however, I would have not to be wish and presentiment merely but insight and prophecy. But judge for yourselves. If it is true that there are sudden conversions whereby in men, thinking of nothing less than of lifting themselves above the finite, in a moment, as by an immediate, inward illumination, the sense for the highest comes forth and surprises them by its splendour, I believe that more than anything else the sight of a great and sublime work of art can accomplish this miracle. And I would believe that, without any gradual approximation beforehand, you may perhaps be met by such a beam of your own sun and turned to religion.

By the first way of finding the Universe, the most abstracted self-contemplation, the most ancient eastern Mysticism, with marvellous boldness that resembled the more recent Idealism among us, linked the infinitely great to the infinitely little and found everything bordering on nothing.

From the contemplation of the masses and their counterparts, again, every religion, the pattern of which is the heavens or elemental nature, has manifestly proceeded. The polytheistic Egypt was long the most perfect nurse of this type of thought. In it we can at least guess that the purest intuition of the original and real may have walked in meek tolerance close beside the darkest superstitions and the most senseless mythology.[5]

And if there is nothing to tell of a religion originating in art that has ruled peoples and times, it is all the clearer that the sense for art has never approached those two kinds of religion without covering them with new beauty and holiness and sweetly mitigating their original narrowness. Thus the ancient sages and poets, and above all, the artists of the Greeks, changed the natural religion into fairer, more gladsome form. In all the mythical representations of the divine Plato and his followers, which you would acknowledge rather as religious than as scientific, we perceive how beautifully that mystical self-contemplation mounts to the highest pinnacle of divineness and humanness. Simply by the ordinary life in the sphere of art and by a living endeavour, sustained by indwelling power and especially by poetic art, he penetrates from one form of religion to the opposite and unites both. One can only marvel, therefore, at the beautiful self-forgetfulness with which in holy zeal, as a just king that does not spare even his too soft-hearted mother, he speaks against art, for, where there was no corruption and no misunderstanding produced by corruption, the work of art was but a free-will service rendered to the imperfect natural religions.

At present art serves no religion, and all is different and worse. Religion and art stand together like kindred beings, whose inner affinity, though mutually unrecognized and unsuspected, appears in various ways.[6] Like the opposite poles of two magnets, being mutually attracted, they are violently agitated but cannot overcome their gravity so as to touch and unite. Friendly words and outpourings of the heart are ever on their lips, but they are always held back, as they cannot find again the right manner and the last reason of their thinking and longing. They await a fuller revelation and, suffering and sighing under the same load, they see each other enduring, with heartfelt liking and deep feeling perhaps, but without the love that truly unites. Will this common burden bring about the happy moment of their union, or from pure love and joy is there to be as you desire a new day for art alone? However it comes, whichever is first set free will certainly hasten, with at least a sister's faithfulness, to aid the other.

But religion of both types not only is without the aid of art, but is, in its own state, worse than of old. The two sources of perception and feeling of the Infinite streamed forth magnificently upon an age when scientific subtilties, without true principles, had not yet corrupted by their commonness the purity of the sense, even though neither may have been rich enough to produce the highest. At present, they are troubled by the loss of simplicity and the ruinous influence of a conceited and false insight. How are they to be purified? Whence are they to have power and fulness for enriching the soil with more than ephemeral products ? To unite their waters in one channel, is the sole means for bringing religion to completion by the way we are now going. That would be an event, from the bosom of which, in a new and glorious form, religion would soon go to meet better times.

See then, whether you wish it or not, the goal of your highest endeavours is just the resurrection of religion. By your endeavours this event must be brought to pass, and I celebrate you as, however unintentionally, the rescuers and cherishers of religion. Do not abandon your post and your work till you have unlocked the recesses of knowledge, and, in priestlike humility, have opened the sanctuary of true science. Then all who draw nigh, and the sons of religion among them, will be compensated for what half knowledge and arrogance have made them lose.

Philosophy, exalting man to the consciousness of his reciprocity with the world, teaching him to know himself, not as a separate individual, but as a living, operative member of the Whole, will no longer endure to see the man who steadfastly turns his eye to his own spirit in search of the Universe, pine in poverty and need. The anxious wall of separation is broken down. The outer world is only another inner world. Everything is the reflection of his own spirit, as his spirit is the copy of all things. He can seek himself in this reflection without losing himself or going outside of himself. He can never exhaust himself in contemplation of himself, for in himself everything lies.

Ethics, in its chaste and heavenly beauty, far from jealousy and despotic pride, will hand him at the entrance the heavenly lyre and the magic glass, that he may see in countless forms the earnest quiet image of the spirit ever the same and may accompany it with divine music.

Natural science sets the man who looks around him to discover the Universe, in the centre of nature, and no longer suffers him to dissipate himself fruitlessly in the study of small details. He can now pursue the play of nature's powers into their most secret recesses, from the inaccessible storehouses of energized matter to the artistic workshops of the organic life. He measures its might from the bounds of world-filled space to the centre of his own Ego, and finds himself everywhere in eternal strife and in closest union. He is nature's centre and circumference. Delusion is gone and reality won. Sure is his glance and clear is his view. Under all disguises he detects it and nowhere rests except in the Infinite and the One. Already I see some distinguished forms return from the sanctuary after initiation into those mysteries, who, having purified and adorned themselves, will come forth in priestly robes.

Can one goddess, then, still linger with her helpful presence? For this, also, time will make us great and rich amends. The greatest work of art has for its material humanity itself, and the Deity directly fashions it. For this work the sense must soon awake in many, for at present, He is working with bold and effective art. And you will be the temple servants when the new forms are set up in the temple of time. Expound the Artist then with force and spirit; explain the earlier works from the later and the later from the earlier. Let the past, the present, and the future surround us with an endless gallery of the sublimest works of art, eternally multiplied by a thousand brilliant mirrors. Let the history of the worlds be ready with rich gratitude to reward religion its first nurse, by awaking true and holy worshippers for eternal might and wisdom. See how, without your aid, the heavenly growth flourishes in the midst of your plantings. It is a witness of the approval of the gods and of the imperishableness of your desert. Neither disturb it nor pluck it up; it is an ornament that adorns, a talisman that protects.

EXPLANATIONS OF THE THIRD SPEECH

(1) Page 123.—This expression appears to contradict the words of Christ which He spoke to His disciples, " Ye have not chosen me, but I have chosen you." Yet the contradiction is only apparent, for on another occasion He asked of His disciples whether they also were deceived as others had been, whereby He acknowledged that their continuance with Him was a free act. Now this is all that is here asserted. In their declaration of steadfastness, we can say, that they chose Him anew as their Master, with a quicker sense and a riper judgment. Also it would be wrong to interpret Christ's words as if they had only special reference to certain persons. This would be a particular sense which I would not defend. It was not by an original divine impulse common to Him and to them, that the kingdom of God was founded. Of subordinate movements in religion, such as reform of the church, this may very well be said, but it was not thus that Peter, as their representative, recognized Him as the profoundest and mightiest. Originally, the emotion was in Him alone ; in them there was only the capacity for having it awakened. What is here said, therefore, entirely agrees with the representation of Christ ; indeed, his relation to His disciples suggested it. Had not Christ set out from the view that every living utterance, however individual, can only awake its response in another in a universal way and that complete attachment to the individuality of another is always a free act, He could not have set His disciples on such a footing of equality as to call them brethren and friends.

(2) Page 124.—What is here said follows naturally from the passage just explained. The best example is found in the oldest Christian history, in the Proselytes from Heathenism, who forsook the Jews who first woke in them the sense of the one Highest Being and went over to Christianity. In every time when the religious life is stirred, as unquestionably it has begun to be among us since this was written, it seems to me specially necessary that all who, either from profession

or from inward call, exercise a marked religious influence, should rise
to this freer view, that they may not wonder why so many who have
received their first impulse from them, should only find their complete
rest in very different views and sentiments. Let everyone rejoice at
waking life, for he thereby approves himself an instrument of the
Divine Spirit, but let none believe that the fashioning of it continues
in his power.

(3) Page 130.—Only by this last trait is the picture of the way of
thinking here described made complete, for these men flee also the letter.
As they admit a moral, political or religious confession only, in so far
as everyone can still think what he will, so no practical rules are
valid except with the proviso of standing exceptions, that everything
following the principle of absolute utility, should stand completely
alone, as nothing through nothing for nothing. Some reader of
another stamp may look askance, however, on an expression that
ascribes a worth, and indeed no small worth, to the letter, for I
make it equal with the other qualities here named, and misunderstandings, specially struggled against at the present day are thus favoured.
I would warn him that such a conscious depreciation of what has
been set too high does not serve truth, but in part produces obstinacy
and in part it favours reaction. Therefore, we would at all times
ascribe a high degree of worth to the letter in all earnest things, in
so far as it is not separate from the spirit and dead. The immediate life in the great unities is too closely shut to be entered by the
letter, for what letter could comprehend, say, the existence of a
people? and in the individual there are elements too fleeting to be
embraced in it, for what letter could express the nature of a single
individual? But the letter is the indispensable selecting discretion,
without which we could only vibrate giddily between the individual and
the great classes. By it the chaotic indeterminate crowd is changed
into the determinate multitude. Nay, in the largest sense the ages
are distinguished by the letter, and it is the master-piece of the
highest wisdom to estimate rightly when human things require a new
letter. Does it appear too early the love for what it is to supplant
rejects it? is it too late, that giddiness has already begun which it
can no more exorcise?

(4) Page 135.—No one will suppose that I regard the manifestations
of an awakened religious life so frequent, especially in Germany at the
present time, as the fulfilment of the hope here uttered. That I do
not regard it in this way, appears clearly enough from what follows,
for a piety revived by greater openness of sense would be of a different type from what we see among us. The impatient uncharitable-

ness of our new Pietists that is not content to withdraw from what it dislikes, but uses every social relation for defamation to the danger of all free spiritual life ; their painful listening for special expressions, in accordance with which they make one man white and another black ; the indifference of most of them to all great historical events ; the aristocratic narrow-mindedness of others ; the general dislike of all science are not signs of an open sense. Rather they are signs of a deep-rooted, morbid state which must be treated with love and also with great firmness, if there is not to be more loss to society in general than gain to individuals. We will not deny that many of the lower class can only be awaked from their stupidity, and of the higher from their worldliness, by this acerb kind of piety, yet we would wish and earnestly labour that this stage should be for most but a transition to a worthier freedom of the spiritual life. This should the more easily be accomplished as it is patent enough how easily men who are concerned with something quite different from true piety, master this form, and how visibly the spirit decays that is long shut up in it.

(5) Page 139.—In the " Glaubenslehre " religion is divided as predominantly active or passive, as concerned with the problem of duty, or absolutely dependent on the Whole, as teleological or æsthetical. With this division the forms of religion here mentioned would not seem to agree, for the most abstracted self-contemplation, or the most objective contemplation of the world may be either active or passive. But I am not seeking to distinguish here the chief forms of religion, I am treating of cultivation of religion by opening of the sense. By this cultivation individuals are not introduced into a definite form of religion, but everyone is rendered capable of discerning the form that best suits him and of determining himself accordingly. Being more concerned to show the chief aspects of sense, I naturally make most prominent those forms in which one or other is most conspicuous. Yet even here it is not meant that subjective reflection has not to do with the objectively observing Ego, or objective observation with a world that awakes and sustains the spiritual life. Hence it would be vain to expect that Christianity be here assigned its place as in the " Glaubenslehre " it is placed under the ethical or teleological. Even in the Speech itself, it is hinted that that historical sense which is the completest union of both directions leads most perfectly to piety. That this sense lies quite specially at the foundation of Christianity, in which everything comes back to the relation of man to the Kingdom of God, requires no proof. It therefore naturally follows that Christianity presents a piety nourished as much by con-

templation of the world, as by self-contemplation, and is best nourished when both are most joined. Of course these are subordinate distinctions of receptivity and are naturally quite subjective and incapable of determining the different forms of Christianity.

(6) Page 140.—This affinity will hardly be denied now by anyone. Nothing but attention to the subject is required to find that, on the one hand, in all arts, all great works are religious representations, and that on the other, in all religions, Christianity not excepted, hostility to art involves barrenness and coldness. In all arts there is a severer, more sustained style and a freer and easier. Religious art mostly upholds the severer style. When religious objects are handled in the light style, the decay of religion is decided and the decay of art quickly follows. The lighter style only maintains its true character as art so long as it finds its mass and harmony in the severer. The more it renounces its connection with the severer style, and therefore with religion, the more certainly and irresistibly it degenerates into over refinement and the art of flattery. Already this has been often repeated in the history of the arts, and in individuals it is being repeated at the present day.

FOURTH SPEECH

THOSE of you who are accustomed to regard religion simply as a malady of the soul, usually cherish the idea that if the evil is not to be quite subdued, it is at least more endurable, so long as it only infects individuals here and there. On the other hand, the common danger is increased and everything put in jeopardy by too close association among the patients. So long as they are isolated, judicious treatment, due precautions against infection and a healthy spiritual atmosphere may allay the paroxysms and weaken, if they do not destroy, the virus, but in the other case the only remedy to be relied on is the curative influence of nature. The evil would be accompanied by the most dangerous symptoms and be far more deadly being nursed and heightened by the proximity of the infected. Even a few would then poison the whole atmosphere ; the soundest bodies would be infected; all the canals in which the processes of life are carried on would be destroyed; all juices would be decomposed ; and, after undergoing such a feverish delirium, the healthy spiritual life and working of whole generations and peoples would be irrecoverably ruined. Hence your opposition to the church, to every institution meant for the communication of religion is always more violent than your opposition to religion itself, and priests, as the supports and specially active members of such institutions are for you the most hated among men.

But those of you who have a somewhat milder view of religion, regarding it rather as an absurdity than as an absolute distraction, have an equally unfavourable idea of all organizations for fellowship. Slavish surrender of everything characteristic and free, spiritless mechanism and vain usages are, you consider, the inseparable consequences of every such institution. It is the skilful work of persons who with incredible success make great gain from things that are nothing, or which at least every other person could have done equally well.

Were it not that I strive to bring you in this matter to the right standpoint, I would very unwillingly expose my heart to you on such a weighty matter. How many of the perverse efforts and the sad destinies of mankind you ascribe to religion, I do not need to recount. In a thousand utterances of the most esteemed among you it is clear as day. And I will not pause to refute those charges in detail and derive them from other causes. Rather let us subject the whole idea of the church to a new consideration, reconstructing it from the centre outwards, unconcerned about how much is fact and experience.

If there is religion at all, it must be social, for that is the nature of man, and it is quite peculiarly the nature of religion. You must confess that when an individual has produced and wrought out something in his own mind, it is morbid and in the highest degree unnatural to wish to reserve it to himself. He should express it in the indispensable fellowship and mutual dependence of action. And there is also a spiritual nature which he has in common with the rest of his species which demands that he express and communicate all that is in him. The more violently he is moved and the more deeply he is impressed, the stronger that social impulse works. And this is true even if we regard it only as the endeavour to find the feeling in others, and so to be sure that nothing has been encountered that is not human.

You see that this is not a case of endeavouring to make others like ourselves, nor of believing that what is in one man is indispensable for all. It is only the endeavour to become conscious of and to exhibit the true relation of our own life to the common nature of man.

But indisputably the proper subjects for this impulse to communicate are the conscious states and feelings in which originally man feels himself passive. He is urged on to learn whether it may not be an alien and unworthy power that has produced them. Those are the things which mankind from childhood are chiefly engaged in communicating. His ideas, about the origin of which he can have no doubts, he would rather leave in quiet. Still more easily he resolves to reserve his judgments. But of all that enters by the senses and stirs the feelings he will have witnesses and participators. How could he keep to himself the most comprehensive and general influences of the world when they appear to him the greatest and most irresistible ? How should he wish to reserve what most strongly drives him out of himself and makes him conscious that he cannot know himself from himself alone ? If a religious view become clear to him, or a pious feeling stir his soul, it is rather his first endeavour to direct others to the same subject and if possible transmit the impulse.

The same nature that makes it necessary for the pious person to speak, provides him also with an audience. No element of life, so much as religion, has implanted along with it so vivid a feeling of man's utter incapacity ever to exhaust it for himself alone. No sooner has he any sense for it than he feels its infinity and his own limits. He is conscious that he grasps but a small part of it, and what he cannot himself reach he will, at least, so far as he is able, know and enjoy from the representations of those who have obtained it. This urges him to give his religion full expression, and, seeking his own perfection, to listen to every note that he can recognize as religious.

Thus mutual communication organizes itself, and speech and hearing are to all alike indispensable.

But the communication of religion is not like the communication of ideas and perceptions to be sought in books.[1] In this medium, too much of the pure impression of the original production is lost. Like dark stuffs that absorb the greater part of the rays of light, so everything of the pious emotion that the inadequate signs do not embrace and give out again, is swallowed up. In the written communication of piety, everything needs to be twice or thrice repeated, the original medium requiring to be again exhibited, and still its effect on men in general in their great unity can only be badly copied by multiplied reflection. Only when it is chased from the society of the living, religion must hide its varied life in the dead letter.

Nor can this intercourse with the heart of man be carried on in common conversation. Many who have a regard for religion have upbraided our times, because our manners are such that in conversation in society and in friendly intercourse, we talk of all weighty subjects except of God and divine things. In our defence I would say, this is neither contempt nor indifference, but a very correct instinct. Where mirth and laughing dwell, and even earnestness must pliantly associate with joke and witticism, there can be no room for what must ever be attended by holy reserve and awe. Religious views, pious feelings, and earnest reflections, are not to be tossed from one to another in such small morsels as the materials of a light conversation. On sacred subjects it would be rather sacrilegious than fitting to be ready with an answer to every question and a response to every address.[2] Religion, therefore, withdraws itself from too wide circles to the more familiar conversation of friendship or the dialogue of love, where glance and action are clearer than words, and where a solemn silence also is understood.

By way of the light and rapid exchange of retorts

common in society divine things cannot be treated, but
there must be a higher style and another kind of society
entirely consecrated to religion. On the highest subject
with which language has to deal, it is fitting that the fulness and splendour of human speech be expended. It is
not as if there were any ornament that religion could not do
without, but it would be impious and frivolous of its heralds,
if they would not consecrate everything to it, if they would
not collect all they possess that is glorious, that religion
may, if possible, be presented in all power and dignity.
Without poetic skill, therefore, religion can only be expressed and communicated rhetorically, in all power and
skill of speech,[3] and in its swiftness and inconstancy the
service of every art that could aid, is willingly accepted.
Hence a person whose heart is full of religion, only opens
his mouth before an assembly where speech so richly
equipped might have manifold working.

Would that I could depict to you the rich, the superabundant life in this city of God, when the citizens assemble,
each full of native force seeking liberty of utterance and full
at the same time of holy desire to apprehend and appropriate what others offer. When one stands out before the
others he is neither justified by office nor by compact; nor
is it pride or ignorance that inspires him with assurance.
It is the free impulse of his spirit, the feeling of heart-felt
unanimity and completest equality, the common abolition of
all first and last, of all earthly order.[4] He comes forward
to present to the sympathetic contemplation of others his
own heart as stirred by God, and, by leading them into
the region of religion where he is at home, he would infect
them with his own feeling. He utters divine things and
in solemn silence the congregation follow his inspired
speech. If he unveils a hidden wonder, or links with prophetic assurance the future to the present, or by new
examples confirms old truths, or if his fiery imagination
enchants him in visions into another part of the world

and into another order of things, the trained sense of the congregation accompanies him throughout. On returning from his wanderings through the Kingdom of God into himself, his heart and the hearts of all are but the common seat of the same feeling. Let this harmony of view announce itself, however softly, then there are sacred mysteries discovered and solemnized that are not mere insignificant emblems, but, rightly considered, are natural indications of a certain kind of consciousness and certain feelings. It is like a loftier choir that in its own noble tone answers the voice that calls.

And this is not a mere simile, but, as such a speech is music without song or melody, there may be a music among the saints that is speech without words, giving most definite and comprehensible expression to the heart.

The muse of harmony, the intimate relation of which to religion has been long known, though acknowledged by few, has from of old laid on the altars of religion the most gorgeous and perfect works of her most devoted scholars. In sacred hymns and choruses to which the words of the poet are but loosely and airily appended, there are breathed out things that definite speech cannot grasp. The melodies of thought and feeling interchange and give mutual support, till all is satiated and full of the sacred and the infinite.

Of such a nature is the influence of religious men upon each other. Thus their natural and eternal union is produced. It is a heavenly bond, the most perfect production of the spiritual nature of man, not to be attained till man, in the highest sense, knows himself. Do not blame them if they value it more highly than the civil union which you place so far above all else, but which nevertheless will not ripen to manly beauty. Compared with that other union, it appears far more forced than free, far more transient than eternal.

But where, in all that I have said of the congregation of

the pious, is that distinction between priests and laity to which
you are accustomed to point as the source of so many evils ?
You have been deluded ; this is no distinction of persons,
but only of office and function. Every man is a priest, in
so far as he draws others to himself in the field he has
made his own and can show himself master in ; every man
is a layman, in so far as he follows the skill and direction
of another in the religious matters with which he is less
familiar. That tyrannical aristocracy which you describe
as so hateful does not exist, but this society is a priestly
nation,[5] a complete republic, where each in turn is leader
and people, following in others the same power that he
feels in himself and uses for governing others.

How then can this be the home of the envy and strife
that you consider the natural consequences of all religious
associations ? I see nothing but unity and, just by means of
the social union of the pious, the gentle mingling of all the
differences found in religion. I have called your attention
to two different types of mind and two different directions
in which specially the soul seeks its highest object. Do
you mean that from them sects must of necessity arise, and
unconstrained fellowship in religion be hindered ? In contemplation, where there is severance because we comprehend only in sections, there must be opposition and
contradiction, but reflect that life is quite different. In
it opposites seek each other and all that is separated in
contemplation is mingled. Doubtless persons who most
resemble will most strongly attract each other, but they
cannot on that account make up a whole by themselves,
for there are all degrees of affinity, and with so many
transitions there can be no absolute repulsion, no entire
separation, even between the remotest elements.

Take any body that by characteristic power has its own
organic structure. Unless you forcibly isolate it by some
mechanical means, it will not be homogeneous and distinct,[6]
but it will show at the extremities transition to the qualities

of another body. Pious persons at the lower stage have a closer union, yet there are always some among them who have a guess of something higher, who, even better than they understand themselves, will be understood by a person belonging to a more advanced society. There is thus a point of union, though it may yet be hidden from them. Again, if persons in whom the one type of mind is dominant, draw together, there will be some among them who at least understand the two types and, belonging in a certain sense to both, are connecting links between two otherwise divided spheres. Thus a person better fitted to put himself in religious communion with nature is not, in the essentials of religion, opposed to a person who rather finds the traces of the Deity in history, and there will never be a dearth of those who walk with equal ease on both ways. And if you divide the great domain of religion otherwise, you will still return to the same point. If unconstrained universality of the sense is the first and original condition of religion, and also, as is natural, its ripest fruit, you can surely see that, as religion advances and piety is purified, the whole religious world must appear as an indivisible whole.

The impulse to abstract, in so far as it proceeds to rigid separation, is a proof of imperfection. The highest and most cultured always see a universal union, and, in seeing it, establish it. Every man is only in contact with his neighbour; but on every side and in every direction he has neighbours and is thus inseparably bound up with the whole. Mystics and physicists in religion; those to whom the Deity is personal and those to whom He is not; those who have risen to a systematic view of the Universe, or those who only see it in its elements or as dim chaos should all be united. A band encloses them all and they cannot be quite separated, except forcibly and arbitrarily. Each separate association is a mobile, integrate part of the whole, losing itself in vague outlines in the whole, and it must ever be the better class of members who feel this truth.   Whence then, if not from pure misunderstanding, is the wild mania for converting to single definite forms of religion that you denounce, and the awful watchword, " No salvation save with us " ? [7]

The society of the pious, as I have exhibited it and as from its nature it must be, is occupied purely with mutual communication, and subsists only among persons already having religion of some kind.   How can it be their business to change the minds of those who already profess to have a definite religion, or to introduce and initiate persons who have none at all?   The religion of this society as such is simply the collective religion of all the pious.   As each one sees it in others it is infinite, and no single person can fully grasp it, for it is in no one instance a unity, not even when highest and most cultivated.   If a man, therefore, has any share in religion, it matters not what, would it not be a mad proceeding for the society to rend from him that which suits his nature, for this element also it should embrace and therefore someone must possess it?   And how would they cultivate persons to whom religion generally is still strange?   Their heritage, the infinite Whole they cannot communicate to them, and any particular communication must proceed from an individual and not the society.   Is there something general, indefinite, something common to all the members that a non-religious person might receive ?   But you know that nothing in a general and indefinite form can actually be communicated. It must be individual and thoroughly definite, or it is nothing.   This undertaking would have no measure and no rule.   Besides, how would the society ever think of going beyond itself, seeing the need which gave it birth, the principle of religious association, has no such bearing ? Individuals join and become a whole ; the whole being satisfied with itself, abides in itself, and has no further endeavour.

Religious effort of this kind, therefore, is never more

than a private business of individuals, and is, if I might so
say, rather in so far as a man is outside the church than
as he is within. When, impelled by sacred feelings, he
must withdraw from the circle of religious association where
the common existence and life in God affords the noblest
enjoyment, into the lower regions of life, he can still bring
all that there occupies him into relation with what to his
spirit must ever remain the highest.[7] On descending among
persons limited to one earthly aim and effort, he is apt to
believe—and let it be forgiven him—that, from intercourse
with gods and muses, he has been transported among a
race of rude barbarians. He feels himself a steward of
religion among unbelievers, a missionary among savages.
As an Orpheus or Amphion he hopes to win many by
heavenly melody. He presents himself among them as a
priestly figure, expressing clearly and vividly his higher
sense in all his doings and in his whole nature. And if there
be any response, how willingly he nurses those first presentiments of religion in a new soul, believing it to be a
beautiful pledge of its growth, even under an alien and
inclement sky, and how triumphantly he conducts the
novice to the exalted assembly ! This activity for the
extension of religion is only the pious longing of the
stranger for his home, the endeavour to carry his Fatherland with him, and find again everywhere its laws and
customs which are his higher, more beauteous life. The
Fatherland itself, blessed and complete in itself, knows
no such endeavour.

After all this, you will possibly say that I seem to be
quite at one with you. I have shown what the church
ought to be. Now, by not ascribing to the ideal church
any of the qualities which distinguish the real, I have, almost
as strongly as you, condemned its present form. I assure
you, however, I have not spoken of what should be, but of
what is,[7] unless, indeed, you deny the existence of what is
only hindered by the limits of space from appearing to the

coarser vision. The true church has, in fact, always been thus, and still is, and if you cannot see it, the blame is your own, and lies in a tolerably palpable misunderstanding. Remember only—to use an old but weighty expression— that I have not spoken of the church militant, but of the church triumphant, not of the church that fights against what the age and the state of man place in its way, but of the church that has vanquished all opposition, whose training is complete. I have exhibited a society of men who have reached consciousness with their piety, and in whom the religious view of life is dominant. As I trust I have convinced you that they must be men of some culture and much power, and that there can never be but very few of them, you need not seek their union where many hundreds, whose song strikes the ear from afar, are assembled in great temples. So close together, you well know, men of this kind do not stand. Possibly anything of the sort collected in one place is only to be found in single, separate communities, excluded from the great church. This at least is certain, that all truly religious men, as many as there have ever been, have not only had a belief, or rather a living feeling of such a union, but have actually lived in it, and, at the same time, they have all known how to estimate the church, commonly so-called, at about its true value, which is to say, not particularly high.

The great association to which your strictures properly apply, is very far from being a society of religious men. It is only an association of persons who are but seeking religion, and it seems to me natural that, in almost every respect, it should be the counterpart of the true church.[8] To make this as clear to you as it is to myself, I must, alas! condescend upon a mass of earthly and worldly things, and wind my way through a labyrinth of marvellous confusions. It is not done without repugnance, but it is necessary, if you are to agree with me. Perhaps if I draw your attention to the different forms of religious association

in the visible and in the true church, you will be convinced
of my opinion in essentials.   After what has been said, you
will, I hope, agree that in the true religious society all
communication is mutual.   The principle that urges us to
give utterance to our own experience, is closely connected
with what draws us to that which is strange, and thus
action and reaction are indivisibly united.   Here, on the
contrary, it is quite different.   All wish to receive, and
there is only one who ought to give.   In entire passivity,
they simply suffer the impressions on their organs.   So
far as they have power over themselves, they may aid in
receiving, but of reaction on others they do not so much as
think.[9]   Does that not show clearly enough the difference
in the principles of association?   They cannot be spoken
of as wishing to complete their religion through others, for
if they had any religion of their own, it would, from the
necessity of its nature, show itself in some way operative
on others.   They exercise no reaction because they are
capable of none; and they can only be incapable because
they have no religion.   Were I to use a figure from science
—from which, in matters of religion, I most willingly
borrow expressions—I would say that they are negatively
religious, and press in great crowds to the few points
where they suspect the positive principle of religion.
Having been charged, however, they again fail in capacity
to retain.   The emotion which could but play around the
surface very soon disappears.   Then they go about in a
certain feeling of emptiness, till longing awakes once more,
and they gradually become again negatively electrified.

In few words, this is the history of their religious life
and the character of the social inclination that runs
through it.   Not religion, but a little sense for it, and a
painful, lamentably fruitless endeavour to reach it, are all
that can be ascribed even to the best of them, even to those
who show both spirit and zeal.   In the course of their
domestic and civil life, and on the larger scene of which

they are spectators, there is much to stir persons with even a small share of religious sense. But those emotions remain only a dim presentiment, a weak impression on a soft mass, the outlines of which at once become vague. Soon everything is swept away by the waves of the active life, and is left stranded in the most unfrequented region of the memory, where it will soon be entirely overlaid by worldly things.

From frequent repetition, however, of this little shock, a necessity at length arises. The dim something in the mind, always recurring, must finally be made clear. The best means, one would think, would be to take time to observe leisurely and attentively the cause. But it is not a single thing which they might abstract from all else, that works on them. It is all human things, and among them the different relations of their life in other departments. Then, from old habit, their sense will spontaneously turn to those relations and once more the sublime and infinite will, in their eyes, be broken up into single, miserable details. Feeling this, they do not trust themselves, but seek outside help. They would behold in the mirror of another person's representation that which in direct perception would soon dissolve.

In this way they seek to reach some higher, more defined consciousness, yet at the end they misunderstand this whole endeavour. If the utterances of a truly religious man awake all those memories, if they have received the combined impression of them, and go away deeply moved, they believe that their need is stilled, that the leading of their nature has been satisfied, and that they have in them the power and essence of all those feelings. Yet they have now as formerly, though it may be in a higher degree, but a fleeting, extraneous manifestation. Being without knowledge or guess of true religion, they remain subject to this delusion, and in the vain hope of at length attaining, they repeat a thousand times the same endeavour, and yet remain where and what they were.[10]

If they advanced, and a spontaneous and living religion were implanted in them, they would soon not wish any more to be among those whose one-sidedness and passivity would no longer accord with their own state. They would at least seek beside them another sphere, where piety could show itself to others both living and life-giving, and soon they would wish to live altogether in it and devote to it their exclusive love. Thus in point of fact the church, as it exists among us, becomes of less consequence to men the more they increase in religion, and the most pious sever themselves coldly and proudly. Hardly anything could be clearer than that man is in this association merely because he is but seeking to be religious, and continues in it only so long as he has not yet attained.[11]

But this proceeds from the way in which the members of the church deal with religion, for suppose it were possible to think of a one-sided communication and a state of willing passivity and abnegation in truly religious men, there could not possibly be in their combined action the utter perversity and ignorance you find in the visible church. If the members of the church had any understanding of religion, the chief matter for them would be that the person whom they have made the organ of religion communicate his clearest, most characteristic views and feelings. But that is what they would not have, and they rather set limits on all sides to the utterances of individuality. They desire that he expound to them chiefly ideas, opinions, dogmas, in short, not the characteristic elements of religion, but the current reflections about them. Had they any understanding of religion, they would know from their own feeling that those matters of creeds, though, as I said, essential to true religious union, can by their nature be nothing but signs that the previously attained results agree, signs of the return from the most personal impressiveness to the common centre, the full-voiced refrain after everything has been uttered with purely individual skill. But of this they know nothing. Those matters for them exist for themselves and dominate special times.[12]

The conclusion is, that their united action has nothing of the character of the higher and freer inspiration that is proper to religion, but has a school-mastering, mechanical nature, which indicates that they merely seek to import religion from without. This they attempt by every means. To that end they are so attached to dead notions, to the results of reflection about religion, and drink them in greedily, that the process that gave them birth may be reversed, and that the ideas may change again to the living emotions and feelings from which they were originally deduced. Thus they employ creeds which are naturally last in religious communication, to stimulate what should properly precede them.

In comparison with the more glorious association which, in my view, is the only true church, I have spoken of this larger and widely extended association very disparagingly, as of something common and mean. This follows from the nature of the case, and I could not conceal my mind on the subject. I guard myself, however, most solemnly against any assumption you may cherish, that I agree with the growing wish that this institution should be utterly destroyed. Though the true church is always to stand open only to those who already have ripened to a piety of their own, there must be some bond of union with those who are still seeking. As that is what this institution should be, it ought, from the nature of the case, to take its leaders and priests always from the true church.[13] Or is religion to be the single human concern in which there are to be no institutions for scholars and beginners?

But indeed the whole pattern of this institution must be different, and its relation to the true church must take an entirely different aspect. On this matter I may not be silent. Those wishes and views of mine are too closely connected with the nature of religious association, and the

better state of things that I imagine, conduces too much
to its glorification for me to reserve my notions. By the
clear-cut distinction we have established, this at least has
been gained, that we can reflect very calmly on all the
abuses that prevail in the ecclesiastical society. You must
admit that religion, not having produced such a church and
not exhibiting itself in such a church, must be acquitted of
every ill it may have wrought and of all participation in
its evil state. So entirely should it be acquitted that the
reproach that it might degenerate into it, should not once
be made, seeing it cannot possibly degenerate where it has
never been.

I grant that in this society a disastrous sectarian spirit
exists and must exist. Where religious opinions are used
as methods for attaining religion, they must, seeing a
method requires to be thoroughly definite and finished, be
formed into a definite whole.[14] And where they are something that can only be given from without, being accepted
on the authority of the giver, everyone whose religious
speech is of a different cast, must be regarded as a dis-
turber of quiet and sure progress, for by his very existence
and the claims involved, he weakens this authority. Nay,
I even grant that in the old Polytheism, where naturally
religion could not be summed up as one, but willingly sub-
mitted to all division and severance, this sectarian spirit
was much milder and more peaceable, and that in the otherwise better times of systematic religion it first organized
itself and displayed its full power. Where all believe they
have a complete system with a centre, the value of details
must be vastly greater.

I grant both; but you will admit that there is no reproach
to religion in general, and there is no proof that the view
of the Universe as system is not the highest stage of
religion. I grant that in this society there is more regard
to understanding and believing, to acting and to perfecting customs than is favourable to a free development of

religious perceptions and feelings, and that in consequence, however enlightened its teaching be, it borders on some superstition and depends on some mythology ; but you will admit, that, in that degree, its whole nature is distant from true religion. I grant that this association can hardly exist without a standing distinction between priests and laity as two different religious orders. Whosoever has cultivated in himself his feeling to dexterity in some kind of presentation, characteristically and completely, cannot possibly continue a layman, or conduct himself as if all this were wanting. He would be free, nay, bound, either to forsake this society and seek the true church, or to allow himself to be sent back by the true church to lead as a priest. This, however, remains certain, that this spirit of division with all that is unworthy in it and all its evil consequences, is not brought about by religion but by the want of religiousness in the multitude.

But here you raise a new objection, which seems once more to roll back those reproaches upon religion. You would remind me that I myself have said that the great ecclesiastical society, I mean this institution for pupils in religion, must take its priests only from the members of the true church, because in itself the true principle of religiousness is wanting. How then can those who are perfect in religion, endure so much that is utterly contrary to the spirit of religion where they have to rule, where all things obey their voice, and they obey only the voice of religion ! Nay, how do they produce so much that is evil, for to whom does the church owe its regulations, if not to the priests ? Or if things are not as they should be, and the government of the dependent society has been rent from the members of the true church, where then is the high spirit that is justly to be expected in them ? Why have they administered so badly their most important province ? Why have they allowed base passions to make that a scourge of humanity, which in the hands of religion would have remained a blessing ? And yet they are the persons whose most joyful and sacred duty, as you confess, is to guide those who need their help !

Truly, alas ! things are not as I maintained they should be. Who would venture to say that all, that even the majority, that even the foremost and notablest of those who for many a day have ruled the great ecclesiastical assembly, have been accomplished in religion or even members of the true church ?

Yet do not take what I say in excuse as mere subterfuge. When you attack religion, it is usually in the name of philosophy, and when you upbraid the church, it is usually in the name of the state. You would defend the politicians of every age on the ground that the interference of the church has made so much of their handiwork imperfect and ill-advised. If now, speaking in the name of the religious, I attribute their failure to conduct their business with better success, to the state and to statesmen, will you suspect me of artifice ? Yet if you will but hear what I have to say of the true source of this evil, you will not, I hope, be able to deny that I am right.

Every fresh doctrine and revelation, every fresh view of the Universe that awakes the sense for it on some new side, may win some minds for religion who by no other way could be introduced into a higher world. To most of them naturally this particular aspect then remains for them the centre of religion. They form around their master a school of their own, a self-existent, distinct part of the true and universal church which yet only ripens slowly and quietly towards union in spirit with the great whole. But before this is accomplished, as soon as the new feelings have permeated and satisfied all their soul, they are usually violently urged by the need to utter what is in them that they be not consumed of the fire within. Thus everyone proclaims the new salvation that has arisen for him. Every object suggests the newly discovered Infinite ; every speech turns into a sketch of their peculiar religious views; every counsel, every wish, every friendly word is an inspired commendation of the sole way they know to salvation. Whosoever knows how religion operates, finds it natural that they all speak, for otherwise they would fear that the stones should surpass them. And whosoever knows how a new enthusiasm works, finds it natural that this living fire should kindle violently around, consume some and warm many, and give to thousands the surface imitation merely of a heart-felt glow.

And it is those thousands that work the mischief. The youthful zeal of the new saints accepts them as true brethren. What hinders, they say all too rashly, that these also should receive the Holy Ghost? Nay, they themselves believe that they have received, and, in joyous triumph, allow themselves to be conducted into the bosom of the pious society. But the intoxication of the first enthusiasm past, the glowing surface burnt out, they show themselves incapable of enduring and sharing the state allotted to the true believers. Compassionately the saints condescend to them, and, to go to their help, relinquish their own higher and deeper enjoyment. Thus everything takes that imperfect form. This comes to pass without outward causes through the corruption common to all human things. In accordance with that eternal order, the corruption most quickly seizes upon the most fiery and active life, that any section of the true church which might arise in isolation anywhere in the world, might not remain apart from all corruption, but be compelled to participate in it and form a false and degenerate church. In all times, among all peoples, in every religion this has happened.

Yet if things were only left quietly to themselves, this state could not anywhere long endure. Pour liquids of various gravities and densities, having small power of mutual attraction, into a vessel; shake them violently together till they seem to form one liquid, and you will see, if only you leave it quietly standing, how they will divide

and only like associate itself to like. So would it have
happened here, for it is the natural course of things. The
true church would quietly have separated itself again to
enjoy the higher, more intimate fellowship of which the
rest are not capable. The bond among those that remained
would then have been as good as loosed, and their natural
dulness would then have had to look for something from
without to determine what should become of them. And
they would not have been forsaken by the members of the
true church. Besides them, who would have had the
smallest call to care for their state? What attraction
would be offered to the regard of other men? What were
to be won or what fame to be obtained from them?

The members of the true church could, therefore, have
remained in undisturbed possession and might have
entered upon their priestly office among them in a new and
better appointed form. Every man would then have
gathered around him those who best understood him, who
by his method could be most strongly stirred. Instead of the
vast association, the existence of which you now bewail, a
great crowd of smaller, less definite societies would have
arisen. In them men would in all kinds of ways, now here,
now there, have tested religion. They would have been only
states to be passed, preparatory for the time when the sense
for religion should awake, and decisive for those who should
be found incapable of being taken hold of in any way.[15]

Hail to those who shall first be called when, the simple
way of nature having failed, the revolutions of human
affairs shall, by a longer, more artificial way, lead in the
golden age of religion! May the gods be propitious to them,
and may a rich blessing follow their labours in their mission
to help beginners, and to smooth the way for the babes to
the temple of the Eternal—labours that in our present unfavourable circumstances yield us such scanty fruit.[16]

Listen to what may possibly seem an unholy wish that I
can hardly suppress. Would that the most distant pre-

sentiment of religion had forever remained unknown to all heads of states, to all successful and skilful politicians ! Would that not one of them had ever been seized by the power of that infectious enthusiasm! The source of all corruption has been, that they did not know how to separate their deepest, most personal life from their office and public character. Why must they bring their petty vanity and marvellous presumption into the assembly of the saints, as if the advantages they have to give were valid everywhere without exception ? Why must they take back with them into their palaces and judgment-halls the reverence due to the servants of the sanctuary ? Probably you are right in wishing that the hem of a priestly garment had never touched the floor of a royal chamber : but let us wish that the purple had never kissed the dust on the altar, for had this not happened the other would not have followed. Had but no prince ever been allowed to enter the temple, till he had put off at the gate the most beautiful of his royal ornaments, the rich cornucopia of all his favours and tokens of honour ! But they have employed it here as elsewhere. They have presumed to decorate the simple grandeur of the heavenly structure with rags from their earthly splendour, and instead of fulfilling holy vows, they have left worldly gifts as offerings to the Highest.

As soon as a prince declared a church to be a community with special privileges, a distinguished member of the civil world, the corruption of that church was begun and almost irrevocably decided. And if the society of believing persons, and of persons desiring belief, had not been mixed after a wrong manner, that is always to the detriment of the former, this could not have happened, for otherwise no religious society could ever be large enough to draw the attention of the governor.

Such a constitutional act of political preponderance works on the religious society like the terrible head of Medusa. As soon as it appears everything turns to stone-

Though without connection, everything that is for a
moment combined, is now inseparably welded together;
accidental elements that might easily have been ejected
are now established for ever ; drapery and body are made
from one block and every unseemly fold is eternal. The
greater and spurious society can no more be separated from
the higher and smaller. It can neither be divided nor dissolved. It can neither alter its form nor its articles of faith.
Its views and usages are all condemned to abide in their
existing state.

But that is not all. The members of the true church
the visible church may contain, are forcibly excluded from
all share in its government, and are not in a position to do
for it even the little that might still be done. There is
more to govern than they either could or would do. There
are worldly things now to order and manage, and privileges
to maintain and make good. And even though in their
domestic and civil affairs, they did know how to deal with
such things, yet cannot they treat matters of this sort as
a concern of their priestly office. That is an incongruity
that their sense will not see into and to which they cannot
reconcile themselves. It does not accord with their high
and pure idea of religion and religious fellowship. They
cannot understand what they are to make out of houses and
lands and riches, either for the true church to which they
belong, or for the larger society which they should conduct.[17]
By this unnatural state of affairs the members of the true
church are distracted and perplexed.

But besides all this, persons are attracted who otherwise
would for ever have remained without. If it is the interest
of the proud, the ambitious, the covetous, the intriguing to
press into the church, where otherwise they would have felt
only the bitterest ennui, and if they begin to pretend
interest and intelligence in holy things to gain the earthly
reward, how can the truly religious escape subjection ?
And who bears the blame if unworthy men replace ripe

saints, and if, under their supervision, everything creeps
in and establishes itself that is most contrary to the spirit
of religion? Who but the state with its ill-considered
magnanimity?

But in a still more direct way, the state is the cause
why the bond between the true church and the visible
religious society has been loosened. After showing to the
church this fatal kindness, it believed it had a right to its
active gratitude, and transferred to it three of its weightiest
commissions.[18] More or less it has committed to the church
the care and oversight of education. Under the auspices
of religion and in the form of a congregation, it demands
that the people be instructed in those duties that cannot
be set forth in the form of law, that they be stirred up to
a truly citizenlike way of thinking, and that, by the power
of religion, they be made truthful in their utterances. As
a recompense for those services, it robs it of its freedom, as
is now to be seen in all parts of the civilized world where
there is a state and a church. It treats the church as an
institution of its own appointment and invention—and
indeed its faults and abuses are almost all its own invent-
ing; and it alone presumes to decide who is fit to come
forward in this society as exemplar and as priest. And do
you still charge it to religion that the visible church does
not consist entirely of pious souls?

But I am not yet done with my indictment. The state
pollutes religious fellowship by introducing into its deepest
mysteries its own interests. When the church, in prophetic devoutness, consecrates the new-born babe to the
Deity and to the struggle for the highest, the state will
take the occasion to receive it from the hands of the church
into the list of its *protégés*. When it gives the stripling
its first kiss of brotherhood, as one who has taken his first
glance into the sacred things of religion, this must also be
for the state the evidence of the first stage of civil independence; [19] if with pious wishes, it consecrates the union of

two persons who, as emblems and instruments of creative
nature, would at the same time consecrate themselves as
bearers of the higher life, it must also be the state's sanction for the civil bond. The state will not even believe
that a man has vanished from this earthly scene, till the
church assures it that it has restored his soul to the Infinite
and enclosed his dust in the sacred bosom of the earth. It
shows reverence for religion and an endeavour to keep
itself perpetually conscious of its own limits, that the state
bows before religion and before its worshippers when it
receives anything from the hands of the Infinite, or returns
it again, but how all this works for the corruption of the
religious society is clear enough. In all its regulations
there is nothing directed to religion alone, nothing even in
which religion is the chief matter. In the sacred speeches
and instructions, as well as in the most mysterious and
symbolical doings, everything has a legal and civil reference,[20]
everything is perverted from its original form and nature.
Hence there are many among the leaders of the church
who understand nothing of religion, but who yet, as servants
of the state, are in a position to earn great official merit, and
there are many among its members who do not even wish
to seek religion, and who yet have interest enough to
remain in the church and bear a part in it.

It is very apparent that a society to which such a thing
can happen, which with false humility accepts favours that
can profit it nothing and with cringing readiness takes on
burdens that send it headlong to destruction ; which allows
itself to be abused by an alien power, and parts with the
liberty and independence which are its birthright, for a
delusion ; which abandons its own high and noble aim to
follow things that lie quite outside of its path, cannot be a
society of men who have a definite aim and know exactly
what they wish. This glance at the history of the ecclesiastical society is, I think, the best proof that it is not strictly
a society of religious men. At most it appears that some

particles of such a society are mixed in it and are overlaid with foreign ingredients. Before the first matter of this boundless corruption could have been admitted, the whole must have been in a state of morbid fermentation in which the few sound portions soon utterly disappeared.

Full of sacred pride, the true church would have refused gifts it could not use, well knowing that those who have found the Deity and have a common joy in knowing Him, have in the pure fellowship in which alone they would exhibit and communicate their inmost nature, really nothing in common the possession of which could be protected by worldly power. On earth they require nothing but a speech by which to make themselves understood and a space in which to be together, things requiring no prince's favour.

But if the true church have nothing to do directly with the profane world, and if there must be a mediating institution whereby to come into a certain contact with it, as it were an atmosphere, both as a medium for purification and for attracting new material, what form must this institution take and how is it to be freed from the corruption it has imbibed? This last question time must answer. Sometime it will certainly be done, but it may be done in a thousand different ways, for, of all sicknesses of man there are various ways of cure. Everything in its place will be tried and have its effect. The goal only I can indicate in order to show you more clearly that here also it has not been religion and its endeavour to which you should have manifested your repugnance.

The fundamental idea of such an auxiliary institution is to exhibit to persons who in any degree have a sense for religion, though because it is not yet apparent and conscious, they are not fit for incorporation into the true church, so much religion as such that their capacity must necessarily be developed. Let us now see what there is in the present state of things that hinders this from taking

place. I will not repeat that the state chooses according to its own wishes which are more directed to the
extraneous matters in the institution, persons to be leaders
and teachers, and that in the view of the state a man
can be a highly intelligent educator and a single-minded
effective teacher of duties to the people without, in the
strict sense of the word, being religiously affected at all,
and that therefore persons whom it reckons among its
worthiest servants, may easily fail utterly. I will grant
that everyone it appoints is truly influenced and inspired
by piety, if you will grant that no artist can communicate
his art to a school with any success, if there is not among
his pupils some equality of preliminary knowledge. This
is more necessary in respect of our subject where the master
can do nothing but point out and exhibit, than in art where
the scholar progresses by exercise and the teacher is chiefly
useful by criticisms. All his work will be in vain if the
same thing is not only intelligible to all, but suitable and
wholesome. The sacred orator must obtain his hearers by
a certain similarity of talents and cast of mind, and not
by rank and file, not as they are counted out to him by
some ancient distribution, not as their houses adjoin, or as
they are set down in the police list.[21]

And assuming that only persons equally near religion
assemble round one master, they may not all be near in
the same way. It is, therefore, most preposterous to wish
to limit any pupil to a single master. There is no one so
universally cultured in religion, nor anyone who can exercise all kinds of influence. No man is in a position to
draw by his representation and speech from all who come
before him the hidden gems of religion to light, for the
sphere of religion is far too comprehensive. Remember
the different ways by which men pass from consciousness
of the individual and particular to the Whole and the
Infinite : remember that, by this very mode of transition,
a man's religion assumes its own distinct character. Think

of the various influences whereby the Universe affects man, of the thousand single perceptions and of the thousand ways of combining them and showing one in the light of the other. Reflect, that if religion is actually to stir a man's own feeling, he must meet it in the definite form that suits his capacity and his point of view. It is, therefore, impossible for any master to be all things to all, and to become to every man what he needs. No one can be a mystic and a scientist at the same time. He cannot be a master in every sacred art whereby religion is expressed, initiated at once into prophecies, visions and prayers, into presentations from history and from experience and into many other things too numerous to mention, all the glorious branches into which the crown of the heavenly tree of priestly art is divided. Master and disciples, therefore, must, in perfect freedom, be allowed to seek and choose what profits them, and no one must in any way be obliged to give except that which he possesses and understands.

But it is not possible for a man to limit his teaching to what he understands as soon as, in the very same transaction, he must have something else in view. Without question, a priestly man can present his religion with zeal and skill as is fitting, and at the same time remain faithful to some civil business and accomplish it effectively. Why then, if it suits, should not a person, having a call to the priesthood, be at the same time a moral teacher in the service of the state ? There is nothing against it. He may do both, only not the one in and through the other ; he must not wear both natures at the same time, not accomplish the two concerns by the one action. The state may be satisfied, if it so pleases, with a religious morality, but religion rejects consciously and individually every prophet and priest that moralizes from this point of view. Whosoever would proclaim religion must do it unadulterated.

It is opposed to every sentiment of honour of a master in

his business, and more particularly of a master in religious purity, if a true priest has to do with the state on such unworthy and impossible conditions. When the state takes other workmen into its pay, whether for the better cultivation of their own talents or to attract pupils, it removes from them all extraneous business, nay, it makes it incumbent upon them to refrain. It recommends them to give themselves chiefly to the special section of their art, in which they believe they can accomplish most, and then it allows their nature full scope. With the artists of religion alone, it does exactly the contrary. They must embrace the whole compass of their subject, and it prescribes to them what school they shall be of and lays upon them unseemly burdens. It will not even, along with attention to its business, grant them leisure for special cultivation of some kind of religious presentation which yet is for them the chief matter, nor free them from burdensome constraints. Even after it has, as in every case it must, set up for itself a school of civil duties,[22] it still will not allow them to follow their own ways. And yet, though it cannot be unconcerned about the priestly works, it employs them neither for use nor for show like other arts and sciences! Away then with every such union between church and state![23] That remains my Cato's utterance to the end, or till I see the union actually destroyed.

Away too with all that has even a semblance to rigid union of priest and laity, whether among themselves or with each other![24] Learners shall not form bodies, for, even in mechanical trades, it can be seen how little that profits. And the priests, I mean as such, shall form no brotherhood among themselves. They shall neither divide their work nor their knowledge according to corporations, but let each man do his own duty without concerning himself about others, or having in this matter closer connection with one than with another. Between teacher and congregation also, there shall be no firm outward band. Accord-

ing to the principles of the true church, the mission of a
priest in the world is a private business, and the temple
should also be a private chamber where he lifts up his voice
to give utterance to religion. Let there be an assembly
before him and not a congregation. Let him be a speaker
for all who will hear, but not a shepherd for a definite
flock.

Only under such conditions, can truly priestly souls take
charge of seekers for religion. Thus only can this preparatory association actually lead to religion and make
itself worthy to be regarded as an adjunct and vestibule of
the true church, for thus only it can lose all that in its present state is unholy and irreligious. By universal freedom
of choice, recognition and criticism, the hard and pronounced distinction between priest and laity will be
softened, till the best of the laity come to stand where the
priests are. All that is now held together by the unholy
bond of creeds will be severed.[25] Let there be no point of
union of this kind, and let none offer the seekers a system
making exclusive claim to truth, but let each man offer his
characteristic, individual presentation. This appears the
sole means for putting an end to the mischief. It is a
poor, if old device, capable only of alleviating the evil for
a moment, when ancient formulas were too oppressive or
were too varied to consort in the same bonds, to cut up the
church by partition of the creed. Like a polypus, each
piece grows again into a whole, and if the character is contrary to the spirit of religion, it is no improvement that
several societies should bear it. The visible religious
society can only be brought nearer the universal freedom
and majestic unity of the true church by becoming a mobile
mass, having no distinct outlines, but each part being now
here, now there, and all peacefully mingling together. The
hateful sectarian and proselytizing spirit which leads ever
farther astray from the essentials of religion, can only be
extinguished when no one, any more, is informed that he

belongs to a distinct circle, and is for other circles of a different faith.

In regard to this society, you see, our wishes are identical. What is obnoxious to you opposes us also. Permit me, however, always to add that this would not have been as it is, if we had only been left alone to occupy ourselves in our own proper work. Our common interest is to have the evil removed, but there is little we can do except to wish and hope. How such a change will take place among us Germans I do not know. Will it be, as in neighbouring countries, only after a great commotion and then everywhere at once? Will the state, by an amicable arrangement and without the death and resurrection of both church and state, break off its unhappy marriage with the church? Or will it endure that another, more virginal institution arise alongside of the one that is for ever sold to it? [26] I do not know.

But till something of this kind do happen, a heavy fate must lie upon all holy souls, who, glowing with religion, would seek to exhibit their most holy things even in the profane world, that something might thereby be accomplished. I will not delude the members of the state privileged order into making much account of what in these circumstances they can accomplish by speech for the dearest wish of their heart. And if many of them believe themselves bound not to be always speaking only of piety, nay, not even frequently to speak chiefly of it and to speak of it alone only on solemn occasions, if they are not to be untrue to their political calling, I know little to say against it.

But this cannot be taken from them, that they can proclaim by a priestlike life the spirit of religion, and this may be their consolation and their best reward. In a holy person everything is significant; in an acknowledged priest of religion everything has a canonical meaning. They may, therefore, in all their movements exhibit the nature of religion. Even in the common relations of life nothing may be lost of the expression of a pious mind. The holy ardour with which they treat everything shows that even in trifles that a profane spirit skims over thoughtlessly, the music of noble feelings resounds in them. The majestic calm with which they equalize small and great, shows that they refer everything to the Unchangeable and in all things alike perceive the Deity. The bright serenity with which they pass every trace of decay, reveals to all how they live above time and above the world. The utmost ease of self-denial indicates how much of the limits of personality they have already abolished. The constantly open and active sense that neither the rarest nor the commonest escapes, shows how unweariedly they seek the Deity and listen for His voice. If in this way the whole life and every movement of soul and body is a priestlike work of art, the sense for what dwells in them may by this dumb speech be awakened in many.

And not content to express the nature of religion, they must also in a similar way destroy the false appearance of it. With childlike ingenuousness, and in the high simplicity of utter unconsciousness, seeing no danger, and feeling no need of courage, they disregard what base prejudices and subtle superstition have surrounded with a spurious glory of sanctity. Unconcerned as the infant Hercules, they let themselves be hissed at from all quarters by the snakes of solemn calumny, being able to crush them quietly in a moment. To this holy service they may devote themselves till better times, and I think that you also will have reverence for this unassuming worth, and will augur well for its influence on men.

But what am I to say to those to whom you refuse the priestly robe because they have not gone through a definite course of science in a definite way? Whither shall I direct them with the social bent of their religion not directed alone to the true church, but also outward to the world? Having no greater scene in which, in any striking way, they might appear, they may rest satisfied with the priestly service of their household gods.[27] One family can be the most cultured element and the truest picture of the Universe. When quietly and securely all things work together, all the powers that animate the Infinite are thus operative; when all advances in quiet joyousness, the high World-Spirit rules in it; when the music of love accompanies all movements, the harmony of the spheres resounds, resounds in the smallest space. They may construct this sanctuary, order it and cherish it. In pious might they may set it up clearly and evidently; with love and spirit they may dispose it. By this means many will learn to contemplate the Universe in the small, obscure dwelling. It will be a Holy of Holies in which many will receive the consecration of religion. This priesthood was the first in the holy and infant world, and it will be the last when no other is any longer necessary.

Nay, at the end of our future culture we expect a time when no other society preparatory for religion except the pious family life will be required. At present, millions of men and women of all ranks sigh under a load of mechanical and unworthy labours. The older generation succumbs discouraged, and, with pardonable inertness, abandons the younger generation to accident in almost everything, except the necessity straightway to imitate and learn the same degradation. That is the cause why the youth of the people do not acquire the free and open glance whereby alone the object of piety is found. There is no greater hindrance to religion than that we must be our own slaves, and everyone is a slave who must execute something it ought to be possible to do by dead force. We hope that by the perfecting of sciences and arts, those dead forces will be made serviceable to us, and the corporeal world, and everything of the spiritual that can be regulated, be turned into an enchanted castle where the god of the earth only needs to utter a magic word or press a spring, and what he requires will be done. Then for the first time, every man will be free-born ; then every life will be at once practical and contemplative ; the lash of the task-master will be lifted over no man ; and everyone will have peace and leisure for contemplating the world in himself. It is only the unfortunate to whom this is wanting, from whose spiritual organs all nourishing forces are withdrawn, because their whole being must be spent untiringly in mechanical service that need individual, fortunate souls to come forward and assemble them about them, to be their eye for them, and in a few swift minutes communicate to them the highest content of a life. But when the happy time comes and everyone can freely exercise and use his sense, at the very first awaking of the higher powers, in sacred youth, under the care of paternal wisdom, all who are capable will participate in religion. All communication that is not mutual will then cease, and the father, well repaid, will lead the stout son, not only into a more joyful world and a lighter life, but straightway into the sacred assembly also of the worshippers of the Eternal, now increased in number and activity.

In the grateful feeling that, when this better time has come, however far off it may still be, the efforts to which you have devoted your days, shall have contributed somewhat to its coming, permit me once more to direct your attention to the fair fruit of your labour. Allow yourselves to be led once more to the exalted fellowship of truly religious souls. It is dispersed and almost invisible, but its spirit rules everywhere, even where but few are gathered in the name of the Deity. What is there in it that should not fill you with admiration and esteem, ye friends and admirers of the good and beautiful ? They are among themselves an academy of priests. The exhibition of the holy life, which for them is the highest, is treated by everyone as his art and study, and the Deity out of His endless riches apportions to each one his own lot. To a universal sense for everything belonging to the sacred sphere of religion, every man joins as artists should, the endeavour to perfect himself in some one department. A noble rivalry prevails, and a longing to produce something worthy of such an assembly makes everyone with faithfulness and diligence master all that belongs to his special section. In a pure heart it is preserved, with concentrated mind it is arranged, by heavenly art it is moulded and perfected. Thus in every way and from every source, acknowledgment and praise of the Infinite resound, everyone bringing, with joyous heart, the ripest fruit of his thinking and examining, of his comprehending and feeling. They are also among themselves a choir of friends. Everyone knows that he is both a part and a work of the Universe, in him also its divine life and working being revealed. He, therefore, regards himself as an object worthy of the attention of others. With sacred reserve, yet with a ready openness that all may enter and behold, he lays bare everything of the relations of the Universe of which he is conscious and what of the elements of humanity takes individual shape in him. Why should they hide anything from one another? All that is human is holy, for all is divine. Again, they are among themselves a band of brothers—or have you perhaps an intenser expression for the entire blending of their natures, not in respect of existence and working, but in respect of sense and understanding? The more everyone approaches the Universe and the more they communicate to one another, the more perfectly they all become one. No one has a consciousness for himself, each has also that of his neighbour. They are no longer men, but mankind also. Going out of themselves and triumphing over themselves, they are on the way to true immortality and eternity.

If in any other department of life, or in any other school of wisdom, you have found anything nobler than this, impart it to me; mine I have given you.

EXPLANATIONS OF THE FOURTH SPEECH

(1) Page 150.—The assertion that scripture alone is sufficent to awake piety, seems to have experience against it, from the sacred writings of all religions down to our books for edification so widely distributed among a certain class, and the small religious pamphlets which are the means chiefly used at present for reaching the people. First, in respect of the sacred writings, only those of monotheistic religions need detain us. The Koran alone has arisen purely as a writing, and it is indisputably to be looked upon mostly as a manual and repertorium of themes for religious compositions, a fact quite in accordance with the unoriginal character of this religion. And the direct, strictly religious influence of the Koran is not to be esteemed very highly. In the very various Jewish codex, the gnomic books especially have something of this purely literary character. The historical section, strictly speaking, has none. The poetical section again in part, as for example a large number of the Psalms, deals immediately with definite occasions and was not produced simply for indefinite use, and is, therefore, not scripture in the strict sense. And who will deny that they produced the effect in this connection of which their present influence as mere scripture is but a shadow ? The prophetic poetry of the earlier period, was for the most part actually spoken, and a not insignificant part has been handed down imbedded in history. As this living traditional power was lost, and the Scriptures became to the Jewish people a learned study, its direct influence was lost, and it became simply the bearer of the living utterances linked to it. The New Testament Scriptures also are, as little as possible, writing in the strict sense of the word. In the historical books the speeches are the most essential, the history being chiefly to give them the movement of life. Even in the history of the Passion the words of Christ are the most sublime and deeply moving parts, and the narrative of pains and agonies might easily produce only a wrong effect. The Acts of the Apostles alone seems

to be an exception, and to have its place in the canon chiefly because it is the root of all church history. But just because it would quite limit the book to this subordinate use, it is repugnant to our feeling when the speeches are regarded as subsequently concocted, as is the fashion of other historical books. Our didactic books, being letters, are as little as possible mere literature, and no one can deny that the influence on the immediate recipients to whom the whole movement of the time was present, must have been much greater. We can only dimly, and then only by learned help, transport ourselves back to those times. Even then, the most vital influence of those writings for our time is that which was borrowed from the synagogue that all living religious utterance is linked to them.

For that reason only, the reading of the Scriptures by the laity continues; otherwise, its influence would not entirely vanish, but it would degenerate into utter vagueness. So vast was the original power of these productions that even now, after they have become entirely literature, a fulness of quickening spirit dwells in them, which is the highest testimony to their divine power; yet the objective side of this influence, the clear understanding, would soon be null for the private use of the laity, but for that connection with the learned exposition. It is, therefore, natural that the Catholic Church, setting little store on preaching, should limit the use of Scripture by the laity. On the other hand, we, believing we dare not so limit it, must make the public exposition of Scripture much more prominent in preaching, and it must always be hurtful to the whole religious life when Scripture is generally made use of for preaching simply as a motto. The reality of the endeavour to rescue the contents of the sacred books from the state of being mere literature, appears from the ready adoption by the most pious Christians of a method that would be in the highest degree unnatural in a work made throughout purely as a book. Single detached passages of Scripture, neither chosen by selection nor by memory, but simply by chance, are used on every occasion, when religious enlightenment or stimulus is needed. This cannot be defended, as it too easily degenerates into magical frivolity, yet it is an endeavour to restore to the religious utterances of holy men a living influence which shall be direct and independent of their effects as a book.

As regards our literature for edification again, which arises for the most part expressly as books, its great influence is not to be denied. The countless editions and the continuance of many of them through a long series of generations speak too clearly. And who does not feel respect for works that, in addition to their vitality, help to guard a great mass of men from the dangerous whirlwind of changing doctrine? Yet it will not be denied that the living word and the religious emotion in a community, have a far higher power than the written letter. On closer consideration also it will be found that the chief influence of practical writings rests less in their completeness than in the multitude of forceful, noble formulas contained, which may embrace many religious moments, and therefore refresh the memory of many things. They also offer a certain assurance that one's own religious emotions are not at variance with the common religious life. Hence the individual, clever work of this kind seldom rejoices in much success. This good witness is only given to able and comprehensive practical works. But the present endeavour of so many well-meaning societies to scatter a multitude of small religious leaflets among the people, that have no right objective character, but utter the most subjective inner experiences in the dead letter of a terminology that neither accords with literary nor religious usage, rests on a deep misunderstanding, and can scarcely have any other result than to bring church matters, the evil of which it presupposes, into still deeper degradation. A multitude of men will be reared who will have manifold hypocrisies, without any actual experience, or who will fall into sad perplexity because their own religious experiences do not accord with the pattern set before them. Is the public church life sick or weak, let each man do his utmost to heal it, but let no man believe it is to be replaced by a dead letter. That the religious life should issue from the circulating library seems to me like handing over the great acts of legislation and executive to irresponsible journals, of which the more numbers and improved editions the better.

(2) Page 150.—Many perhaps, who formerly cherished the well-meant wish that the sociality which had become vain and frivolous should have new life put into it by an admixture of the religious element, have already applied the proverb to themselves that with time we may easily have too much of what earlier we zealously desired. Confusion and trouble enough have arisen from treating religious subjects in brilliant circles in the form of conversation, in which the personal element too easily preponderates. I wrote then from my youthful experiences among the Moravians. They had special meetings for the distinct object of religious conversation. An absent person of a different mind could not there readily be discussed, yet I have never heard anything of real life and worth, and I believe I have here quite rightly grasped the general principle. Our wish should, therefore, be not so much that in our free sociality religious subjects

should be treated, as that a religious spirit should rule. And this wish will certainly not fail as soon as a considerable part of society consists of religious men.

(3) Page 151.—Since this was written I have had almost thirty years' conduct of office, a period within which every man must come as near his ideal as he can. A greater contrast between that description, and what I myself have accomplished in that time in the domain of religious speech would be hard to imagine. Were there really such a difference of theory and practice, my only apology would be that, as it was given to Socrates, other wisdom being denied, to know that he knew nothing, the higher not being granted me, I was content with plain speech rather than strive for false ornamentation. Yet it is not quite so. My practice has been based on the distinction that is drawn later in this Speech between the existing church and the true church. In the former all discourse, whatever be its subject-matter, must have a didactic character. The speaker would bring something to consciousness in his hearers, which indeed he assumes to exist in them, but does not suppose would develop of itself in this exact way. Now the more the didactic character appears, the less room there is for ornament, and for this purpose a blessing undoubtedly rests on unadorned speech. In another religious art, the same thing appears. Who would think of taking the pious poetry, in all its power and magnificence, that is suited for glorifying God in a circle of thoroughly cultured religious men, of which we have many splendid examples in our Klopstock and our Hardenberg, and making it the standard in collecting a church hymn-book?

(4) Page 151.—It can hardly be necessary for me here to guard myself against being misinterpreted, as wishing to banish all order from the assembly of the truly pious, and make them like many fanatical sects that arrange nothing beforehand for their meetings, but leave everything to the moment. On the contrary, the higher the style of religious utterance, the more it exhibits an artistically organized unity, the more it requires a rigid order. This only is meant that everything belonging to civil order must be left outside, and all things must be fashioned on the foundation of an original, universal equality. I hold this the essential condition of all prosperity in such a fellowship, not less in the actually existing church than in the ideal. Every fellowship is destroyed by disorder, and an order that is made for another society is disorder. If the distinction between priest and laity is not to be sharply drawn, how much less is a difference to apply among the laity themselves that belongs to a

quite different sphere. If a member of the congregation, even though outwardly he may stand in some relation of guardian to it, assumes the right, because he is distinguished in the civil society, to interfere and have priestly functions in directing the body and arranging the meetings, any other member, however low his station in the civil society, would have the same right, and true and fitting order would be at an end.

(5) Page 153.—Every reader familiar with Scripture, will here think of the Apostle Peter, who exhorts all Christians to train themselves into a holy priesthood, and assures them all that they are a royal priesthood. This is, therefore, a truly Christian expression. The view here set forth of the equality of all true members of the religious community, so that none are to be made merely recipient and the exclusive right of utterance given to one, is also a truly Christian view. Christianity has recognized its true goal in that prophetic saying that all should be taught of God. Suppose this goal attained by the whole community, so that there was no more need to awake religion in others, then, leaving out of sight the education of the young, there could be no distinction among members, save such as the passing occasion required. If then we find in all religious forms, from the earliest antiquity, the distinction between priest and laity in force, we are driven to assume, either that there was an original difference, a religiously developed stock that had joined a rude race and had never succeeded in raising it to its own fulness of religious life, or that the religious life had developed so unequally in a people that it had become necessary, if it were not again to be scattered, to organize the more advanced for more effective operation on the rest. In this latter case the more it succeeds the more superfluous this organization will become. The Christian priesthood is manifestly of this kind. This narrower use of the word I never quite justify to myself, for we in the Protestant community are quite agreed how far the expression generally can have no validity in Christianity. The need for this narrower priesthood only gradually made itself felt. This is the more apparent that, at the beginning, the apostolic character itself involved no special pre-eminence in the community. But this smaller body, chosen from the community, came to acquire a position apart from the religious enthusiasm of the others, because the history of Christianity and in particular the intimate knowledge of original Christianity necessarily became an object of science. In this scientific information all had to have some share, if their communications were to be in conscious agreement with history. This distinction could never disappear till all Christians were

familiar with this science. Even though this is not to be looked for, the validity of this distinction must ever more and more be limited to the sphere in which finally alone it can have a reason.

(6) Page 153.—This assertion, from which I afterwards draw the conclusion that the external religious society should be as mobile a body as possible, seems to contradict what I have exhaustively developed in the Introduction to the "Glaubenslehre," §§ 7–10. Here I say that in religious communication there are no entire separations and definite boundaries except by a mechanical procedure, that is a procedure which is in a certain sense arbitrary and not founded in the nature of the matter. There I say that the different pious communions that appear in history stand to one another, partly, as stages of development, the monotheistic being the highest, and, partly, as different in kind, according as the natural or the ethical in human life predominated. Further, I distinguish the individual type of common piety, partly externally, by its historical origin, and partly internally, as characteristic variation of any faith of one stage and one kind. It will not suffice to say that in the "Glaubenslehre" communion is secondary, and that the primary aim was to discover from their contents the characteristic features of the different types of faith, particularly of Christianity, for this involves dealing with the Christian church as a definitely bounded society. The two passages are rather to be harmonized as follows : On the one side, I grant here that certain bodies of communion are formed organically, which agrees with the assertion in the "Glaubenslehre" that every distinct communion has a historical point of departure which dominates the organic development. Did this point of departure not also presuppose an inner difference, these bodies would only be distinguished by number or by size, and the superiority given by favouring circumstances, like the fruits of one stem. Were their boundaries to touch they would naturally grow together, and could only be again mechanically divided. On the other side, in the "Glaubenslehre," an inner difference in the types of faith, whereby the communions are divided, is maintained. But it is only difference in the subordination and mutual relations of the separate parts, which does not involve any greater degree of communion than is here represented. The whole attempt there made would be in vain, if from one type of faith it were not possible to understand another. But if it is understood in its inner nature, its modes of externalizing itself, its services must be capable not only of being understood by a spectator, but in some degree of being appropriated. Persons to whom this is impossible, can in any communion be only the un-

cultured. Now that is simply what is here maintained, that the separating impulse, when it makes a hard and fast cleavage, is a proof of imperfection. Again, as the uncultured do not alone, but only along with the cultured, form the communion, the assertions there made also agree with this that the religious communion, though divided and organized, would yet in another respect be only one but for mechanical interference either of sword or letter. Does it not appear to us violent and irreligious, when the members of one communion are forbidden to frequent, with a view to edification, the services of another? Yet only by such an utterly mechanical procedure could the communions be quite separated.

(7) Pages 155 and 156.—It was doubtless serviceable to establish that the wild mania for proselytizing is nowhere founded in religion itself. But there seems to be too much here, for mild proselytizing also, every endeavour to draw from another form to one's own, every endeavour to implant religion in souls still without piety, seems to be rejected. Against the witness of all history, against the clear words of the Founder Himself, no less than against my own statements in the " Glaubenslehre," about the relation of Christianity to other forms of religion, it appears to be maintained that the spread of Christianity in the world did not proceed from the pious Christian sense. But this good endeavour is always in some way connected with the notion, here uniformly rejected, that salvation, either altogether or in a much higher degree, is not to be found outside a definite religious communion as it is found inside. True and false do not seem to be here sufficiently distinguished. If the assertion that proselytizing work is entirely inadmissible, is a just consequence of the previously accepted theory of the religious communion, the error must be sought in the theory. On going back upon it we find what solves the difficulties, that the spread of our own form of religion is a natural and permissible private business of the individual. Though there is in the strict sense only one universal religious communion, in which all the different forms of religion mutually recognize each other, in which transference of a follower of one form to another seems to be a wish to impair the whole by destroying its manifoldness, it is manifest that here also much is naturally destroyed, which can only happen in an inferior stage of development. Hence it is regarded by the experienced as simply a point of transition, and it cannot be wrong to accelerate and guide the progress. Wherefore, the more the adherents of one form of religion are compelled to regard many other forms simply as such transitions, the more powerfully will the work of proselytizing organize itself among them.

This should most apply to the monotheistic religions in general, and in the broadest sense to Christianity. And this holds from the present standpoint, as it is more fully dealt with in the " Glaubenslehre," as the issue of a more scientific course of thought. The work of proselytizing presupposes the one graduated communion. As Paul did in Athens, regarding the Hellenic idolatry, to assign it a value and obtain a link of connection for the communication of his own piety, it must always be done. This community of two forms of religion shows itself at all points wheresoever a like effort at assimilation is developed. We can therefore say that this is the true distinction between praiseworthy zeal for conversion that would recognize the faintest traces of religion and purify and build up a piety already begun, and that wild irreligious mania for conversion which easily degenerates into persecution. The former begins with unprejudiced and loving comprehension even of the most imperfect kind of faith, the latter believes it is exalted above any such endeavour. Further, it is not to be understood with too painful accuracy that proselytizing can only be the private business of the individual. The individual stands here opposed to the all-embracing communion. Hence associations of individuals, nay, a whole mode of faith can be regarded as individuals. The maxim "nulla salus," again has for the great communion of the pious an absolute verity, for without any piety it can acknowledge no salvation. Only in so far as one religious party utters it against another, does it work destructively, which is to say, in so far as a universal communion is denied. Hence it clearly goes along with the wild mania for conversion. The special truth of this in Christianity is dealt with in the " Glaubenslehre," in full agreement with these views.

(8) Page 157.—The propensity, found in all great forms of religion, at all times, in varying degree and under the most different shapes, to form smaller and warmer societies within the great one, rests undeniably on the presumption that the great society has fallen into deep corruption. This expresses itself in separatism which accepts generally the type of doctrine, but will have nothing to do with the regulations of the religious society. Manifestly therefore, it must maintain that the regulations of the society are independent of its doctrine, and determined by something alien, and that in consequence the members of the religious society are in a state of sickness. After what is said above about the social nature of piety, no one will believe that I am here speaking of separatist piety. On the contrary, it is rather of the endeavour to found closer associations more accordant with the idea of the true church. But this praise associa-

tions only deserve when they unfold a rich productiveness in religious communication, not when they are founded on a narrow and exclusive letter, and reject the idea of one all-embracing communion. Is this the case and productiveness is weak or quite fails, the state of sickness is not to be denied. Hence among all similar societies the Moravian Brethren, who have at least produced a characteristic type of poetry, are always pre-eminent. Religious speech also among them has more scope and variety, for, besides the general assembly, the community is divided up in various ways. A very beautiful scheme at least is not to be denied, and if the result is less rich, a deficiency in the cultivation of talent may be to blame. In other directions also this society has taken a good and praiseworthy course. It has rejected that exclusiveness of the letter which keeps the two chief branches of the Protestant Church apart, and stands in manifold relations to the whole of this church according as occasion offers. In its missionary efforts, moreover, in which it must be acknowledged to excel, it has displayed a pure and right tact and a happy readiness in reaching the most imperfect states of religion and awaking receptiveness for the high spirit of Christianity. Where the sense for such closer union is awakened, the contempt of the recognized church, in its existing state, is natural. But this contempt is here ascribed to all who, in a higher sense, are religious and the next step is, that from this state the endeavour must go forth to improve the great outward society itself and bring it nearer its natural union with the true church.

(9) Page 158.—This description may very well be quite in accordance with the form which our assemblies for divine service, broadly considered, showed at that time. In any case it was the result of an immediate impression. Yet the consequence that the principle of communion in these assemblies is entirely different from what has actually been developed, is not to be drawn straightway, but only under the following limitations. Further on, page 178, family worship is assigned to members of the true church, who do not have the requisite endowments for coming forward in personal activity and priestly function in the outward religious society, that they may there satisfy their impulse to communicate. Now persons who are in this position cannot, despite outward appearance, be merely passive and receptive in the assemblies of the church. They carry the work of the church further, and their activity is actually in the assembly. Thus when public and family worship are regarded as one, the whole of the larger assembly appears as an active organism. This activity would also have its influence in the

assembly if several families were to join for a pious purpose, if the leader of the assembly had this inner productiveness of its members before his mind. Wherefore, the consequence would only be rightly drawn where no religious communication had developed itself in domestic life and family intercourse, a thing seldom found at that time in our country. Further, religious communication is also an art, not determined by piety only, but by training also. Hence entire equality and reciprocity are not possible. Compare great representations in any art. In music, for example, the composer is not the only person, but the performers also, from the leading instrument to the most subordinate accompanyist. Then there must be the maker of the musical instruments, and the audience too, if they are connoisseurs, do not merely receive, but each one in his own way also has his work. Similarly we must acknowledge that in the assemblies of the church the greatest number can only contribute to the representation of the whole as accompanying artists. Thus one-sidedness only fully appears when such co-operation entirely fails, either the piety doing nothing but absorb, or the speaking and working being offered simply from a profane artistic sense without religious spirit.

(10) Page 159.—If this were taken quite exactly, the result would certainly be that the visible church would exist only through its own nullity, through its incapacity to bring the religious feeling to any high degree of keenness. But that it is not to be taken exactly is manifest, because otherwise this cold and proud withdrawal from the visible church would be praised, in direct contradiction to the previous contention that this great religious society is by no means to be dissolved. Yet here, as in all similar human things, there are gradations, founded in the original constitution of the individual. Persons of different grades are directed by nature to one another, but it is only a shallow view that one simply affects the other, as if one could simply by working on another implant religion in him. Religion is original in every man, and stirs in every man. In some, however, it keeps pace with the whole individuality of the person, so that, in every manifestation of the pious consciousness, this individuality appears; in others, again, religion only appears under the form of the common feeling. And this may be so even in persons otherwise of marked individuality. The religious emotions are linked to the common states of things, and find in the common presentation their satisfaction. Were persons of more individual emotion now to withdraw from those common forms of presentation, both parties would suffer loss. What would become of the common presentations unfertilized by individual emotions we can see in the ecclesiastical

societies in which individuality generally is in the background, and all rests on steadfast formulas. The Armenian and Greek churches, unless, indeed, the latter be now receiving a new impulse, appear to be quite dead, and only to be moved mechanically. The individual again, however strong and characteristic his life may be, who leaves the common ground, gives over the largest range of his consciousness, and, if the true church nowhere shows itself in actuality, nothing remains for him but an isolated, separatist existence, always decaying from want of a larger circulation.

(11) Page 160.—Seeing that in this passage the view that dominates this whole Speech is here presented most decisively and compactly, it may be best to say what remains to be said in explanation and justification of it. The whole matter resolves itself into the right representation of the relation between the perfectly mutual communication, here regarded as the true church, and the actually existing religious communion. The state of this communion is acknowledged to be capable of such an improvement as is described further on p. 166. This being assumed, the question stands thus : Should there be in this educational society, besides the priestly work which only those fully cultured religiously should exercise, a special communion of such persons corresponding to the idea of the church to which the members of the visible religious society might, in the measure of their progress, go over ? Now the greatest masters are required for the greatest representations. We have seen every master, who would have his full effect, requires subordinate artists and a worthy, an informed, a responsive audience. Further, great masters are too rare, and too much dispersed to fashion alone this twofold sphere. What remains for us then but to say that, in corporeal and visible form, such a society is nowhere to be found on earth. The best of this kind to be actually discovered, is that improved type of the existing church, those societies in which a skilful master gathers around him a number of kindred souls whom he fires and fashions. The more the members of this circle advance and fashion that twofold sphere, the more such a company is a great presentation of religion. For those who are the soul of such a presentation, there is the higher fellowship which consists in mutual intercourse and insight. The other members share in so far as they succeed in raising themselves to the possibility of such enjoyment of forms strange to them. The idea of the true church here given is not realized therefore in one single instance, but, as has been indicated on p. 154, by the peaceful cosmopolitan union of all existing communions, each being as perfect as possible after its own manner.

This idea, belonging as it does to the completion of human nature, must be developed more fully in the science of ethics. Two objections to it, however, may be easily set aside. First, how does this agree with the call attributed to Christianity in the " Glaubenslehre" to absorb all other kinds of faith, for were all one, that cosmopolitan union for communicating and for understanding different faiths would not exist. But this has already been answered. All naturally existing different characteristics in Christianity would not disappear, but would always develope itself in a subordinate way, without injury to its higher unity. At present Christianity exhibits no outward unity, and the highest we can wish to see is just such a peaceful union of its various types. We have no reason to believe that it will ever exhibit an outward unity, but, even if it did, it would still be such a cosmopolitan union. But, secondly, can it be said that what is here called the true church has ever actually existed in any one instance ?   When the Apostles of Christ scattered to preach the Gospel and break bread in the houses and the schools, they exercised the priestly office among the laity in the visible church, and when they were by themselves in the upper-room to praise God and the Lord, what were they but that true church ?   In this Speech also it is pointed out not indistinctly (p. 165), that this kind of existence has been always renewed and has never quite vanished from the true church.   And, certainly, if there has ever been any one instance of the true church it was then.   But something was wanting, something held in this Speech to be essential to the true church, greatness and majesty of presentation. This consciousness of inadequacy was, humanly speaking, among the motives for the wider expansion of Christianity. Yet this instance, despite its short continuance, showed that the imperfect church only springs from the perfect. But having once disappeared, the enormous expansive power of Christianity made its reappearance impossible, and the true church can never again be found except in that cosmopolitan union.

The highest spiritual communion of the most perfect saints is thus conditioned by the communion of the more perfect with the less perfect.   But if this latter communion is of a better type, and can be the only foundation for the former, does it deserve the reproach that only inquirers enter it, and only those who are not yet pious stay in it ?   This may still be said, only not as a reproach. All who enter, and not only the more receptive and imperfect, seek some one to inspire and encourage them, but the more advanced also seek helpers for such a presentation as can be recognized as proceeding from the spirit of the true church.   Through this common work they seek advancement in outward mastery as well as inward power and truth. Hence none of the members of the church have attained, they are only attaining. But if to this combination in its best form, a combination of the perfect be opposed who seek nothing beyond the joy of contemplation, because everyone is already what he can be, this can be nothing but just that cosmopolitan union. In it everyone is valued simply according to his present state and attainments, and cannot expect to be immediately forwarded in his own peculiar sphere by contemplating extraneous things. But if the description of the true church were the immediate association of the more perfect, it would need to be understood literally of the church triumphant, for only in it can an absolutely mutual communion that is without inequality and without progress, be thought of. There, on the contrary, there is only so much of the true church as there is true life and reproductive development in the existing religious communions.

(12) Page 160.—Two reproaches are made here against the present regulation of the church. The former evil has doubtless caused far more confusion at various times, but the latter has always given me a painful feeling of the undeveloped state of the society. I mean the regulation, that for our holiest symbol, the Lord's supper, though it is, in most larger communions at least, in the most natural way, the crown of each service, previous meditation and preparation are required on each occasion from the participants. Clearly no one will deny that it would be the finest effect of the whole service, if very many present were attuned for celebrating this sacred meal. But this fairest blossom of devoutness is lost. How often, on the other hand, with all previous meditation and preparation, inward and outward disturbance may enter, and diminish the full blessing. Now just because of the previous preparation it may not be easy to put off the participation. Is not this way of doing a speaking proof of how little influence upon the heart we believe the matter itself to be capable, and how we treat all Christians, without exception, as unreliable novices? It will be a happy time when we dare to cast aside this caution and welcome to the table of the Lord everyone whom a momentary impulse conducts thither. . . . Still more confusion, however, arises from the other misunderstanding here mentioned, which is that not only do the clergy among themselves estimate themselves by the standard of a creed, but the laity also presume to deliver judgment on the clergy by the same standard. Nay, a right is acknowledged in the congregation to require that their clergy shall teach them according to the letter of the creed.

In other matters, if anything is prepared for my use I must be allowed, if I will, to determine myself how it shall be prepared, seeing I alone can rightly judge of my necessity. It is, however, quite otherwise with doctrine, for, if I am in a position to judge how a doctrine on any subject is to be set forth if it is to be useful to me, I do not require teaching, but can myself give it, or at most I require to be reminded. This claim, therefore, is the more preposterous the sharper the line is drawn between clergy and laity. Were all on the same level, indeed, it might be easier to suppose an agreement to abide by a common type. It is also the more absurd the more the teaching of the clergy is, as, God be thanked, it still is everywhere in the Evangelical Church a free outpouring of the heart, and the chief worth is not set on the repetition of fixed formularies as in the Romish or Greek Churches. If the laity, whether singly as patrons of a church or congregation, or combined as state officials, or as a congregation, decide what accords with the letter of the creed, and how far its authority is to apply to the teaching, it is peculiarly preposterous. The letter of the creed has had its sole origin with the clergy, who certainly did not wish to be themselves limited by it in their dealings with the laity. The laity are only through the instruction of the clergy even in a position to understand the letter of the creed. This preposterousness appears at its height when the head of a state personally believes he has by his position justification and qualification for deciding on the creed of another communion, when he believes he can judge of the relation of the clergy to it and what religious communications, the religiousness of which is quite strange to him, may tend to forward its interests. The Chinese Emperor, for example, tolerates Christianity, but provides through his mandarins that no party swerve from its own creed. There is, however, one consolation, that on this point there can be nothing but improvement.

(13) Page 161.—This state of things is, in many respects, most prominent in the Romish and Greek Churches. Nor is it merely because the distinction between priest and laity is there most pronounced. The clergy are not limited to the duty in the congregations; only for the secular clergy is this the chief concern. For the others it is only secondary. First of all they are to live in high religious contemplation. The clergy thus in their inward association form the true church. The laity are simply those who by them have been formed to piety, and who therefore stand under continual spiritual guidance, while the highest triumph is for some to become capable of reception into that closer sphere of the religious life. That the principle of

this theory exists in the Catholic Church we should have to acknowledge, even though, in other respects, the most glaring opposition
between the two classes had not again appeared. And I do not rest
on the imperfect result, on the bad state of the clergy, on the irreligious vacuity of the cloister life. In that case we could only say at
most that the attempt to present the true church, separate from
those who are only being taught in religion, has not succeeded. The
chief point is that the failure is based in the principle. In practice
the clergy and monastics are often deeply involved in all worldly
matters, but, according to the idea, the contemplative life is quite
separated from the active, the latter being declared quite incompatible with the higher religious stage. Judging the consequences
from all that has hitherto taken place, it is not to be doubted that
Protestantism is, in this regard, a return to the right way of presenting the true church, and that it bears more also of its image.

(14) Page 161.—A misunderstanding is here easily possible, as if
systematic theology had its only source in the corruption of religion.
Elsewhere I have plainly enough declared that, so soon as any religion
attains any greatness, it must construct for itself a theology, of which
system—an exhibition of the closest connection of the religious principles and dogmas—has been and must remain a natural and essential
part. But here I speak only of the false interest taken often by the
whole church in the connection of doctrine. Clearly this is based
only on that corruption. The system as a whole and in its sections,
which can only be fully understood in connection with the whole,
should remain the exclusive possession of those who in this particular respect have had a scientific training. It is their concern,
because on the one side it enables them to scan the whole circumference of possible subjects of religious communication and presentation, and to assign each its place, and on the other it serves as a
critical norm for testing all religious utterances by the precise
expression, whereby it is easier to discover whether anything that
cannot be reduced to this expression is mere confusion or conceals
something contrary to the spirit of the whole. As both interests lie
quite outside the horizon of all the other members of the church, they
should not be affected by anything exclusively bearing on them. If
there is anything in the public or social utterance that immediately
injures their pious consciousness, they have no need of further
witness from any system. But if they can be injured by what is
contained only in scientific terminology, then this is just that corruption here shown, whether they have lost themselves in unseemly
conceit of wisdom, or are called in blind zeal by theological dispu-

tants to help in crushing some dangerous man. How beautiful would it be if theologians would begin the change and warn the laity of all kinds against all participation in dogmatic strifes, and point them to the good belief that there are pious theologians enough to arrange the matter.

(15) Page 162.—This is easy to correct from the preceding explanations. If what is here called the true church has no separate manifestation, neither is there, in a literal sense, a passing sojourn in the actually existing communion. Exclusiveness alone is passing, so that outside of his own communion everyone advanced in piety may be also capable in a certain sense of sharing in the cosmopolitan union of all. Similarly the word *decisive* is not to be taken literally as if the incapable should be quite outside of all religious fellowship, either being put out or keeping out. This the pious neither could nor should do, nor even suffer to be done. Since they seek to give their presentations of religion the widest and deepest influence, they can let no one depart. Still less can they exclude, for an absolute incapacity can never be acknowledged. They must always look for a time when an element common to all men shall be developed, and for some yet untried art that may favour its development. Yet it remains true that the person in whom religiousness, in the form nearest and most congenial to him, is awakened only after such long and painful effort can hardly attain that higher development and free enjoyment. .

(16) Page 166.—A great preference is here exhibited for the smaller communions as against the great ecclesiastical institutions. One side only doubtless is brought into prominence. This is difficult to avoid, at least in an oratorical connection, when attention has to be drawn to an utterly neglected or greatly depreciated subject. The preference, however, rests on the following reasons. First, on the greater variety that can be manifested in the same time and space. In the great bodies either no variety is allowed to grow, or it is hidden, or discoverable only by close observers. In the religious sphere, moreover, more than anywhere else, points of union arise which cannot long continue, but which, though fleeting, may produce something strong and characteristic. If now only great church institutions exist, these germs are all lost, or at least reach no clear and complete organization. The other leading reason is, that the smaller ecclesiastical societies, because they awake less apprehension, are freer, and are less seldom put in wardship by the civil authority. When I first wrote this, America seemed to me a marvellously active theatre, where everything took this shape, and where, in conse-

quence, I thought that, more than anywhere else, our own beloved Fatherland not excepted, the freedom of the religious life and of the religious society was assured. Since then the development has confirmed the anticipation. Unions are freely made and dissolved. They divide themselves. Smaller parts separate from a greater whole, and smaller wholes draw together. Thus they seek a centre around which to form a greater unity. The freedom of Christian development is so great that many communions, as the Unitarian, would appear to us, I believe wrongly, outside of Christianity. In such a breaking up of Christianity there might be a fear that it would gradually lose its great historical form, and its scientific stability come to be quite forgotten. But the prospect is better since science has advanced and institutions have been founded for the propagation of Christian learning. Only one thing is to be lamented—at least so it appears to us from the distance—the British spirit has so much taken the upper hand and the German keeps on receding. For those free states, therefore, such a German immigration as would establish an abiding influence, were to be wished. . . . Now, however, that I have been more weaned from the smaller society and have grown more into the larger institution I would not speak so decisively. In England, for example, it is most evident that it would stand ill with Christianity, either if the Episcopal Church were quite dissolved and scattered among the smaller societies, or if it absorbed them all and existed alone. Similarly we must conclude that if the religious life in its whole variety and fulness would develope in the broad compass of Christianity, both great institutions and small societies must exist together as they have almost always done, so that the institution must be resolved into small societies and from them be again produced. Disorganizing elements it must surrender to them, and from them again it must be enriched and strengthened. After this exposition of the matter, no one will ask how this preference for smaller religious societies is consistent with a lively participation in the union of the two Protestant ecclesiastical societies, that would not only make one greater out of two smaller, but manifestly cause the smaller at least to disappear. The following alone I would add. The difference of doctrine has always appeared to me insignificant, but there has manifestly been a difference of spirit between the two communions. Without that, such a division could not have arisen from motives otherwise so insignificant. This difference has not yet by any means quite disappeared. Now this involves onesidedness on the part of both, and the time now appears to be come for a more vigorous effort to diminish these limitations by complete combination of differences and by friendly proximity. This could better be accomplished by union, by a life in freedom more bound and in the bonds more free. Besides, it seemed high time to provide that a recurrence of envy between the two might not render impossible the strong resistance which is becoming necessary against the manifold suspicious endeavours of the Romish Church.

(17) Page 166.—A person who has spoken as urgently as I have done in the fourth collection of my sermons for once moremaking the whole care of the poor a business of the ecclesiastical association, appears to know quite well to what all property and money endowments might be devoted. But even the most extensive care of the poor requires only a secure yearly income. Wherefore, if the congregational tie is secure, and the spirit that rules in it embraces an active goodwill for this subject, this business also can be carried on satisfactorily without any such possession. Other things being equal, it will, indeed, be carried on better. On the one side all capital can be better used by private people, and on the other this possession adds a foreign element to the pure character of a congregation and introduces an estimate of its members other than the purely religious.

(18) Page 169.—By this complaint I in nowise meant that the state should not in many and in most important things rely chiefly on the power of the religious sentiments and on the agreement of its own interests with their natural working. But I meant that in so far as it believes it must so rely, it is to be desired that the state do not interfere in a manner hurtful to the pure effect of these sentiments. Now this happens without fail, when there is any positive intermeddling. The state may on the one side assume the religious sentiment of its members and rejoice confidingly in its working. It then reserves the right to withdraw this assumption in respect of an individual who does not manifest this working, or when this deficiency shows itself in a decisive majority of a religious society, it inquires how far the defect has its root in the principles of the society and modifies its assumption accordingly. But so long as it has no ground for withdrawing its trust, it must know that the organization of the society proceeds from the very sentiment, from which it expects good result, and that in the nature of the case only those in whom this sentiment is strongest will have most influence in forming and guiding the society. It must, therefore, leave the sentiment free to operate, allowing the organization of the society to take its own course without its guidance. This must continue till the result gives ground for lessening the state's confi-

dence. If a state has this confidence only in one particular form of religiousness, it follows this course with the society in which it exists, and regulates its conduct towards the others by the greatness of its distrust, varying up to complete intolerance. A state relies on one religious society and accords it a high degree of independence; another it watches more closely, and itself decides on its organization. Now in reason this can have no other ground than that the state gives the latter society less confidence. A marvellous phenomenon cannot be thought of, as if a state would watch more closely the religious society to which the sovereign himself belonged and limit it in its free activity more than any other. This case of confidence in the religious sentiment is, for our present inquiry, the first point. The second is the opposite case, when the state looks for no good effect in respect of anything falling within its own sphere from the religious sentiment of its members. Even then there seems to be no consistent course, except to allow religion to manifest itself as an amusement to which the state is indifferent, taking care, as with other private associations, that no harm arises to the civil community. Applying this now to education, the matter here in discussion and the matter to which everything comes back, there seem to be the following consequences. The religious education of man will never, as such, be the whole education of man All training in which the religious society does not, as such, interest itself, as for example the academic and higher scientific, lies outside of its domain. Perhaps the church has earlier thought of education than the state. The state will then say, " I see that you have the institutions for educating the youth, but they do not suffice me. I will add what fails but will then take them under my guidance." If the church dares to speak and understands its own good, it will reply, " Not so, but for all deficiency make your own institutions and we, as citizens, will honourably contribute our utmost to their success. Within our special limits, however, leave us our own to care for ourselves, and only omit from yours that for which you think ours will suffice." Does the state, nevertheless, do by force the contrary, there will be an element in the highest degree undesirable to the church, and it will feel it an injury even when this gives the doubtful privilege of a certain influence on many things whereon, by the natural course of things, it would have none. . . With the teaching of human duties in civil life, which is nothing but a continuous education of grown-up people, it is the same. That this is needed by the state admits of no doubt, all the more if it does not proceed naturally from the public life. The state finds now that there is teaching of this kind in the exercises and utterances of the religious society existing in its midst. It willingly resolves to spare an institution of its own for this object. The religious society is pleased to render this service to the common good. But the state says, " I will make use of your teaching, but to make sure that it completely reaches my purpose, I must prescribe to you what you are not to forget to speak of, and what you shall recall from history at fixed times, and I must make arrangements to know that this is actually done." The church will then, if it dare, certainly say, " By no means, for there would then be much teaching not belonging to our department, and in respect of history it is repugnant to us, for example, to recall joyfully certain days when you were victorious over another state, while our society in that state must observe a discreet silence, and should rejoice on other days when you were defeated, and which we again must pass over. Both days are alike to us, and we must, in our own way, make the same use both of what is to your honour and to your shame. With this use you may well be content, but for that special purpose make another arrangement, for we cannot assist." And if the state gives no heed to these representations, it injures the personal freedom of its members where it is holiest and most inviolable. . . . The third matter here mentioned, the taking of oaths, properly belongs to the second, but is specially mentioned because of the special manner in which the state brings the church to its aid. An injury has here also been inflicted. The different small societies of non-swearers are allowed a simple affirmation instead of an oath, but the great church, specially favoured by the state, is exhorted to preach on the sacredness of oaths, and its members must take them in the pre-scribed manner or lose all the privileges involved. There may, however, be many among them who, fearing the plain prohibition of Christ, are troubled in conscience about swearing, and among the teachers there may also be many who cannot get over the literal inter-pretation of those words, and who think it irreligious to come to the help of the state in such a manner. How can it be that such an injury to religious freedom should not be felt very painfully ? These fuller explanations, it is to be hoped, will justify the wish expressed in the text, that the state should employ what is useful to it in the ar-rangements of the church only in so far as consists with uninjured freedom.

(19) Page 269.—Of the three points here lamented, two are only burdensome because they witness to the dependence of the church or the state. The sacred acts of baptism and solemnization

of marriage are made to appear as done by the clergy, first of all, as servants of the state, in the name of the state. Without question this is one reason why the way they are carried out betrays so little of a Christian or indeed of a religious character. If inscription in the civil register were a purely civil act, no one could regard baptism as merely a legal formality, accompanied occasionally by a stately speech. And if the marriage contract were first concluded purely civilly, and the blessing of the church were purely an act of the members of a congregation, it would soon appear that marriages are best where a special value is set on this additional outward consecration. But the worst is, the point between. An Evangelical Christian state unites many civil qualifications with admission to the sacrament. In many instances it demands attestations of this act. It acts with the best intention towards the youth, seeking to guard them against the religious negligence of their parents or guardians. But how much are the consciences of pious clergymen burdened; how often must they, quite against their conviction, declare religious instruction and closer supervision at an end. Even were a great number of baptized Christians to remain all their lives without participation in the other sacrament, as is the case in North America, it does not appear that this would be a misfortune. Rather it would have the advantage that the Christian church would not appear responsible for the lives of the grossest men, while the strife about the right of exclusion from the congregation would be spared. In Protestant Europe only the grossest would be outside, for the continued participation in divine service would sooner or later supply what they had lost at that time when confirmation usually takes place. As in the American free states it might furthermore happen with us that the children of Christian parents, who set no great store on the fellowship of the church, would remain unbaptized. They would then have no link with the church. This might well happen, though with us such an anti-Christian zealotism would be very rare. But to hinder the real loss that would hence arise, the state should not be required to impose baptism by force, but it should begin early to protect the freedom of conscience of the children even against the parents. These complaints appear plainly capable of remedy, but only by a great difference of form in all those concerns that relate to the connection of church and state. If the example of the free states in the other hemisphere alone were considered, and everything in the condition of the church charged as consequences of what is here postulated, it would unquestionably be unfair. There are these imperfections inseparable from a young and very dissimilar population that have been gathered from all quarters, which will be thrown off without the necessity of essential change in these matters.

(20) Page 170.—That in all religious doings the predominance of legal or civil relations is a departure from the original nature of the matter, especially if it occasions pecuniary transactions between the clergy and the members of the congregation, requires no further discussion. Yet it appears as if this complaint would never be removed so long as a state, as such, confesses its adherence to any one religious society, or even if it believes it can require all its members to belong to some society. In the former case, if a law declares that only in one church is there the greatest fulness of that sentiment which can maintain this state and be the fullest security against all its possible foes, it would follow that the whole maintenance of the state would be entrusted only to the members of this society. In the present state of social relations this can only continue as a law where the great body of the people belong to that society, the rest being only clients and strangers. But even in Catholic countries such a state of matters no longer exists, and it does not seem as if, in the present position of affairs, a state would easily be able to confess absolute and undivided adherence to one religious society. The south European states, which have anew proclaimed the Catholic religion to be the religion of the state, will not, even though their position is favourable and Protestants are only found scattered as clients, be able for many generations of tranquillity to adhere without harshness and injustice to this system. It is quite different when, without law and in consequence of the natural effect of public opinion, all that is essential in the government of the state falls to the adherents of one society. Such a transaction is not a state's confession, and we must wish that it may long continue. But if adherence to one society is now a passing state of things, is it a right maxim for the state, without deciding which, to require that its citizens belong to some one? Let it be granted that irreligious men are neither profitable for the civil union, nor to be relied upon. But would they be made religious by being compelled to confess adherence to any one religious society? Manifestly the only way to make irreligious men really religious is to strengthen the influence of religious men upon them as much as possible. For this end the state cannot work more effectively than by allowing all the religious societies within its domain to operate with the fullest freedom. This freedom they will never feel till those intermeddlings cease.

(21) Page 172.—With this exposition, which rests on a very meagre

experience, I can no longer agree. And first, in respect of capabili-
ties, it appears as if the people and the cultured would have a very
unequal enjoyment of a religious utterance on which, according to
the demands made above, all the flowers of speech are to be expended.
But all true eloquence must be popular throughout. It is affecta-
tion that chooses either expressions or combinations of thought
unsuited to the majority, and the cultured also must be capable of
guidance by a thoroughly popular diction. A division of hearers in
respect of capacity is not required by the nature of the subject, but
by the consciousness of imperfection in the artists. It is only a
different kind of imperfection when one man speaks better for the
people and another for the higher ranks. But in the second
place, in respect of mental type, it is indeed not to be denied that
the differences of the audience must be contained in very narrow
limits, if a religious utterance is to have a large and happy result.
But it must be a wrong assumption, that in a multitude united in
other matters and woven together in a common life, we must have
very different religious peculiarities, and indeed so marvellously
different that on the one side they are not strong enough to form a
religious society of their own, and on the other they are so markedly
singular that they cannot appropriate a religious utterance of
another type. Only in great cities could elements so different be
brought into a small compass, and here every one has an easy choice,
selecting the presentations of religion that can strengthen and
quicken him. But suppose the people are considered in relation to
the different forms of religion afterwards mentioned. It will always
be found that in whole districts, through many generations, the
religious life has been prevailingly mystic, or more linked to history,
or influenced by understanding and reflection. Exceptions are rare,
and those who are not religious according to the dominant type are
less religious altogether. If, therefore, the easy selection of the gay
world in great cities were not troubled by narrow partiality for the
ministrants, and on the other hand all religious orators strove only
after true popularity, on this point, at least, our present state would
be tolerable enough.

(22) Page 174.—That the state, besides what it confides to the
church, must provide an educational institution of its own, be it for
the younger generation or for the less educated portion of the people,
is here regarded as absolutely necessary. This contention shows the
speaker's decision on the much discussed question of the relation of state
and church to what in the widest sense of the word is called school.
In part the state may continue to rely on the religious associations.

Yet it must be content to exercise only a negative supervision over their institutions. For the rest it is the duty of the state to arrange and care. Where there is any kind of religious association, that the awaking of the higher spiritual be not hindered, there is also in the homes a uniform discipline for taming sensuality, which is in every way useful for the civil life. But if the state requires a special discipline to produce certain habits in its citizens suited to the time, it must not come from the church. The proper feeling of its necessity being universally diffused, the state may rely on the work of the families, not as elements of the religious but of the civil society. If this feeling is not sufficiently diffused, the state must make public provision. All that is academic in education is of this kind, for it cannot and, being quite foreign to it, should not even appear to proceed from the church. Further, wherever a system of religious communication exists, there must be common instruction of the youth in all that bears upon understanding the religious speech and the creed. This is properly the church parish school. In Christendom it is for transmitting religious ideas, and among Protestants for some small understanding at least of the Scriptures. Has the state confidence that an effective communication of moral ideas and the germs of mental development will be given at the same time, it may rely on the church school for those objects. But everything statistical, mathematical, technical and such like is foreign to the church school. If the ecclesiastical and the civil community are identical, the ecclesiastical and the civil school may for some good reason be united in one institution. But the state no more acquires the right thereby to conduct the ecclesiastical school, than the church to conduct the civil. Finally, every religious fellowship that has a history requiring, for comprehending its development, attainments that belong to the sphere of science and learning, needs an institution to maintain and encourage such attainments. This is the church academy. All other sciences are foreign to the church. Suppose there exist in the state, either being maintained by the state or being independent bodies, academies for general science, and suppose the church has confidence that their methods are suited to its requirements, it may find it expedient to unite with them its own special academy. But the expediency must be determined by the church, and neither by the state nor by the scientific bodies. The church may neither found a claim on this union to general superintendence of scientific institutions, nor give up its right to manage its own academy. These are the principles then on which church and state are to act together or act apart. But to acknowledge these principles towards one church and not towards another is the worst possible inconsistency. It must necessarily pain the slighted church that incurable disagreement should arise between their religious and their political feeling.

(23) Page 174.—Well said of every such relation! and in this view I still stand firm. Nay, I stand firmer, the more lamentable complications I see arising from this dependence of the church on the state. These complications were less thought of then, for the only thing of the kind so rapidly came to grief on the dominant tendency of the time. Yet it is impossible that the church should be without any union with the state. That appears even where the church is freest. The least is that the state treat the religious societies like any other private society. As a general principle of association it takes knowledge of them and puts itself in a position to interfere in case they should cherish anything prejudicial to the common freedom and safety. With this least, however, it is seldom possible to escape, as appears even in North America where the church is freest. The freer the churches are the easier it happens that some dissolve and some combine. Now even though they may have no possessions except the most absolutely necessary means for meeting together, there are difficulties of settlement in which the state is the natural arranger and umpire. Had this and no other relation existed between church and state at the time of the Reformation, the present curious position of affairs would not have come to pass, that in lands almost entirely Protestant the Catholic Church is well endowed and secured, while the Evangelical Church is referred to a changeable and often doubtful good will. Every further union of church and state should be regarded as a private agreement for the time being. The more of these transactions there are the more it will seem that a church-communion in one state becomes the church of the land, and becomes more divided from its brethren in the faith in other states. The less there are, the more a communion, though spread over many states, may appear an undivided whole, and the more marked is the independence of the church from the state. Within these limits, all existing relations are permissible, and it belongs to completeness that at some time and place they have all had historical existence. On the contrary, what transcends these limits is of evil.

(24) Page 174.—This rejection of all closer connection among the congregations of the same faith and of all religious associations, rests solely on the presupposition that every existing church is only a visible appendage of the true church. It is, therefore, right, only in so far as the presupposition is right. Since I wrote this I have

shown myself a zealous defender of synodal government which is
manifestly included in this rejection. In part I have abandoned
the presupposition. By observation and joyful experience I have
reached the conviction that truly believing and pious persons exist
in adequate number in our congregations, and that it is good to
strengthen as much as possible their influence on the rest. This
result naturally flows from well-ordered combinations. In part
also, life in our time soon conducts to the view that every improvement that is to succeed must be ushered in from all sides at once.
This involves that men should in many respects be treated as if
they already were what they ought to be. Otherwise it would be
necessary to wait on and on and no beginning would be possible.
But according to my view the sole warrant for such closer combinations is that the participators are members of the true church, in
which the distinction between priests and laity is only to serve the
occasion and cannot be permanent. Wherefore, I could only defend
a constitution that rested on this equality and any other in the
Evangelical Church there could never be. Where synodal unions
consist purely of the clergy, they seem either by the state commis-
sion and purely consultative, or literary and friendly, rather than
ecclesiastical, and constitutional. A constitutional priestly government becomes only the Catholic Church. The foundation stone of
that church is the higher personal religious worth of the priests, and
its first principle that the laity, only by their mediation, enjoy
their share in the blessings of the church. The last assertion
ventured in this passage, that there should be no outward bond
between teachers and congregation, depends still more on the
presupposition that the congregation still require to be led to
religion. This could only be done on condition of the most complete
spontaneousness. Who is then to impose this outward bond?
Neither the state nor a corporation of the clergy, if this spontaneousness is to exist. The congregations cannot, for they cannot judge of
those who must first communicate to them the ability to judge the
worth in question. Hence this bond can only be entered on and
upheld where the spirit of piety in the congregations can be assumed,
and where those who can guide and limit this judgment are regarded as having come forth from the congregation. Herein are
contained the principles for determining in different circumstances
the firmness or the freedom of the bond.

(25) Page 175.—On the limits of the binding power exercised by
creeds, I have lately declared myself more fully, though with special
reference to the Evangelical Church. I here call this bond unholy

when it is regarded in the ordinary way, and I am still of this opinion. Than unbelief nothing is more unholy to the pious. Of unbelief an abundance underlies the maxim that teachers of religion, and even teachers of theology, should be bound by the letter of a written confession. It is unbelief in the power of the common spirit in the church, when men are not convinced that alien elements in individuals will not, by the living power of the whole, be either assimilated or enveloped and made harmless, but believe external force is required to cast it out. It is unbelief in the power of the word of Christ and of the Spirit that declares Him, when men do not believe that every time has naturally its own fitting interpretation and application of it, when they believe we must adhere to the production of another age. It can never again befall us that the spirit of prophesy should become dumb. The Sacred Scripture itself has obtained its position, and will retain it only by the power of free belief and not by outward sanction.

(26) Page 176.—The feeling that ecclesiastical matters as they then existed in the greater part of Germany, and still exist, little altered, could not continue as they were, has since become much more general and definite. Yet how the matter will turn is still not much clearer. This alone can be foreseen, that if an Evangelical Church is not soon put in a position in which a fresher public spirit can be developed in it, and if the restrictive treatment of our universities and our open spiritual intercourse is longer continued, the hopes we cherished will be fruitless blossom, and the fair dawn of the recent time has only betokened storm. Living piety and liberal courage will ever more and more disappear from the clerical order. Dominion of the dead letter from above and uneasy spiritless sectarianism from below will approach. From their collision a whirlwind will arise that will drive many helpless souls into the outstretched net of Jesuitism, and deaden and weary the great masses to utter indifference. The signs that proclaim this are clear enough ; but everyone should on every occasion declare that he sees them as a testimony against those who heed them not.

(27) Page 178.—This limitation will seem to many too narrow. A profound and extensive cultivation of the mind, and a rich inward experience may very well exist where the theological erudition, that is the essential condition of the office of church teacher, is wanting. Should such gifts be limited in their religious working to the narrow circle of the domestic life ? Could not and should not such men, even when they cannot lead in public religious assemblies, yet work by the living word in freer, wider circles ? Should not the enormous influence

which they can obtain through the written word be pointed out to them? To this I have a twofold answer. First, all that, as free sociableness, most resembles the family connection, links itself naturally to the domestic life. The work of exhibiting there the character of a liberal-minded religious life is not insignificant. It is a duty hitherto neither sufficiently understood nor sufficiently exercised. If it were, there could not possibly be such a marked contrast in a great part of Germany, particularly among the higher and more refined circles, between the interest taken in religious formulas and theological disputes, and the domestic and social life in which no trace of a decisive religious character appears. Here, then, is a great sphere for the pious sense. But larger assemblies, exceeding the limits and the nature of the social life, yet not aiming at forming a congregation, in short conventicles, are always miserable half and between affairs, that have never contributed much to the advancement of religion, but have rather produced and cherished what is morbid. Secondly, in respect of religious influence by the written word, it would certainly be a great evil if the clerical order were to possess a monopoly. Nay, it does not seem to me consistent with the spirit of the Evangelical Church, that they should exercise a general censorship. But while there should be the greatest freedom, it is an entirely different question whether everyone should venture to communicate his religious views and sentiments in this way; and whether it would be expedient that it should happen often is very much to be doubted. The harm from the flood of mediocre romances and children's books may very well be compared with the harm from the mass of mediocre religious writings. Nay, they are manifestly a desecration, which the former are not. Even superior talent falls more easily into mediocrity, for what is to have attraction and effect is the subjective apprehension of universally known objects and relations. Only a high degree of unaffected originality, or a true inspiration, coming from the inmost depths of a reflective mind, or from the stimulating power of a life, nobly active, can succeed. Otherwise there can be nothing but mediocrity. With religious songs, indeed, it is different. Among us a large proportion of them has been composed by laymen of all classes. Many that a severe judge would call only mediocre, have passed into church use, and have attained thereby a kind of immortality. Two circumstances assist. First, every hymn book has only a very limited sphere, and here much may be good that has not all the qualities demanded by absolute publicity. Many of those productions would doubtless have long perished, and been forgotten, had they required to maintain themselves as pure literary works. Secondly, in the public use of hymns so many other things assist. The author does not produce the effect alone. He is supported by the composer by whom, more or less, everything that has the same metre and is known to all has harmony and effect ; he is supported by the congregation who put their piety into the execution, and by the liturgies that assign the work of the poet its right place in a larger connection.

FIFTH SPEECH

THE RELIGIONS

MAN in closest fellowship with the highest must be for you all an object of esteem, nay, of reverence. No one capable of understanding such a state can, when he sees it, withhold this feeling. That is past all doubt. You may despise all whose minds are easily and entirely filled with trivial things, but in vain you attempt to depreciate one who drinks in the greatest for his nourishment. You may love him or hate him, according as he goes with you or against you in the narrow path of activity and culture, but even the most beautiful feeling of equality you cannot entertain towards a person so far exalted above you. The seeker for the Highest Existence in the world stands above all who have not a like purpose. Your wisest men say that, even against your will, you must honour the virtuous who, in accordance with the laws of the moral nature, endeavour to determine finite concerns by infinite requirements. And were it even possible for you to find something ridiculous in virtue itself, because of the contrast between the limited powers and the infinite undertaking, you still could not deny esteem to one whose organs are open to the Universe, who is far from strife and opposition, exalted above all imperfect endeavour, responsive to the Universe and one with it. You cannot despise when you see man in this supreme moment of human existence and the clear beam is reflected in its purity upon you.

But whether the picture of the nature and of the life of religion I have drawn has claimed your esteem I do not inquire. Because of false conceptions and devotion to non-essentials esteem is too often refused, but I am sure of the power of the subject, as soon as it is freed from its distorting drapery. Nor do I ask whether my thoughts on the coherence of this indwelling capacity with all that is sublime and godlike in our nature, have stimulated you to an intenser study of our nature and possibilities. I also pass the question, whether you have taken the higher standpoint I showed you, and have recognized from thence, in that nobler fellowship of spirits, so much misjudged, wherein everyone freely surrenders himself, not regarding the glory of his self-will, nor the exclusive possession of his deepest, most secret individuality, that he may regard himself as a work of the eternal, the all-fashioning World-Spirit, even the holy of holies of fellowship, higher far than any earthly fellowship, holier than the tenderest tie of friendship. In short, I do not ask whether all religion, in its infinity, its divine power, has compelled you to adoration, for I leave the matter itself to work upon you.

At present I have something else to deal with, a new opposition to vanquish. I would, as it were, conduct you to the God that has become flesh; I would show you religion when it has resigned its infinity and appeared, often in sorry form, among men; I would have you discover religion in the religions. Though they are always earthly and impure, the same form of heavenly beauty that I have tried to depict is to be sought in them.

The divisions of the church and the difference of religion are almost always found together. The connection seems inseparable. There are as many creeds and confessions as churches and religious communions. Glancing at this state of things, you might easily believe that my judgment on the plurality of the church must also be my judgment on the plurality of religion. You would, however, entirely mistake my opinion. I condemned the plurality of the church, but my argument presupposed the plurality of religion. I showed from the nature of the case that in the church all rigid outline should be lost, that all distinct partition should disappear. Not only did I hold that all should be one indivisible whole in spirit and sympathy, but that the actual connection should have larger development and ever approach the highest, the universal unity. Now if there is not everywhere plurality of religion, if the most marked difference is not necessary and unavoidable, why should the true church need to be one? Is it not that everyone in the religion of others may see and share what he cannot find in his own? And why should the visible church be only one, if it is not that everyone may seek in it religion in the form best fitted to awake the germ that lies asleep in him? And if this germ can only be fertilized and made to grow by one definite kind of influence, it must itself be of a definite kind.

Nor can these different manifestations of religion be mere component parts, differing only in number and size, and forming, when combined, a uniform whole. In that case every one would by natural progress come to be like his neighbour. Such religion as he acquired would change into his own, and become identical with it. The church, this fellowship with all believers which I consider indispensable for every religious man, would be merely provisional. The more successful its work, the quicker would it end—a view of the institution I have never contemplated. I therefore find that multiplicity of the religions is based in the nature of religion.

That no man can perfectly possess all religion is easy to see. Men are determined in one special way, religion is endlessly determinable. But it must be equally evident that religion is not dismembered and scattered in parts by random among men, but that it must organize itself in manifestations of varying degrees of resemblance. Recall the several stages of religion to which I drew your attention. I said that the religion of a person, to whom the world reveals itself as a living whole, is not a mere continuation of the view of the person who only sees the world in its apparently hostile elements. By no amount of regarding the Universe as chaotic and discrete can the higher view be attained. These differences you may call kinds or degrees of religion, but in either case you will have to admit that, as in every similar case, the forms in which an infinite force divides itself is usually characteristic and different.

Wherefore, plurality of religions is another thing than plurality of the church. The essence of the church is fellowship. Its limit, therefore, cannot be the uniformity of religious persons. It is just difference that should be brought into fellowship.[1] You are manifestly right when you believe that the church can never in actuality be completely and uniformly one. The only reason, however, is that every society existing in space and time is thereby limited and losing in depth what it gains in breadth, falls to pieces. But religion, exactly by its multiplicity, assumes the utmost unity of the church. This multiplicity is necessary for the complete manifestation of religion. It must seek for a definite character, not only in the individual but also in the society. Did the society not contain a principle to individualize itself, it could have no existence. Hence we must assume and we must search for an endless mass of distinct forms. Each separate religion claims to be such a distinct form revealing religion, and we must see whether it is agreeable to this principle. We must make clear to ourselves wherein it is peculiar. Though the difference be hidden under strange disguises, though it be distorted, not only by the unavoidable influence of the transitory to which the enduring has condescended, but also by the unholy hand of sacrilegious men, we must find it.

To be satisfied with a mere general idea of religion would not be worthy of you. Would you then understand it as

it really exists and displays itself, would you comprehend
it as an endlessly progressive work of the Spirit that
reveals Himself in all human history, you must abandon
the vain and foolish wish that there should only be one
religion ; you must lay aside all repugnance to its multiplicity ; as candidly as possible you must approach everything that has ever, in the changing shapes of humanity,
been developed in its advancing career, from the ever
fruitful bosom of the spiritual life.

The different existing manifestations of religion you call
positive religions. Under this name they have long been
the object of a quite pre-eminent hate. Despite of your repugnance to religion generally, you have always borne more
easily with what for distinction is called natural religion.
You have almost spoken of it with esteem.

I do not hesitate to say at once that from the heart I entirely deny this superiority. For all who have religion at
all and profess to love it, it would be the vilest inconse-
quence to admit it. They would thereby fall into the
openest self-contradiction. For my own part, if I only
succeeded in recommending to you this natural religion,
I would consider that I had lost my pains.

For you, indeed, to whom religion generally is offensive,
I have always considered this preference natural. The so-
called natural religion is usually so much refined away, and
has such metaphysical and moral graces, that little of the
peculiar character of religion appears. It understands so
well to live in reserve, to restrain and to accommodate
itself that it can be put up with anywhere. Every positive
religion, on the contrary, has certain strong traits and a
very marked physiognomy, so that its every movement,
even to the careless glance, proclaims what it really is.

If this is the true ground of your dislike, you must now
rid yourself of it. If you have now, as I hope, a better
estimate of religion, it should be no longer necessary for
me to contend against it. If you see that a peculiar and

noble capacity of man underlies religion, a capacity which, of course, must be educated, it cannot be offensive to you to regard it in the most definite forms in which it has yet appeared. Rather you must the more willingly grant a form your attention the more there is developed in it the characteristic and distinctive elements of religion.

But you may not admit this argument. You may transfer all the reproaches you have formerly been accustomed to bestow on religion in general to the single religions. You may maintain that there are always, just in this element that you call positive, the occasion and the justification of those reproaches, and that in consequence the positive religions cannot be as I have sought to represent, the natural manifestations of the true religion. You would show me how, without exception, they are full of what, according to my own statement, is not religion. Consequently, must not a principle of corruption lie deep in their constitution ? You will remind me that each one proclaims that it alone is true, and that what is peculiar to it is absolutely the highest. Are they not distinguished from one another by elements they should as much as possible eliminate? In disproving and contending, be it with art and understanding, or with weapons stranger and more unworthy, do they not show themselves quite contrary to the nature of true religion ? You would add that, exactly in proportion as you esteem religion and acknowledge its importance, you must take a lively interest in seeing that it everywhere enjoys the greatest freedom to cultivate itself on all sides. You must, therefore, hate keenly those definite religious forms, that hold all their adherents to the same type and the same word, withdraw the freedom to follow their own nature and compress them in unnatural limits. In contrast, you would praise mightily the superiority in all these points of the natural to the positive religions.

Once more I say, I do not deny that misunderstandings and perversions exist in all religions, and I raise no objections to the dislike with which they inspire you. Nay, I acknowledge there is in them all this much bewailed degeneration, this divergence into alien territory. The diviner religion itself is, the less would I embellish its corruptions, or admiringly cherish its excrescences. But forget for once this one-sided view and follow me to another. Consider how much of this corruption is due to those who have dragged forth religion from the depths of the heart into the civil world. Acknowledge that much of it is unavoidable as soon as the Infinite, by descending into the sphere of time and submitting to the general influence of finite things, takes to itself a narrow shell. And however deep-rooted this corruption may be, and however much the religions may have suffered thereby, consider this also : if the proper religious view of all things is to seek even in things apparently common and base every trace of the divine, the true and the eternal, and to reverence even the faintest, you cannot omit what has the justest claims to be judged religiously.

And you would find more than remote traces of the Deity. I invite you to study every faith professed by man, every religion that has a name and a character. Though it may long ago have degenerated into a long series of empty customs, into a system of abstract ideas and theories, will you not, when you examine the original elements at the source, find that this dead dross was once the molten outpourings of the inner fire ? Is there not in all religions more or less of the true nature of religion, as I have presented it to you ? Must not, therefore, each religion be one of the special forms which mankind, in some region of the earth and at some stage of development, has to accept ?

I must take care not to attempt anything systematic or complete, for that would be the study of a life, and not the business of a discourse. Yet you must not be allowed to wander at hazard in this endless chaos. That you may not be misled by the false ideas that prevail; that you may estimate by a right standard the true content and essence of any religion; that you may have some definite and sure procedure for separating the inner from the outer, the native from the borrowed and extraneous, and the sacred from the profane, forget the characteristic attributes of single religions and seek, from the centre outwards, a general view of how the essence of a positive religion is to be comprehended and determined.

You will then find that the positive religions are just the definite forms in which religion must exhibit itself—a thing to which your so-called natural religions have no claim. They are only a vague, sorry, poor thought that corresponds to no reality, and you will find that in the positive religions alone a true individual cultivation of the religious capacity is possible. Nor do they, by their nature, injure the freedom of their adherents.

Why have I assumed that religion can only be given fully in a great multitude of forms of the utmost definiteness? Only on grounds that naturally follow from what has been said of the nature of religion. The whole of religion is nothing but the sum of all relations of man to God, apprehended in all the possible ways in which any man can be immediately conscious in his life. In this sense there is but one religion, for it would be but a poverty-stricken and halting life, if all these relations did not exist wherever religion ought to be. Yet all men will not by any means apprehend them in the same way, but quite differently. Now this difference alone is felt and alone can be exhibited while the reduction of all differences is only thought.

You are wrong, therefore, with your universal religion that is natural to all, for no one will have his own true and right religion, if it is the same for all. As long as we occupy a place there must be in these relations of man to the whole a nearer and a farther, which will necessarily determine each feeling differently in each life. Again, as long as we are individuals, every man has greater receptiveness for some religious experiences and feelings than for others. In this way everything is different. Manifestly then, no single relation can accord to every feeling its due. It requires the sum of them. Hence, the whole of religion can be present only, when all those different views of every relation are actually given. This is not possible, except in an endless number of different forms. They must be determined adequately by a different principle of reference to the others, and in each the same religious element must be characteristically modified. In short, they must be true individuals.

What determines and distinguishes these individuals, and what, on the other hand, is common to all their component parts, holds them together, and is their principle of adhesion, whereby any given detail is to be adjudged to its own type of religion, are implied in what has been already said. But this view can only be verified by the existing historical religions, and of them it is maintained that all this is different, and that such is not their relation to one another. This we must now examine.

First, a definite quantity of religious matter is not necessarily, in the same degree, a definite form of religion.

This is an entire misunderstanding of the nature of the different religions. Even among their adherents it is general, and causes manifold opposite and false judgments. They suppose that because so many men acknowledge the same religion, they must have the same body of religious views and feelings. Their fellow-believers must have the same opinions and the same faith as they have, and this common possession must be the essence of their religion. The peculiarly characteristic and individual element in a religion is not easy to find with certainty from instances, but, however general the idea may be, if you believe that it consists in including a definite sum of religious intuitions and feelings, and that as a consequence the positive religions are prejudicial to the freedom of the individual in the development of his own religion, you are in error. Single perceptions and feelings are, as you know, the elements of religion, and it can never lead to the character of any one religion to regard them as a mere heap, tossed together without regard to number, kind or purpose.

If now, as I have sought to show, religion needs to be of many types because, of every relation different views are possible, according as it stands related to the rest, how would we be helped by such a compendium of some of them that could define none? If the positive religions were only distinguished by what they exclude, they could certainly not be the individual manifestations we seek. That this is not their character, however, appears from the impossibility of arriving from this point of view at a distinct idea of them.

As they continue to exist apart, such an idea must be possible, for only what commingles in fact is inseparable in idea. It is evident that the different religious perceptions and feelings are not, in a determinate way, awakened by one another or interdependent. Now, as each exists for itself, each can lead, by the most various combinations, to every other. Hence, different religions could not continue long beside one another, if they were not otherwise distinguished. Very soon each would supplement itself into uniformity with all others.

Even in the religion of any one man, as it is fashioned in the course of life, nothing is more accidental than the quantity of religious matter that may arrive at consciousness. Some views may set and others may rise and come to clearness, and his religion in this respect is ever in flux. Much less can the boundary, which in the individual is so changeable, be permanent and essential in the religion of several associated individuals. In the highest degree it must be an unusual and accidental occurrence that, even for a little time, several men remain in the same circle of perceptions and advance along the same path of feeling.[2]

Hence, among those who determine their religion in this way, there is a standing quarrel about essentials and non-essentials. They do not know what is to be laid down as characteristic and necessary, and what to separate as free and accidental; they do not find the point from which the whole can be surveyed; they do not understand the religion in which they live and for which they presume to fight; and they contribute to its degeneration, for, while they are influenced by the whole, they consciously grasp only the detail. Fortunately the instinct they do not understand, guides them better than their understandings, and nature sustains what their false reflections and the doing and striving that flow from them would destroy.

If the character of any special religion is found in a definite quantity of perceptions and feelings, some subjective and objective connection, binding exactly these elements together and excluding all others, must be assumed. This false notion agrees well enough with the way of comparing religious conceptions that is common but is not agreeable to the spirit of religion. A whole of this type would not be what we seek to give religion in its whole compass a determinate shape. It would not be a whole, but an arbitrary section of the whole ; it would not be a religion, it would be a sect. Except by taking the religious experiences of one single person, and necessarily of only one short period of his life, as the norm for a society, it could hardly arise. But the forms which history has produced and which are now actually existing are not wholes of this sort. All sectarianism, be it speculative, for bringing single intuitions into a philosophical coherence, or ascetic, for reaching a system and determinate series of feelings, labours for the utmost uniformity among all who would share the same fragment of religion. Those who are infected with this mania certainly do not lack activity, and if they have never succeeded in reducing any one positive religion to a sect,[3] you will have to acknowledge that the positive religions must be formed on another principle and must have another character.

You will see this even more clearly by thinking of the times that gave them birth. You will recall how every positive religion, in its growth and bloom, when its peculiar vigour was most youthful, fresh and evident, did not concentrate and exclude, but expanded and pushed fresh shoots and acquired more religious matter to be wrought up in accordance with its own peculiar nature.

Therefore religions are not fashioned on this false principle. It is not one with their nature, it is a corruption that has crept in from the outside, as hostile to them as to the spirit of religion generally. Their relation to it which is a standing warfare, is another proof that they actually are constituted as individual manifestations of religion should be.

Just as little could the general differences of religion suffice to produce a thoroughly definite individual form. The three ways of being conscious of existence and of its totality, as chaos, system and elemental diversity, so often mentioned, are very far from being so many single and distinct religions. Divide an idea to infinity if you will, you cannot thereby reach an individual. You only get less general ideas which may, as genus and species, embrace a mass of very different individuals. To find the character of individual beings, there must be more than the idea and its attributes. But those three differences in religion are only the usual division according to the current scheme of unity, diversity and totality. They are types of religion but not religious individualities, and the need to seek for this individuality is by no means satisfied by the existence of religion in this threefold way. It is clear as day that there are many distinct manifestations of religion belonging to each type.

Just as little are the personal and the opposing pantheistic modes of conception two such individual forms.[4] They
go through all three types of religion and, for that reason
alone, cannot be individualities. They are simply another
principle of division. Only recently we agreed that this
antithesis rests simply on a way of regarding the religious
feeling, and of ascribing to its phenomena a common object.
Hence the fact that any particular religion inclines more
to one form of representation and expression than to the
other, no more determines its individuality than it would
its worth and the stage of its development. The individual
elements of religion are as indefinite, and none of the various
ways of regarding them are realized, because either the one
or the other thought accompanies them. This may be seen
in all purely deistic manifestations of religion. Though
they desire to be considered quite definite, you will find
everywhere that all religious feelings, and especially what
is most dwelt on—all views of the movements of humanity
in the individual, of the highest unity of mankind, of everything in the mutual relations of men that lies beyond each
man's good pleasure, are utterly indefinite and ambiguous.
The personal and the pantheistic conceptions, therefore,
are only very general forms that may be further determined
and individualized in various ways.

Perhaps you may seek this further determination by
uniting the two modes of conception with the three modes
of intuition. You would reach narrower sub-divisions, but
not a thoroughly definite and individual whole. Neither
naturalism[5]—meaning perception of the world limited to
elemental diversity, without the conception of a personal
consciousness and will in the various elements—nor pantheism, nor polytheism, nor deism are single and definite
religions, such as we seek. They are simply types within
which there have been, and there will still be, very many
genuine individualities developed.[6]

Let me say then at once, that the only remaining way

for a truly individual religion to arise is to select some one
of the great relations of mankind in the world to the Highest
Being, and, in a definite way, make it the centre and refer
to it all the others. In respect of the idea of religion, this
may appear a merely arbitrary proceeding, but, in respect
of the peculiarity of the adherents, being the natural expression of their character, it is the purest necessity.
Hereby a distinctive spirit and a common character enter
the whole at the same time, and the ambiguous and vague
reach firm ground. By every formation of this kind one
of the endless number of different views and different
arrangements of the single elements, which are all possible
and all require to be exhibited, is fully realized. Single
elements are all seen on the one side that is turned towards
this central point, which makes all the feelings have a common tone and a livelier closer interaction.

The whole of religion can only be actually given in the
sum of all the forms possible in this sense. It can, therefore, be exhibted only in an endless series of shapes that are
gradually developed in different points of time and space,
and nothing adds to its complete manifestation that is not
found in one of those forms. Where religion is so moulded
that everything is seen and felt in connection with one
relation to the Deity that mediates it or embraces it, it
matters not in what place or in what man it is formed or
what relation is selected, it is a strictly positive religion.
In respect of the sum of the religious elements—to use a
word that should again be brought to honour—it is a heresy,[7]
for from many equals one is chosen to be head of the rest.
In respect, however, of the fellowship of all participants and
their relation to the founder of their religion who first
raised this central point to clear consciousness, it is a school
and a discipleship.

But if, as is to be hoped, we are agreed that religion
can only be exhibited in and by such definite forms, only
those who with their own religion pitch their camp in some

such positive form, have any fixed abode, and, if I might so say, any well-earned right of citizenship in the religious world. They alone can boast of contributing to the existence and the progress of the whole, and they alone are in the full sense religious persons, on one side belonging by community of type to a kindred, on the other being distinguished by persistent and definite traits from everyone else.

But many perhaps who take an interest in the affairs of religion may ask with consternation, or some evil-disposed person may ask with guile, whether every pious person must connect himself with one of the existing forms of religion. Provisionally, I would say, by no means. It is only necessary that his religion be developed in himself characteristically and definitely. That it should resemble any great, largely accepted, existing form is not equally necessary. I would remind him that I have never spoken of two or three definite forms, and said that they are to be the only ones. Rather, they may evermore develope in countless numbers from all points. Whosoever does not find himself at home in an existing religion, I might almost say whosoever is not in a position to make it if he had not found it,[8] must belong to none but should be held bound to produce a new one for himself. Is he alone in it and without disciples, it does not matter. Everywhere there are germs that cannot arrive at any more extended existence, and the religion of one person may have a definite form and organization, and be quite as genuinely a positive religion as if he had founded the greatest school.

In my opinion, then, you will see that the existing forms should not in themselves hinder any man from developing a religion suitable to his own nature and his own religious sense. The question of abiding in one of them or of constructing a religion of one's own, depends entirely on what relation developes in a man as fundamental feeling and middle-point of all religions.

This is my provisional answer, but if he will hear more I would add that, except by misunderstanding, it would be very difficult to find oneself in such a position. A new revelation is never trivial, and merely personal, but always rests on something great and common. Hence adherents and fellow-believers have never failed the man really called to institute a new religion. Most men, following their nature, will belong to an existing form, and there will be only few whom none suffices.

Yet—and this is my chief point—the authority being the same for all, the many are no less free than the few, and do no less fashion something of their own. If we follow any man's religious history, we find first dim presentiments which never quite stir the depths of the heart, and, being unrecognized, again disappear. Around every man, especially in earlier days, they doubtless hover. Some hint may awaken them, and they may again vanish without reaching any definite form and betraying aught characteristic. Afterwards it first comes to pass that the sense for the Universe rises once for all into clear consciousness. One man discovers it in one relation, another in another. Hereafter all things are referred to this relation, and so group themselves around it. Such a moment, therefore, in the strictest sense, determines every man's religion. Now I hope you will not consider a man's religion less characteristic, less his own, because it lies in a region where already several are collected. In this similarity you are not to find a mechanical influence of custom or birth, but, as you do in other cases, you are to recognize a common determination by higher causes. This agreement is a guarantee of naturalness and truth, and cannot, whether one is first or last, be hurtful to individuality. Though thousands before him and after him referred their religious life to one relation, would it, therefore, be the same in all?

Remember that every definite form of religion is exhaustless for any one man. In its own way it should embrace the whole, a thing too great for any man. And not only so, but in itself there exist endless varieties of cultivation which are, as it were, subordinate types of religion. Is there not here work and scope enough for all? I, at least, am not aware that any religion had succeeded in so taking possession of its territory, and had so determined and exhibited everything therein, according to its own spirit, that, in any one professor of distinguished gifts and individuality of mind, nothing is wanting to perfection. Only to few of our historical religion has it been granted, even in the time of their freedom and higher life, to develope rightly and perfectly the neighbourhood of the middle-point, and, in even a few forms, to give individual impress to the common character. The harvest is great but the labourers are few. An infinite field is opened in each of those religions, wherein thousands may scatter themselves. Uncultivated regions enough present themselves to every one who is capable of making and producing something of his own.[9]

The charge that everyone who allows himself to be embraced in a positive religion, can only be an imitator of those who have given it currency and cannot develope himself individually, is baseless. This judgment no more applies here, than it would to the state or to society. It seems to us morbid or quixotic for any one to maintain that he has no room in any existing institution, and that he must exclude himself from society. We are convinced that every healthy person will, in common with many, have a great national character. Just because he is rooted in it and influenced by it, he can develope his individuality with the greatest precision and beauty. Similarly, in religion only morbid aberration so cuts off a man from a life in fellowship with those among whom nature has placed him, that he belongs to no great whole. Somewhere, on a great scale, everyone will find exhibited or will himself exhibit what for him is the middle-point of religion. To every such common sphere we ascribe a boundless activity that goes into detail, in virtue of which all individual characteristics issue from its bosom. Thus understood, the church is with right called the common mother of us all.

To take the nearest example, think of Christianity as a definite individual form of the highest order. First there is in our time the well known outward division, so definite and pronounced. Under each section there is then a mass of different views and schools. Each exhibits a characteristic development, and has a founder and adherents, yet the last and most personal development of religiousness remains for each individual, and so much is it one with his nature that no one can fully acquire it but himself. And the more a man, by his whole nature, has a claim to belong to you, ye cultured, the more religion must reach this stage in him, for his higher feeling, gradually developing and uniting with other educated capacities, must be a characteristic product.

Or if, after unknown conception and rapid birth-pangs of the spirit, the higher feelings develope, to all appearance suddenly, is not then a characteristic personality born with the religious life? There is a definite connection with a past, a present and a future. The whole subsequent religious life is linked in this way to that moment and that state in which this feeling surprised the soul. It thus maintains its connection with the earlier, poorer life, and has a natural uniform development. Nay more, in this initial consciousness there must already be a distinctive character. Only in a shape and only under circumstances thoroughly definite, could it so suddenly enter a life already developed. This distinctive character, then, every subsequent moment displays and is thus the purest expression of the whole nature. The living spirit of the earth, rending itself from itself as it were, links himself as a finite thing to one definite moment in the series of organic evolutions and a new man arises, a peculiar nature. His separate existence is independent of the mass and objective quality either of his circumstances or his actions. It consists in the peculiar unity of the abiding consciousness that is linked to that first moment, and in the peculiar relation to it which every later moment preserves. Wherefore, in that moment in which in any man a definite consciousness of his relation to the highest Being has, as it were, original birth, an individual religious life originates.

It is individual, not by an irreversible limitation to a particular number and selection of feelings and intuitions, not by the quality of the religious matter. This matter all who have the spiritual birth at the same time and in the same religious surroundings have in common. But it is individual by what he can have in common with no man, by the abiding influence of the peculiar circumstances in which his spirit was first greeted and embraced by the Universe, and by the peculiar way in which he conducts his observation and reflection on the same. This character and tone of the first childhood of his religion are borne by the whole subsequent course of his views and feelings, and are never lost, however far he may advance in fellowship with the Eternal Fountainhead.

Every intelligent finite being announces its spiritual nature and individuality by taking you back to what I may call a previous marriage in him of the Infinite with the finite, and your imagination refuses to explain it from any single prior factor, whether caprice or nature. In the same way you must regard as an individual everyone who can point to the birthday of his spiritual life and relate a wondrous tale of the rise of his religion as an immediate operation of the Deity, an influence of His spirit. He must be characteristic and special, for such an event does not happen to produce in the kingdom of religion vain repetition.[10] Everything that originates organically and is self-contained can only be explained from itself. If its origin and individuality are not regarded as mutually explanatory and identical, it can never be quite understood. Thus you can only understand the religious person in so far as you know how to discover the whole in the notable moment that began his higher life, or from the developed manifestation can trace back this uniform character to the first, dimmest times of life.

All this being well considered, it will not be possible for you, I believe, to be in earnest with this complaint against the positive religions. If you still persist in it, it can only be from prejudice, for you are far too careless about the matter to be justified by your own observation. You have never felt the call to attach yourselves to the few religious men you might be able to discover. Though they are ever attractive and worthy enough of love, you have never tried by the microscope of friendship, or even of closer sympathy, to examine more accurately how they are organized both by and for the Universe.

For myself I have diligently considered them, I have sought out as patiently and studied them with the same reverent care that you devote to the curiosities of nature, and it has often occurred to me whether you would not be led to religion simply by giving heed to the almighty way in which the Deity builds up, from all that has otherwise been developed in man, that part of the soul in which He specially dwells, manifests His immediate operation, and mirrors Himself, and thus makes His sanctuary quite peculiar and distinct, and if you only noticed how He glorifies Himself in it by the exhaustless variety and opulence of forms. I, at least, am ever anew astonished at the many notable developments in a region so sparsely peopled as religion. Men are distinguished by all degrees of receptivity for the charm of the same object and by the greatest difference of effect, by the variety of tone produced by the preponderance of one or other type of feeling, by all sorts of idiosyncrasies of sensitiveness and peculiarity of temperament, and the religious view of things nevertheless is perpetually prominent. Again I see how the religious character of a man is often something quite peculiar in him, strongly marked off to the common eye from everything else shown in his other endowments. The most quiet and sober mind may be capable of the strongest, most passionate emotions; a sense most dull to common and earthly things feels deeply even to sadness, and sees clearly even to rapture and prophecy; a heart most timid in all worldly matters testifies even by martyrdom to the world and to the age. And how wonderfully is this religious character itself fashioned and composed. Culture and crudeness, capacity and limitation, tenderness and hardness are in each, in a peculiar way, mixed and interwoven.

Where have I seen all this? In the peculiar sphere of religion, in its individual forms, in the positive religions which you decry as utterly wanting in variety. I have seen it among the heroes and martyrs of a definite faith in a way for which the friends of natural religion are too cold, among enthusiasts for living feeling, in a way they hold as too dangerous, among the worshippers of some new sprung light and individual revelation. There I will show you them, there at all times and among all peoples. Nowhere else are they to be met. No man as a mere single being can come to actual existence. By the very fact of existence he is set in a world, in a definite order of things, and becomes an object among other objects, and a religious man, by attaining his individual life, enters by this very fact into a common life, which is to say into some definite form of religion. The two things are simply one and the same divine act, and cannot be separated. If the original capacity of a man is too weak to reach this highest stage of consciousness, by fashioning itself in a definite way, the stimulus must also be too weak to initiate the process of a characteristic and robust religious life.

And now I have rendered you my account. It is for you now to tell me how, in respect of development and individuality, it stands with your boasted natural religions. Show me among its professors an equally great variety of strongly marked characters. For myself I must confess that I have never found among them anything of the sort. Your boast of the freedom that this kind of religion gives its adherents to develope themselves religiously according to their own sense, seems merely of freedom to remain undeveloped, freedom neither to be, nor to see, nor to feel anything at all that is definite. Religion plays in their mind far too wretched a role. It is as if religion had no pulse, no vasculary system, no circulation, and so had no heat, no assimilative power. It has no character of its own, no peculiar presentation. Everywhere it shows itself dependent upon the cast of a man's morals and sensibility. In union with them, or rather meekly following them, it moves idly and sparingly, and is only perceptible when it is patiently, and, as it were by drops, separated from them.

Many estimable and strong religious characters, indeed, I have met, whom the adherents of the positive religions, not without wondering at the phenomenon, regard as adherents of natural religion. But on closer view they recognized them as their confrères. Such persons have always swerved somewhat from the original purity of the religion of reason, and have accepted something arbitrary, as it is called, something positive.

But why do those who respect natural religion at once distrust everyone who introduces any characteristic feature into his religion? They also would have uniformity, though at the opposite extreme from sectarianism, the uniformity of indefiniteness. So little is any special personal cultivation through the positive religions to be thought of, that its most genuine adherents do not even wish the religion of man to have any history of its own at all or to commence with any notable event. Too much there has been already for their taste, moderation being for them the chief matter in religion, and all who can boast of religious emotions issuing suddenly from the depths of the heart, come at once into the evil repute of being in-

fected by baleful enthusiasm. By little and little men are
to become religious, just as they become wise and prudent
and everything else they should be. All must come to
them by instruction and education. There must be
nothing that could be regarded as supernatural or even as
singular.

I would not say that in making instruction and education
everything, natural religion has pre-eminently fallen into
the evil of being mixed with metaphysics and morals, nay,
of being changed into them : but this at least is clear, that
its adherents have not started from any living self-contemplation and allowing nothing to mark their cast of thought,
whereby in any characteristic way men might be affected,
they have no sure middle-point. The belief in a personal
God, more or less anthropomorphic, and in a personal immortality, more or less dematerialized and sublimated—the
two dogmas to which they reduce everything—depends, as
they know themselves, on no special way of viewing or
comprehending. Hence, any one who joins them is not
asked how he came to his faith, but how he can demonstrate
it. Thus they assume that he must have reached everything by demonstration. Any other and more definite
middle-point you would have difficulty in indicating. The
little that their meagre and attenuated religion does contain is of great ambiguity. They have a providence in
general, a righteousness in general, a divine education in
general. Now it is in this perspective and fore-shortening,
now in that, so that the value of everything is perpetually
changing. Or if there is any common reference to one
point, it is to something alien to religion, such as how to
remove obstacles from morality, or sustain the desire for
happiness, or something else about which, in ordering the
elements of their religion, truly religious men have never
asked. Their scanty religious possessions are thereby still
more scattered and dispersed.

This natural religion, then, does not unite its religious

elements by one definite view and is no definite religious form, no proper individual representation of religion. Those who profess it have in its territory no definite dwelling, but are strangers whose home, if indeed they have any, must be elsewhere. They remind one of the thin and dispersed mass said to float between the worlds, which is here attracted by one and there by another, but not enough by any to be swept into its rotation. Why it exists the gods may know. It must be to show that the indefinite also can have a certain existence. Yet it is properly only a waiting for existence, to which they can only attain by the power of some force stronger and of a different kind from any they have been subjected to heretofore. More I cannot ascribe to them than the dim presentiments that precede that living consciousness in which religious life comes to visibility for man. There are certain dim impulses and conceptions that have no coherence with a man's individuality and only, as it were, fill up the vacant spaces. They originate only in the collective life, and are uniformly the same in all. The religion of men of this kind is thus the inarticulate echo of the piety around them.

At the highest it is natural religion in the sense in which men used to speak of natural philosophy and natural poetry. The name was applied to such productions as lacked originality, and which, without being clumsy, conscious imitations, were but crude utterances of superficial endowments. The epithet was meant to distinguish them from the works of living, plastic science and art.

The better part found only in the productions of the religious societies, they do not wait for with longing, they do not esteem it more highly because they cannot reach it, but they oppose it with all their might. The essence of natural religion consists almost entirely in denying everything positive and characteristic in religion and in violent polemics. It is the worthy product of an age, the hobby of

which was that wretched generality and vain soberness
which in everything was most hostile to true culture. Two
things are hated supremely, a commencement in anything
extraordinary and incomprehensible, and subsequently any
suggestion of a school. This same corruption you will find
in all arts and sciences. Into religion also it has forced
its way, and its product is this empty formless thing. Men
would be self-produced and self-taught in religion, and they
are rude and uncultured, as is common with such persons.
For characteristic production they have neither power nor
will. Every definite religion they resist because it is a
school, and if they should light on anything whereby a
religion of their own might be fashioned, they would be as
violent against it, seeing that from it also a school might
arise.

Hence their resistance to the positive and arbitrary is
resistance to the definite and real. If a definite religion
may not begin with an original fact, it cannot begin at all.
There must be a common ground for selecting some one
religious element and placing it at the centre, and this
ground can only be a fact. And if a religion is not to be
definite it is not a religion at all, for religion is not a name
to be applied to loose, unconnected impulses. Recall what
the poet says of a state of souls before birth. Suppose
someone were to object to come into the world because he
would not be this man or that, but a man in general ! The
polemic of natural religion against the positive is this
polemic against life and it is the permanent state of its
adherents.

Go back then, if you are in earnest about beholding
religion in its definiteness, from this enlightened natural
religion to those despised positive religions. There everything appears active, strong and secure, every single
intuition has its definite content and its own relation to the
rest, and every feeling has its proper sphere and its peculiar
reference. You find somewhere every modification of

religiousness and every mental state in which religion can place men, with each of its effects somewhere complete. Common institutions and single utterances alike testify that religion is valued almost to forgetfulness of all else. The holy zeal with which it is contemplated, communicated and enjoyed, and the child-like longing with which new revelations of heavenly power are expected,[11] guarantee that no element visible from this standpoint shall be overlooked, and that nothing has disappeared without leaving a monument. Consider the variety of forms in which every single kind of fellowship with the Universe has already appeared. Do not be scared either by mysterious darkness or by wonderful dazzling grotesque traits. Do not admit the delusion that it may all be imagination and romance. Dig ever deeper where your magic rod has once pointed, and without fail you will bring forth the heavenly stream to the light of day.

But regard also the human which is to receive the divine. Do not forget that religion bears traces of the culture of every age and of the history of every race of men. Often it must go about in the form of a servant, displaying in its surroundings and in its adorning the poverty of its home and its disciples. You must not overlook how it has often been stunted in its growth from want of room to exercise its powers, and how from childhood it has pined miserably from bad treatment and ill-chosen nourishment.

And if you would comprehend the whole, do not abide by the various forms of religion that for centuries have shone and have dominated great peoples, and have been glorified in many ways by poets and sages. Recollect that what is historically and religiously most noteworthy is often distributed among but few, and remains hidden to the common eye.[12]

But when, in this way, you have wholly and completely within your vision the right object, it will ever remain a difficult business to discover the spirit of the religions and from

it to interpret them. Once more I warn you not to try to
deduce it as an abstraction from the elements common to
all the adherents. You will wander into a thousand vain
researches, and come in the end not to the spirit of the religion but to a definite quantity of matter. You will remember that no religion has quite reached actuality, and that
you cannot know it until, far removed from seeking it in
a narrow space, you are able to complete and define it in
the way it would develope if its scope had been large enough.
And as this applies to every positive religion, it applies to
every period of it and to every subordinate form of it. You
cannot enough impress it upon yourselves that it all resolves
itself into finding the fundamental relation. Without that,
knowledge of details is unavailing, and you have not found
it till all details are fast bound in one.

Even with this principle of research as a touchstone, you
will be exposed to a thousand errors, for much will meet
you to withdraw your eyes from the true path. Above all,
I beseech you, never forget the difference between the
essence of a religion, in so far as it is a definite form and
representation of religion in general and its unity as a
school.

Religious men are throughout historical. That is not
their smallest praise, but it is also the source of great misunderstandings. The moment when they were first filled
with that consciousness which they have made the centre
of their religion is always sacred for them. Without reference to it, they never speak of what for them is characteristic in religion and of the form to which in themselves it
has attained. You can easily imagine, then, how much more
sacred still the moment must be in which this infinite
intuition was first of all set up in the world as the foundation and centre of one peculiar religion. To it the whole
development of this religion in all generations and individuals is historically linked. Now this sum of the religion,
and the religious culture of a great body of mankind, is

something infinitely greater than a man's own religious life, and the little mirror of this religion which he personally exhibits. This fact then is glorified in all ways ; every ornament of religious art is heaped upon it. It is worshipped as the greatest and most blessed miracle of the Highest. Men never speak of their religion, nor ever exhibit any of its elements except in connection with this fact.

As a consequence nothing is more natural than that this fact should be confused with the fundamental intuition of the religion. This has misled almost everyone and distorted the view of almost all religions. Never forget that the fundamental intuition of a religion must be some intuition of the Infinite in the finite, some one universal religious relation, found in every other religion that would be complete, but in this one only placed in the centre.

I beg you also not to regard everything found in the heroes of religion or in the sacred sources as religion. Do not seek in everything the decisive spirit of that religion. Nor do I exclude trifles merely, or things that on any estimate are foreign to religion, but things often mistaken for it. Recollect how undesignedly those sources were prepared, so that it was impossible to provide for the exclusion of everything not religion. And recall how the authors lived in all sorts of circumstances in the world, and could not say at every word they wrote, this does not belong to the faith. When they speak worldly wisdom and morality, or metaphysics and poetry, therefore, do not at once conclude that it must be forced into religion, or that in it the character of religion is to be sought. Morality, at least, should be everywhere only one, and religion which should not be anywhere one, cannot be distinguished by the differences of morality, which are always something to be got rid of.[13]

Above all I beg you not to be misled by the two hostile principles that everywhere, and almost from the earliest times, have sought to distort and obscure the spirit of religion. Some would circumscribe it to a single dogma, and exclude everything not fashioned in agreement with it, others, from hatred to polemics, or to make religion more agreeable to the irreligious, or from misunderstanding and ignorance of the matter, or from lack of religious sense, decry everything characteristic as dead letter. Guard yourselves from both. With rigid systematizers or shallow indifferentists you will not find the spirit of a religion. It is found only among those who live in it as their element, and ever advance in it without cherishing the folly that they embrace it all.

Whether with these precautions you will succeed in discovering the spirit of the religions I do not know. I fear religion is only comprehensible through itself, and that its special architecture and characteristic difference will not become clear till you yourselves belong to some one religion.

How you may succeed in deciphering the rude and undeveloped religions of remote peoples, or in unravelling the manifold, varied religious phenomena lying wrapped up in the beautiful mythologies of Greece and Rome, I care very little. May your gods guide you! But when you approach the holiest in which the Universe in its highest unity and comprehensiveness is to be perceived, when you would contemplate the different forms of the highest stage of religion which is not foreign or strange, but more or less existent among ourselves, I cannot be indifferent as to whether or not you find the right point of view.

Of one form only I should speak, for Judaism is long since dead. Those who yet wear its livery are only sitting lamenting beside the imperishable mummy, bewailing its departure and its sad legacy. Yet I could still wish to say a word on this type of religion. My reason is not that it was the forerunner of Christianity. I hate that kind of historical reference. Each religion has in itself its own eternal necessity, and its beginning is original. But the beautiful childlike character of Judaism charms me. This is so entirely overlaid, and we have here such a notable example of the corruption and utter extinction of religion in a great body in which it formerly existed, that it will well repay a few words. Remove everything political and moral as well, so God will, whereby this phenomenon is supposed to be characterized. Forget the experiment of joining the state to religion, if I should not say to the church; forget that Judaism was, in a certain sense, an order founded on an ancient family history and sustained by priests. Regard only its strictly religious elements, and then say what is the human consciousness of man's position in the Universe and his relation to the Eternal that everywhere shines through. Is it anything but a relation of universal immediate retribution, of a peculiar reaction of the Infinite against every finite thing that can be regarded as proceeding from caprice? In this way everything is regarded, growth and decay, fortune and misfortune. Even in the human soul freedom and caprice interchange with immediate operation of the Deity. All other recognized attributes of God express themselves in accordance with this principle, and are always regarded in their bearing upon it. The Deity is throughout represented as rewarding, punishing, disciplining single things in single persons. When the disciples asked Christ, " Who has sinned, this man or his parents? " the religious spirit of Judaism appeared in its most pronounced form, and his answer : " Think ye that these have sinned more than others? " was his polemic against it.

The universal interweaving of parallelism, therefore, is not an accident, nor the value set on dialogue. All history, being an abiding interchange between this attraction and this repulsion, is presented as a colloquy in word and deed between God and man, and what unity there is, is only from the uniformity of this dealing, and hence the sacredness of the tradition in which the connection of this great dialogue was contained, the impossibility of attaining religion, except through initiation into this connection, and hence also, in later times, the strife among the sects about the possession of this intercourse.

Just because of this view, it came to pass that the gift of prophecy was developed in Judaism as in no other religion. Even Christians are, in comparison, mere learners. The whole idea of the religion is in the highest degree childlike. It could only work on a narrow scene, without complications, where the whole being simple, the natural consequences of actions would not be disturbed or hindered. The more the adherents of this religion advanced on the scene of the world and had relations with other peoples, the more difficult did the exhibition of this idea become. Imagination had to anticipate the word which the Almighty would speak, and, abolishing intervening time and space, bring the second part of the same transaction immediately before the eyes. That is the essence of prophecy, and the effort after it was necessarily a prominent feature of Judaism, so long as it was possible to hold fast the fundamental idea and original form of the Jewish religion.

The belief in the Messiah was its highest product, its noblest fruit, but also its last effort. A new sovereign must come to restore Zion, wherein the voice of the Lord was dumb, to its original splendour. By the subjection of the peoples to the old law, the simple course of patriarchal times, broken by the unpeaceful association of peoples, the opposition of their forces, and the difference of their customs, should again become general. This faith has long persisted, and, like a solitary fruit, after all life has vanished, hangs and dries on the withered stem till the rudest season of the year.

The limited point of view allowed this religion, as a religion, but a short duration. It died, and as its sacred books were closed, the intercourse of Jehovah with His people was looked upon as ended. The political association linked with it dragged on still longer a feeble existence. Till very much later its external part endured, and was that unpleasant phenomenon, a mechanical motion from which life and spirit have long vanished.

The original intuition of Christianity is more glorious, more sublime, more worthy of adult humanity, penetrates deeper into the spirit of systematic religion and extends itself further over the whole Universe. It is just the intuition of the Universal resistance of finite things to the unity of the Whole, and of the way the Deity treats this resistance. Christianity sees how He reconciles the hostility to Himself, and sets bounds to the ever-increasing alienation by scattering points here and there over the whole that are at once finite and infinite, human and divine. Corruption and redemption, hostility and mediation, are the two indivisibly united, fundamental elements of this type of feeling, and by them the whole form of Christianity and the cast of all the religious matter contained in it are determined. With ever-increasing speed the spiritual world has departed from its perfection and imperishable beauty. All evil, even this that the finite must decay before it has completed the circuit of its existence, is a consequence of the will, of the self-seeking endeavour of the isolated nature that, everywhere rending itself from its connection with the Whole, seeks to be something by itself. Death itself has come on account of sin. The spiritual world, going from bad to worse, is incapable of any production in which the Divine Spirit actually lives. The understanding being darkened has swerved from the truth; the heart is corrupt and has no praise before God; the image of the Infinite in every part of finite nature has gone extinct.

In accordance with this state of the spiritual world, all dealings of Divine Providence are calculated. They are never directed to the immediate results for feeling; they do not consider the happiness or suffering which they produce ; they are not even for hindering or forwarding certain actions. They are simply calculated to check corruption in the great masses, to destroy, without mercy, what can no more be restored, and with new powers to give birth to new creations. Wherefore He does signs and wonders that interrupt and shake the course of things, and sends ambassadors, with more or less of divine spirit indwelling, to pour out divine powers upon men.

And when man does seek through self-consciousness to enter into fellowship with the unity of the Whole, the finite resists him, and he seeks and does not find and loses what he has found. He is defective, variable and attached to details and non-essentials. He wills rather than gives heed, and his aim vanishes from his eyes. In vain is every revelation. Everything is swallowed up by the earthly sense, everything is swept away by the innate irreligious principle. The Deity finds ever new devices. By His power alone, ever more glorious revelations issue from the bosom of the old. He sets up ever more exalted mediators between Himself and men. In every later ambassador the Deity unites with humanity ever more closely, that men may learn to know the Eternal Being. Yet the ancient complaint that man cannot comprehend what is from the Spirit of God is never taken away.

This is how Christianity most and best is conscious of God, and of the divine order in religion and history. It manipulates religion itself as matter for religion. It is thus a higher power of religion, and this most distinguishes its character and determines its whole form. Because it presupposes a widely-extended godlessness it is through and through polemical. It is polemical in its outward communication, for, to make its deepest nature evident, every corruption must be laid bare, be it in morals or in thinking. Above all it must expose the hostility to the consciousness of the Highest Being, which is the irreligious principle itself. Relentlessly it unmasks every false morality, every bad religion, every unhappy union of both for mutual covering of nakedness. Into the inmost secrets of the corrupt heart it presses and illumines, with the sacred torch of personal experience, every evil that creeps in darkness. Almost its first work on appearing was to destroy the last expectation of its pious contemporaries, saying it was irreligious and godless to expect any other restoration than restoration to purer faiths, to the higher view of things and to eternal life in God. Boldly it led the heathen beyond the separation they had made between the world of the gods and the world of men. Not to live and move and have the being in God is to be entirely ignorant of Him. If this natural feeling, this inner consciousness is lost amid a mass of sense impressions and desires, no religion has yet entered the narrow sense. Everywhere, then, its heralds tore open the whited sepulchres and brought the dead bones to light. Had these first heroes of Christianity been philosophers, they would have spoken as strongly against the corruption of philosophy. They never failed to recognize the outlines of the divine image. Behind all distortions and degradations they saw hidden the heavenly germ of religion. But as Christians they were chiefly concerned with the individual who was far from God and needed a mediator.

Christianity, moreover, is as sharply and strongly polemical within its own borders, and in the inmost fellowship of the saints. Just because religion is nowhere so fully idealized as in Christianity, through its original postulate, perpetual warfare against all that is actual in religion is presented as a duty that can never be sufficiently fulfilled. And just because the ungodly is everywhere operative, because all actuality together appears unholy, an infinite holiness is the aim of Christianity. Never content with its attainments, it seeks, even in its purest productions, even in its holiest feelings, traces of irreligion and of the tendency of all finite things to turn away from the unity of the

Whole. In the tone of the highest inspiration an ancient writer criticizes the religious state of the community; in simple openness the great apostles speak of themselves. And this is how every man is to walk in the sacred circle. He is not only to be an inspired man and a teacher, but in humility he is to present himself also to the universal testing. Nor shall anything be spared, not even what is most loved and dear; nor shall anything be indolently put aside, not even what is most generally acknowledged. Though without it be praised as holy and be set up before the world as the essence of religion, within it must be subjected to a severe and repeated test. Thus impurities are to be removed, and the splendour of the heavenly colours to shine more clearly in every pious impulse of the spirit.

In nature you often see a compound mass, as soon as its chemical powers have overcome outside resistance or reduced it to equilibrium, take to fermenting, and eject one and another element. So it is with Christianity, it turns at last its polemical power against itself. Ever anxious, lest in its struggle with external irreligion it has admitted something alien, or may yet have in itself some principle of corruption, it does not avoid even the fiercest inward commotions to eject the evil.

This is the history of Christianity that is rooted in its very nature. "I am not come to bring peace, but a sword," the Founder Himself said. His gentle soul could not possibly have meant that He was come to occasion those bloody commotions, so utterly contrary to the spirit of religion, or that wretched strife of words that deals with dead matter which living religion does not admit. But what He did foresee, and in foreseeing command, were those holy wars that spring necessarily from the essence of His teaching, and which, as bitterly as He describes, rend hearts asunder and dissolve the most intimate relations of life.

But not only are the elements of Christianity themselves subjected to this perpetual sifting; in their unbroken existence and life in the spirit there is an insatiable longing for ever stricter purification, ever richer fulness. Irreligion is thought to dominate every moment in which the religious principle is not evident in the mind. Religion has no other opposite than just the absence of religious purpose : every interruption of religion is irreligion. If the mind is for a moment without intuition and feeling of the Infinite, it at once becomes conscious of hostility and remoteness. Christianity then demands as first and essential that piety be a constant state. It scorns to be satisfied, even with the strongest displays of it, as soon as it only rules certain portions of the life. Piety should never rest, and there should never be anything so absolutely opposed as to be inconsistent with it. From all finite things we should see the Infinite. We should be in a position to associate religious feelings and views with all sentiments, however they may have arisen, and with all actions, whatever be their object. That is the true highest aim of mastery in Christianity.

How the fundamental view in Christianity, the view to which all others are referred, determines the character of its feelings is easy to discover. What do you call that feeling of an unsatisfied longing which is directed towards a great object, and which you are conscious is infinite? What impresses you on finding the sacred and the profane, the noble with the common and the mean intimately united? And what is the mood that urges you at times to assume the universality of this combination, and to search for it everywhere? With Christians this holy sadness is not occasional, but is the dominant tone of all their religious feelings. That is the only name which the language affords me. It accompanies every joy and every pain, every love and every fear. Nay, in its pride and in its humility it is the ground tone. If you can reconstruct the depths of a spirit from single features, undisturbed by foreign elements that have come from who knows where, you will find this feeling throughout dominant in the

Founder of Christianity. If a writer, who has left but a few leaves in a simple speech is not too unimportant for your attention, you will discover this tone in every word remaining to us from his bosom friend.[14] And if ever a Christian has allowed you to listen in the sanctuary of his soul, you have certainly caught just the same tone.

Such is Christianity. Its distortions and manifold corruptions I will not spare, for the corruptibility of every holy thing, as soon as it becomes human, is part of its fundamental view of the world. And I will not go farther into the details of it. Its doings are before you, and I believe I have given you the thread that, guiding you through all anomalies, will make the closest scrutiny possible. From first to last look only at the clearness, the variety, and the richness with which that first idea has been developed.

When, in the mutilated delineations of His life I contemplate the sacred image of Him who has been the author of the noblest that there has yet been in religion, it is not the purity of His moral teaching, which but expressed what all men who have come to consciousness of their spiritual nature, have with Him in common, and which, neither from its expression nor its beginning, can have greater value, that I admire; and it is not the individuality of His character, the close union of high power with touching gentleness, for every noble, simple spirit must in a special situation display some traces of a great character. All those things are merely human. But the truly divine element is the glorious clearness to which the great idea He came to exhibit attained in His soul. This idea was, that all that is finite requires a higher mediation to be in accord with the Deity, and that for man under the power of the finite and particular, and too ready to imagine the divine itself in this form, salvation is only to be found in redemption. Vain folly it is to wish to remove the veil that hides the rise of this idea in Him, for every beginning in religion, as elsewhere, is mysterious. The prying sacrilege that has attempted it can only distort the divine. He is supposed to have taken His departure from the ancient idea of His people, and He only wished to utter its abolition which, by declaring Himself to be the Person they expected, He did most gloriously accomplish. Let us consider the living sympathy for the spiritual world that filled His soul, simply as we find it complete in Him.

If all finite things require the mediation of a higher being, if it is not to be ever further removed from the Eternal and be dispersed into the void and transitory, if its union with the Whole is to be sustained and come to consciousness, what mediates must not again require mediation, and cannot be purely finite. It must belong to both sides, participating in the Divine Essence in the same way and in the same sense in which it participates in human nature. But what did He see around Him that was not finite and in need of mediation, and where was aught that could mediate but Himself? " No man knoweth the Father but the Son, and He to whom the Son shall reveal Him." This consciousness of the singularity of His knowledge of God and of His existence in God, of the original way in which this knowledge was in Him, and of the power thereof to communicate itself and awake religion, was at once the consciousness of His office as mediator and of His divinity.

I would not speak of Him as standing opposed to the rude power of His foes without hope of longer life, for that is unspeakably unimportant. But when, forsaken in the thought of being silenced for ever, without seeing any outward institution for fellowship among His own actually set up, when in the face of the solemn splendour of the old corrupt system that had so mightily resisted Him, when surrounded by all that could inspire awe and demand subjection, by all that, from childhood, He had been taught to honour, sustained by nothing but that feeling, He uttered without delay that Yea, the greatest word mortal ever spake, it was the most glorious apotheosis, and no divinity can be more certain than that which He Himself thus proclaimed.[15]

With this faith in Himself, who can wonder at His assurance that He was not only a mediator for many, but would leave behind a great school that would derive their religion from His? So certain was He that before it yet existed He appointed symbols for it. This He did in the conviction that they would suffice to bring the band of His disciples to a secure existence. Nay, so sure was He that already He had spoken among His own, with prophetic enthusiasm, of the immortalization of His memory.

Yet He never maintained He was the only mediator, the only one in whom His idea actualized itself. All who attach themselves to Him and form His Church should also be mediators with Him and through Him. And He never made His school equivalent to His religion, as if His idea were to be accepted on account of His person, and not His person on account of His idea. Nay, He would even suffer His mediatorship to be undecided, if only the spirit, the principle from which His religion developed in Himself and others were not blasphemed.

His disciples also were far from confusing this school with His religion. Pupils of the Baptist, still only very imperfectly initiated into the nature of Christianity, were, without anything further, regarded and treated by the apostles as Christians and reckoned genuine members of the community. And it should be so still. Everyone who, in his religion, sets out from the same cardinal point, whether his religion originates from himself or from another, is, without respect of school, a Christian. It will naturally follow that when Christ with His whole efficacy is shown him he must acknowledge Him, who has become historically the centre of all mediation, the true Founder of redemption and reconciliation.[16]

Nor did Christ say that the religious views and feelings He Himself could communicate, were the whole extent of the religion that should proceed from this ground-feeling. He always pointed to the living truth which, though only "taking of His," would come after Him. Similarly with His disciples. They never set limits to the Holy Spirit. His unbounded freedom and the absolute unity of His revelations are everywhere acknowledged by them.

And when, the first bloom of Christianity being past and it was appearing to rest from its works, those works, so far as they were contained in the sacred scriptures, were regarded as a finished codex of religion, it was only brought about by those who took the slumber of the Spirit for death —religion, as far as they were concerned, being dead. All who still feel the life of religion in themselves or perceive it in others, have ever protested against this unchristian proceeding. The sacred scriptures have, by their native power, become a bible, and forbid no other book to be or to become a bible. Anything written with like power they would willingly allow to be associated with themselves. Nay, should not every later utterance of the whole church, and therefore of the Divine Spirit, append itself confidently, even though there be ineffaceably in the first fruits of the Spirit a special holiness and worth ? [17]

In accordance with this unlimited freedom, this essential infinity, then, this leading idea of Christianity of divine mediating powers has in many ways been developed, and all intuitions and feelings of the indwelling of the Divine Being in finite nature have within Christianity been brought to perfection. Thus very soon Holy Scripture in which, in its own way, divine essence and heavenly power dwelt, was held as a logical mediator to open for the knowledge of God the finite and corrupt nature of the understanding, while the Holy Spirit, in a later acceptation of the word, was an ethical mediator, whereby to draw near to the Deity in action. Nay, a numerous party of Christians declare themselves ready to acknowledge everyone as a mediating and divine being who can prove, by a divine life

or any impress of divineness, that he has been, for even a
small circle, the first quickening of the higher sense. To
others Christ has remained one and all, while others have
declared that their mediators have been their own selves
or some particular thing. Whatever failure there may
have been in form and matter, the principle is genuinely
Christian, so long as it is free. Other human situations
have, in their relation to the central point of Christianity,
been expressed by feelings and represented by images, of
which there is no hint in the speeches of Christ or elsewhere
in the sacred books. Hereafter there will be more, for
the whole being of man is not yet by any means embodied
in the peculiar form of Christianity, but, despite of what
is said of its speedy, its already accomplished overthrow,
Christianity will yet have a long history.

For why should it be overthrown? The living spirit of
it, indeed, slumbers oft and long. It withdraws itself into
a torpid state, into the dead shell of the letter, but it ever
awakes again as soon as the season in the spiritual world
is favourable for its revival and sets its sap in motion.
Thus in oft repeated cycle it renews itself in various ways.
The fundamental idea of every positive religion, being a component part of the infinite Whole in which all things must
be eternal, is in itself eternal and universal, but its whole
development, its temporal existence may not, in the same
sense, be either universal or eternal.   For to put the centre
of religion just in that idea, it requires not only a certain
mental attitude, but a certain state of mankind.   Is this
state, in the free play of the universal life, gone, never to
return, that relation which, by its worth, made all others
dependent on it, can no longer maintain itself in the feeling,
and this type of religion can no more endure.   This is the
case with all childlike religions, as soon as men lose the
consciousness of their essential power.   They should be
collected as monuments of the past and deposited in the
magazine of history, for their life is gone, never to return.

Christianity, exalted above them all, more historical and more humble in its glory, has expressly acknowledged this transitoriness of its temporal existence. A time will come, it says, when there shall no more be any mediator, but the Father shall be all in all. But when shall this time come? I, at least, can only believe that it lies beyond all time.

One half of the original intuition of Christianity is the corruptibleness of all that is great and divine in human things. If a time should come when this—I will not say can no more be discovered, but no more obtrudes, when humanity advances so uniformly and peacefully, that only the navigator who calculates its course by the stars knows when it is somewhat driven back on the great ocean it traverses by a passing contrary wind, and the unarmed eye, looking only at what is taking place, can no more directly observe the retrogression of human affairs, I would gladly stand on the ruins of the religion I honour.

The other half of the original Christian faith is that certain brilliant and divine points are the source of every improvement in this corruption and of every new and closer union of the finite with the Deity. Should a time ever come, when the power that draws us to the Highest was so equally distributed among the great body of mankind, that persons more strongly moved should cease to mediate for others, I would fain see it, I would willingly help to level all that exalteth itself. But this equality of all equalities is least possible. Times of corruption await all human things, even though of divine origin. New ambassadors from God will be required with exalted power to draw the recreant to itself and purify the corrupt with heavenly fire, and every such epoch of humanity is a palingenesis of Christianity, and awakes its spirit in a new and more beautiful form.

And if there are always to be Christians, is Christianity, therefore, to be universal and, as the sole type of religion, to rule alone in humanity? It scorns this autocracy.

Every one of its elements it honours enough to be willing to see it the centre of a whole of its own. Not only would it produce in itself variety to infinity, but would willingly see even outside all that it cannot produce from itself. Never forgetting that it has the best proof of its immortality in its own corruptibleness, in its own often sad history, and ever expecting a redemption from the imperfection that now oppresses it, it willingly sees other and younger, and, if possible, stronger and more beautiful types of religion arise outside of this corruption. It could see them arise close beside it, and issue from all points even from such as appear to it the utmost and most doubtful limits of religion. The religion of religions cannot collect material enough for its pure interest in all things human. As nothing is more irreligious than to demand general uniformity in mankind, so nothing is more unchristian than to seek uniformity in religion.

In all ways the Deity is to be contemplated and worshipped. Varied types of religion are possible, both in proximity and in combination, and if it is necessary that every type be actualized at one time or another, it is to be desired that, at all times, there should be a dim sense of many religions. The great moments must be few in which all things agree to ensure to one among them a wide-extended and enduring life, in which the same view is developed unanimously and irresistibly in a great body, and many persons are deeply affected by the same impression of the divine. Yet what may not be looked for from a time that is so manifestly the border land between two different orders of things ? If only the intense crisis were past, such a moment might arrive. Even now a prophetic soul, such as the fiery spirits of our time have,[18] turning its thoughts to creative genius, might perhaps indicate the point that is to be for the future generations the centre for their fellowship with the Deity. But however it be, and however long such a moment may still linger, new developments of religion, whether under Christianity or alongside of it, must come and that soon, even though for a long time they are only discernible in isolated and fleeting manifestations. Out of nothing a new creation always comes forth, and in all living men in whom the intellectual life has power and fulness, religion is almost nothing. From some one of the countless occasions it will be developed in many and take new shape in new ground. Were but the time of caution and timidity past! Religion hates loneliness, and in youth especially, which for all things is the time of love, it wastes away in a consuming longing. When it is developed in you, when you are conscious of the first traces of its life, enter at once into the one indivisible fellowship of the saints, which embraces all religions and in which alone any can prosper. Do you think that because the saints are scattered and far apart, you must speak to unsanctified ears? You ask what language is secret enough—is it speech, writing, deed, or quiet copying of the Spirit? All ways, I answer, and you see that I have not shunned the loudest. In them all sacred things remain secret and hidden from the profane. They may gnaw at the shell as they are able, but to worship the God that is in you, do you not refuse us.

EXPLANATIONS OF THE FIFTH SPEECH

(1) Page 213.—As the question of the multiplicity of religion and unity of the church, treated in earlier passages, is here expressed in short compass, I would take the occasion to add something to the explanations of this seemingly paradoxical statement. First, in every type of faith it is the narrower brethren who would make the society so exclusive, that on the one hand they would absolutely take no part in the religious exercises of other types of faith, and would remain in entire ignorance of their nature and spirit ; and on the other, for the slightest deviation, they are ready to found a distinct society. The more liberal and noble again seek to have an affectionate appreciation of the mind of strange fellow believers, not only as spectators, but as far as may be by active participation in the divine services that have as their chief purpose the exhibition of this mind. Had this not taken place among the members of the two Evangelical churches, there could not be, even where they most mingle, any thought now, more than three hundred years ago, of union. A Catholic could more easily be edified by the whole Evangelical service, in which he would only miss much that in another way is made up to him, than a Protestant with the Catholic service which, as it exhibits in the most positive way the difference between the two types of faith, cannot be the expression of his own. Even for a Protestant, however, there is a way of taking part in much, by recasting, adjusting, translating in one's own heart, that is not indifferentism. Only the Protestant who has done this can boast of understanding the Catholic type, and of having guarded his own faith when put to the touch-stone of contrast. This leads us to the second point. The endeavour to found an all-embracing society is the true and blameless principle of tolerance. Though the possibility of such a society may be remote if you take it quite away, nothing would remain but to regard the different types of religion as an unavoidable evil. It is just like the mutual toleration between differently constituted states. It continues

because intercourse is still possible. When this ceases intolerance enters, and a supposed right is assumed to interfere in the affairs of other people. This can only be done by an act, by a government, taking outward destructive action, and never by reasoning or even by plausibility. Only the narrow-minded, however, assume such a right. The more liberal seek everywhere to open up intercourse, and to make manifest thereby the unity of the human race. Their love to the constitution of their Fatherland does not in the least suffer, and in religion also true tolerance is far removed from all indifferentism.

(2) Page 220.—This expression savours strongly of the time when this book was written. There was then no great common interest: every man estimated his own condition according to his individual circumstances, without the smallest trace of public spirit; and the French Revolution itself, though already it had largely developed as a historical event, was regarded by us in a way thoroughly selfish and in the highest degree different and vacillating. Only at a later time, in the days of calamity which were the days of glory, did we again learn the power of common sentiments, and then the consciousness and the consolation of common piety returned. At present the patriotic and the religious sentiment may easily be measured by each other. Where empty words, instead of the deed looked for, are given in the concerns of the Fatherland, piety is also empty, however zealous its pretence; and where the interest in the improvement of our condition breaks up into morbid factions, piety again degenerates into sectarianism. It appears then that a quickening of natural, healthy public spirit contributes more to clearness in religion than all critical analysis. As is indicated by what follows in the Speech, analysis, wanting this impulse, is too apt to become sceptical. When the great social interests are weakened, piety is lamed and perplexed. Hence the religious societies that have a tendency to obscurity, do well to keep clear of all contact with other forms of religion.

(3) Page 221.—I have made slight changes here, rejecting a capricious play on words that I might be more historical. The manifold divisions of one and the same type of faith are manifestly not all of equal worth. Such as recast the whole in a characteristic way have a natural worth, and have a good right to exist. All splits, however, about single points of small importance, as most of the separations from the great body of the church in the first centuries, owe their existence simply to the obstinacy of the minority. While they deviate in one point they may not, however, unless kept in breath by persistent polemies, neglect the rest. Those only are most called

sects, and deserve only a name that indicates willing exclusion who absorb themselves in a few devious views and allow all the rest to grow strange. Such sects always rest on one narrow but forcible personality.

(4) Page 222.—On the position assigned to this difference I hope I have already sufficiently declared myself. This representation, however, of the antithesis between the personal and the pantheistic, as going through all three stages, gives me an opportunity to explain the matter from another side. In the polytheistic stage this antithesis is undeniable, only it is less clear as in everything imperfect antitheses are less pronounced. Even when all that is known of their history is put together, most of the gods of Hellenic mythology have little unity. For explanation it is necessary to go back to the rise of their service to their different countries and the character of the myths there prevalent. The personality being slight, the forms readily become symbolical. Many of foreign origin have received native names and are quite symbolical, such as the Ephesian Diana, which is a pure representation of the universal life, *natura naturans,* the direct opposite of the idea of personality. In the Egyptian and Indian systems the basis is either symbolic or hieroglyphic, and there is no personality underneath. Such a purely symbolical representation of first causes has properly no conscious gods, but is really pantheistic. The dramatic or epic representation of the relation of the symbolic or hieroglyphic being, however, produces an appearance of personality. The two forms of polytheism, the personal and pantheistic, thus appear to mingle, but in principle they are easy to distinguish. Analogy would show that the same antithesis exists in the chaotic stage or fetichism. Here, however, it is more difficult to recognize and exhibit, there being but larvæ of the gods which only by a later development become psychic.

(5) Page 222.—I include in naturalism all the forms of religion usually known as worship of nature. They are all, in the sense given above, impersonally polytheistic. The worship of the stars is not an exception. Even the worship of the sun is only apparently monotheistic, for a wider knowledge of the system of the world must at once reduce it to worship of the stars, and, therefore, to polytheism. This departure from common usage has the disadvantage that the words naturalist and naturalism are employed among us for something quite different. I can only defend myself by hoping that every reader who does not think of the ancient usage, but of the present connection, will easily understand the expression employed and find it appropriate. Still I would have refrained, if the manner

in which naturalism and rationalism were used almost synonymously as the opposite of supernaturalism had not even then so much displeased me. Even at that time I had the opinion, to which I have since given expression on different occasions, that it caused confusion. There is some sense, and more perhaps than is usually thought, in opposing reason to revelation, but there is no ground for a contrast between nature and revelation. For this antithesis the biblical foundation, to which a Christian will always return, entirely fails, and the more a matter is discussed from such a standpoint the more perplexed it will become.

(6) Page 222.—The expectation that some polytheistic religions would yet develope was not expressed at random. It rested on the view also hinted at in the Introduction to my " Glaubenslehre," that many polytheistic systems have manifestly arisen from smelting together small idolatrous clan religions, and that they are of higher value than their elements. As long as races exist that have only a fetich worship such an occurrence is possible, and at a time when Christian missions had almost gone to sleep, I regarded this as the natural road to improvement for the most rude societies. This probability has since greatly diminished, and it has grown more likely that they also can be taken hold of directly by Christianity.

(7) Page 223.—At one time the expression heretic was honourable Among the Greeks the schools of the philosophers and physicians, the home of all the science and art of the time, were so called. And to come nearer to our subject the different dogmatic schools of the Jews also bore among the Hellenists the same name. In ecclesiastical language the established faith of the church is no longer the orthodox or catholic heresy. Yet the exclusive use of the word for what is to be rejected does not rest on etymology. Probably it has arisen because with a different reference it is used in this bad sense in scripture. Here I use it of the positive religions in the sense in which it was used of the Hellenic schools, which together contained the whole national philosophy. It must be a bad philosophical system indeed that has not caught some truly philosophic element, and in some way sought to refer to it all other elements. The same holds of the positive religions, and we may conclude that if they were all developed there would be contained in the sum of them the whole religion of the human race.

(8) Page 224.—This *make* is, of course, to be understood with a certain limitation. In writing it I lived in the good confidence that every one would complete it for himself. For example, it could not be my meaning that he alone is a true Christian who could himself have

been Christ had not Christ already been before him. But this must be admitted, that any man is a Christian only in so far as in pre-christian times he would among the Jews have held and transmitted the messianic idea, and among the heathen been convinced of the insufficiency of sensuous idolatry, only in so far as, by the feeling of his need for redemption, Christianity had attracted him and drawn him to itself. What follows shows clearly enough how little I was serious with the statement that some or perhaps many could have the germs of quite new types of religion outside of the historical forms, and that it should be their duty to bring them to the light.

(9) Page 226.—Though I hope this passage, in its connection, could not easily be misunderstood, I would not leave it without a slight correction of both sense and expression. The expression has a certain appearance of giving countenance to the idea that it is possible, in the sphere of religion to proceed to discovery or by set purpose to produce something. Everything that is new, in particular if it is to be true and unadulterated, must issue spontaneously, as by inspiration, from the heart. This appearance, however, will not deceive those who hold fast the expression and the connection of the whole. In the second place, the sense appears to be presented too broadly and with too little regard to the great difference in various forms of religion. Every religion of the highest stage, and especially one that has constructed for itself a complete theology, must be in a position to review its whole domain. It is the business of systematic theology to draw such a map of it, that not only everything that has come to actuality in that form of religion finds its place, but that every possible place be indicated. And when such a map is looked at, we will not easily find any place empty, only some parts better filled, some less. None but subordinate forms of religion and smaller sects fail to aim at completeness. I have already shown why these sects have a natural inclination not to deal with the whole mass of religious matter, and in the smaller religious forms individuals may differ too little to be able fully to complete one another.

(10) Page 228.—This book bears throughout the marks of opposition, and those who can call up that time will easily see that I am here chiefly defending the cause of those who refer the beginning of their religious life to one definite moment. Yet this is by no means a mere attempt to reduce the opponents of this view to silence, in the good assurance that they could not defend themselves. Singularly I have had to defend this position against an able man, now long departed, who was a distinguished teacher in a religious society I

greatly value, and whose whole practice really rested on this assumption of definite moments of grace. He asked me if I actually believed in such moments and considered them necessary, so that a gradual imperceptible growth of religious life would not suffice me. He raised an objection from an experience that must have struck all attentive readers of the lives of men who have been awakened. They have moments when they receive the assurance of divine grace, when they are born to a personal, individual religious life. But, sooner or later, to most of them times of relaxation come, when this certainty is again lost. Moments of confirmation must follow, and it may be easily doubted whether the first or the second experience is the true commencement. From this doubt it follows that the truth is only in the gradual progress which the first moment prepared for, and the second and third confirmed. I reminded him of what I would here again recall, that I did not consider this the only form, but acknowledged also the imperceptible rise and growth. The inner truth, however, I held to be the union of both, one being more prominent in one case and the other in another. It was, however, one thing to postulate such moments and another to require that everyone should be able to specify it and have consciousness of the time. This idea I have further developed in a sermon. Thus we came to agree. To the way, however, in which the matter is here presented as an extraordinary moment with each life produced from it necessarily quite individual, two objections may be raised. First, even in the early times of the church, by the preaching of the apostles, there were Christian awakenings in large numbers together, and even yet, at times, not only among members of other faiths, but particularly among Christians whose piety has succumbed to worldly cares and occupation, such awakenings are, as it were, epidemic, and cannot, therefore, be regarded as extraordinary. Wherefore, secondly, it is probable that all it produces is not extraordinary and individual, more especially as these awakenings often appear as reactions against uniform, extensive indifference and licentiousness. This conclusion is supported by experience. At different times we find, just among those who hold by such authentic decisive moments, only one wearisomely uniform type of piety and the same, somewhat confused phraseology about the state of the soul that is conjoined with it. But this is connected with the uncertainty of those moments, and it is not in this sense that I contrast a life suddenly awaked with a life gradually developed. In a gradual development, the common elements dominate. By their power the individual elements are moulded and subordinated. Characteristic features are rarer and less pronounced. But the religiousness that rests apparently on a moment of awakening has the same character. Even those who effect the conversions have usually only one traditional type, which, from its very limitation to a few strong formulas, is fitted to arouse the indifferent, whether they are callous or have suffered defeat. Just because their view requires such a moment, their persistent demand actually prepares for it. By the repetition of such moments, though only in a quite general and originally passing manner, consciousness of personal worthlessness and of divine grace increase together, and a religious life is gradually established. This is the undeniable blessing that rests on this method. Yet the life adheres rigidly to that type, and is consequently careful and troubled and but sparingly equipped. If persons having such a history remain modestly in their own circle, they are for us worthy comrades. When they are highly cultured in an earthly sense and find themselves happy in this stage of religion, it is a phenomenon both elevating and humbling. But it is to none of those persons I refer here, for they have not developed an individual life. The moments I refer to are of quite a different stamp. They come to pass only where a religious tendency exists though chaotic and indefinite. They are not the result of external influences, rather they are prepared for by the ever renewed feeling that everything offered from without is precarious and inadequate. By quiet thought and aspiration the positive is fashioned from that negative, the inmost self is taken hold of by the divine, and then, comprehending itself, it more or less suddenly comes forth. These are rare occurrences, but even the most careless observer cannot deceive himself into believing that he can exhaustively describe them by one general name.

(11) Page 235.—Of course it is not new revelations outside the circuit of any given religion that are here meant. A longing for such revelations could not exist in any positive religion, for even its longing must naturally bear its own characteristic form. Even the messianic hopes of the Jews were not a longing for something beyond Judaism, though they were afterwards fulfilled by the appearing of Christ. In the measure of its vitality every religion has a desire to find in itself something divine yet unknown. Hence the historical consistency of any faith that is to have an extended influence for a long time is determined by its possession of some principle to which everything new may be referred. Where this fails unity tends to dissolution. Even if despite this principle there should still be divisions the largest sections will abide by it. In this sense we can say the strife between the Greek and Roman Churches is between

the original and the translation, and that the strife between them both and the Evangelical Church is between scripture and tradition.

(12) Page 235.—On similar grounds this passage requires a slight explanation. It might appear as if the great historical religions were put in the shade and the noteworthy sought only in smaller modifications. In the political sphere, indeed, we are somewhat accustomed to such a procedure. Many constitutions of great peoples appear to us clumsy or insignificant, while the form of government of single towns with small dominion are admired and studied by historians as masterpieces of political art. But it is otherwise in the religious sphere. A strong religious life, even if hedged in by narrow forms, sooner or later breaks through the limits of nationality. This even Judaism did, and nothing in this sphere with character and strength can remain small for ever. But I am speaking here especially of what takes place within the great forms of religion, particularly Christianity. Here it is quite otherwise. What most easily finds an entrance with the multitude becomes great and extended, which is usually that mean between extremes which is only to be reached by active attention on every side. Now this involves to some extent a direction of the attention without, that does not encourage an inward and characteristic development. This is the dominant character of what in the ancient sense of the word we call catholic. As this is chiefly thought of when the character and development of Christianity are under discussion, it seemed to me right to direct the attention of earnest inquirers away from what impresses by its size to what was smaller. But it was less to heretical parties that are marked by special partialities than to individuals in the greater church who cannot manage to adhere to mediocrity, or if you will to circumspection, whereby alone the individual retains a distinguished place among the catholic, but who prefer their inward freedom, and are not vexed by obscurity.

(13) Page 237.—It has never seriously been my opinion that the doctrine of ethics should everywhere be one and the same. It will suffice, if I here adduce what is universally accepted. It appears to me that morality never can be everywhere the same, as all times witness that it never has been. Its form is essentially speculative, and never can be the same till speculation in general is everywhere the same. Of this, despite the great fruitfulness of the last centuries in philosophy of universal validity, there is not yet any appearance. Nor can its content be the same, even if everyone who dealt with ethics set out from pure humanity, for he only sees it through the

medium of his age and his personality. Wherefore, any doctrine of morals of universal application can contain only the most general truths in formulas of varying worth. Hence the universal application is always rather apparent than real. Still the position here maintained is so far right, in that ethics applies another standard to these differences than religion. It begins by subordinating the individual and therefore the characteristic to the general. Only by this subordination does the characteristic gain a right to make itself valid. Suppose it possible to have as correct or even exactly the same system built on the opposite mode of procedure, it would never reach the universal feeling and anywhere give it effect. In religion on the contrary, everything issues from the individual life, and the more individual the more effective, and all common elements arise simply from observing affinity and connection. Hence many who are not yet conscious of their difference can adhere to one kind of religion. Many, even when they are conscious of their difference, if only their apprehension of human relations is the same, may, it is true, accept one doctrine of morals, yet there may be found among the adherents of one religion such marked difference that it is impossible for them to have even a common moral doctrine.

(14) Page 246.—Nothing betrays less sense of the nature of Christianity and of the person of Christ Himself than the view that John has mixed much of his own with the speeches of Jesus. It even betrays small historical sense and understanding of what brings great events in general to pass, and of the nature the men must have on whom they are founded. This assertion was formerly but a whisper, but after strengthening itself in quiet, and providing itself with critical weapons, it makes a bolder venture, and now John did not write the gospel at all, but a later writer invented this mystic Christ. But we are left to find out for ourselves how a Jewish rabbi of philanthropic disposition, somewhat Socratic morals, a few miracles, or what others took for miracles, and a talent for striking apothegms and parables, a man to whom, according to the other evangelists, some follies will have to be forgiven, a man who could not have held water to Moses and Mahommed, could have had such an effect as to produce a new religion and a new church. But this must be fought out in a learned manner, and the friends and adorers of the Johannine Son of God are doubtless already girding themselves. The sadness of the Christians of which I have spoken can be traced in Christ in the other evangelists also, as soon we learn to understand them rightly through John. I have said that this sadness is the ground-tone in the pride as in the humility of the Christian. It may appear that, though it

is generally agreed that something exists which may be described as pride which is not to be blamed, it is somewhat venturesome to call it a Christian state of mind. In the Christian disposition, humility is so essential and so predominant, that in this sphere it does not appear as if there could be anything resembling pride, even though in civil morals we would not blame it. I will not shield myself by saying that I have also put fear and love together. As love is the mark of the Christian, and perfect love casts out fear, I might say that I was thinking of a human, that is an imperfect state of things. But my meaning was this. There must be distinguished in the Christian his personal consciousness over against Christ from his personal consciousness in fellowship with Christ. The former, even after the divine spirit of goodness has accomplished much in him, can be nothing but humility, but the later, consisting in the acquisition of all Christ's perfections, must be of quite the opposite nature. Now I know no other term that would express the contrast more strongly. To point out this feeling I only need to recall all the glorification of the Christian church in our New Testament books. But that even in this pride there should be sadness about the still narrow limits in which fellowship with Christ is actually felt, is a matter of course.

(15) Page 248.—It is always dangerous, especially as here before unbelievers, to rest faith in Christ on any one thing in Him. Something apparently similar may only too readily be compared with it, and its inner and essential difference may not be easy to detect. Many an enthusiast has thought greatly of himself and died in that faith. How often has an error been defended with the firmest conviction at the risk of life! Such a rooted error, if indeed the proper object of the faith is not the truth to which the error has attached itself, rests only on an idiosyncrasy which cannot extend far. But of this self-consciousness of Christ, the faith of the whole company of His disciples and the joy of all the martyrs of this faith are the reflection. Such a power the self-deception of any one soul never exercised. Consider also that this claim did not have to do merely with inner phenomena of the consciousness about which men could easily deceive themselves, nor with some prospect in the distant future, which offers free play to fancy. Christ had to believe that, under unfavourable circumstances, open and easily surveyed, the divine power of this abiding consciousness would approve itself. Still the vindication of faith by any one thing is always incomplete, and to attempt to plant it thereby in another is always hazardous.

(16) Page 248.—The conclusion of this exposition that, *Christ is the*

centre of all mediation, should connect all the details in it and complete what appears insufficient. Still I would not have the reader overlook what I wish to make prominent. At that time the distinction between the teaching of Christ and the teaching about Christ was hailed as a great discovery. Even allowing its validity to some extent, the idea of mediation must in every way be reckoned the teaching of Christ. Our teaching about Christ is nothing but the ratification and application of that teaching of Christ as it is fashioned by faith and sealed by history. And if I distinguish His school from His religion it is only, as the conclusion shows quite clearly, a different consideration of the same matter from different points of view. The religion of Christ is that the idea of redemption and mediation is the centre of religion. The application, so far, however, as the reference of this idea to a person was a historical process—and on this reference the whole historical existence of the doctrine as well as of the society rests—I call, by an expression now generally used, His school. That this was for Christ only secondary appears from what is here adduced, and also from the fact that at first the kingdom of God, and He who was to come was announced, and only afterwards He is spoken of as having come. Again, when it is said further back that Christ has become a mediator for many, it is to be remembered that Christ Himself said that "He would give his life a ransom for many." A particularist meaning is not to be drawn from my words, or at least only in accordance with my view set forth elsewhere. This is, that the actually experienced relation of man to Christ is limited, and ever will be, even when Christianity spreads over the whole earth. On the other hand, I acknowledge a purely inward and mysterious relation of Christ to human nature generally, which is absolutely general and unlimited.

(17) Page 249.—Many of the members of our church will perhaps consider what is here said of the Scriptures to be Catholic, and Catholics will consider it hyper-protestant; the constitution of the Scriptures by the church not being acknowledged, but the volume being declared not yet finished. This is said only in a tentative way, to distinguish clearly the shell of the matter from the kernel. If there could be a book from an author like Mark or Luke or Jude, with all the marks of authenticity, we would hardly agree unanimously to receive it into the canon. Yet it would show its native biblical power and be bible in fact. Just this power has been the ground for determining the practice of the church, and the ecclesiastical deliverance only confirmed it. How imperceptible the transition

from the canonical to the apocryphal, and both in power and purity, how in strength and beauty many productions of the church approach the canonical, no Protestant with experience and love of history will deny.

(18) Page 252.—This is not an addition which I now make for the first time. It was meant for the second edition, but as it seemed to me too much of a challenge I again erased it. Now that those times are past, it can stand as a monument of the impression made on me and doubtless on many. It was not that the surfeit of a senseless Christianity at that time appeared in many as irreligion, for it was to the honour of Christianity that they believed that where Christianity was nothing religion generally was nothing. But among not a few there was an endeavour to provide for natural religion, an external existence, a thing already shown in England and France to be a vain endeavour. There was also an itch for innovation that, dreaming of a symbolized or gnostic Heathenism, of a return to ancient mythologies as of a new salvation, rejoiced at the thought of seeing the fanatical Christ vanquished by the calm and cheerful Zeus.

EPILOGUE

BEFORE parting with you, let me add a word about the conclusion of my Speech. Perhaps you think that it had been better suppressed, because now, after several years, it is apparent that I was wrong in adducing as a proof of the power of the religious sentiment that it was in the act of producing new forms. As nothing of the sort has anywhere come to pass, did I not wrongly presume to guess what they would be ? If you think so, you have forgotten that prophecy only deserves its name, in so far, as it is the first fore-runner of the future. It is an indication of what is to be, and in it, to the eyes of the prophet's kindred, the future is already contained. But the more the thing prophesied is great and comprehensive, and the more the prophesying itself is in the genuine lofty style, the less can the fulfilment be near. As in the far distance the setting sun makes, from the shadows of great objects, vast magic shapes on the grey east, prophecy sets up only in the far distance the shapes of the future which it has fashioned from the past and the present. Wherefore, what I said was in no sense to be to you a sign to prove the truth of my Speech, which should rather be clear to you by itself. I had no wish to prophesy, even if the gift had not been wanting, for it would have availed me nothing to point you to a distant future.

All I wished was partly to demand, not of you, but of some others, half in irony, whether they could perhaps produce that of which they appear to boast, and partly I hoped to lead you to trace for yourselves the course of the fulfilment. I was sure you would there find, what I would willingly show you, that, in the very type of religion, which in Christianity you so often despise, you are rooted with your whole knowing, doing and being. You would see that you cannot get away from it, and that you seek in vain to imagine its destruction without the annihilation of all that you hold dearest and holiest in the world—your whole culture and mode of life, your art and science.

From this it follows that, as long as our age endures, nothing disadvantageous to Christianity can come forth, either from the age or from Christianity itself, and from all strife and battle it must issue renewed and glorified. This was my chief purpose, and you can see that I could not have meant to attach myself to some expressions of able and superior men, from which you understand that they wish to re-introduce the Heathenism of Antiquity, or even to create a new mythology, and by it to manufacture a new religion. In my opinion, rather, you can recognize, in the way that everything connected with such an endeavour is void and without result, the power of Christianity.

Above all, it is necessary that you understand what I have said of the fortunes of Christianity. This is not the place to expound and defend or even largely indicate my views, but I shall make a simple explanation that may prevent me from being classed, in the usual way of referring everything to schools and parties, with persons with whom, in this respect at least, I have nothing in common.

From the first there has almost always been some pronounced antithesis in Christianity. As is natural, it always has a beginning, a middle, and an end. The hostile elements gradually separate, the division reaches a climax, and then gradually subsides until it fully disappears in another antithesis that has meantime been developing. This has marked the whole history of Christianity, and at present Protestant and Catholic are the dominant antithesis in

Western Christendom. In each the idea of Christianity
has characteristic expression, so that, only by conjoining
both, can the historical phenomenon of Christianity correspond to the idea of Christianity. This antithesis, I say, is
still in operation and persists. Were I to interpret for
you the signs of the time, I would say it has reached the
turn of the tide, but has not appreciably diminished or disappeared.[1] Let no one, therefore, be indifferent, but let every
man consider to what side he and his Christianity belong,
and in which church he can lead a religious and edifying
life. And none who are happy in having a healthy, strong
nature, and who follow it, can go astray.[2]

At present there are some who appear to rescue themselves from the Protestant into the Catholic Church. I am
not speaking of those who in themselves are nothing and
are dazzled like children by glitter and show, or are talked
over by monks. But there are some to whom I myself
have formerly drawn your attention who are somewhat-
able poets and artists who are worthy of honour ; and a
host of followers, as is the fashion nowadays, has followed
them. The reason given is that in Catholicism alone there
is religion, and in Protestantism only irreligiousness, a
godlessness growing out of Christianity itself. Let that
man be honoured by me who ventures on such a step solely
on the conviction that he is following his nature. But if
his nature is only at home in that form of Christianity,
surely traces of this natural constitution will appear in his
whole life. It must be capable of proof that his act has
only completed outwardly what inwardly and spontaneously
was strictly contemporaneous and anterior.

There is another class also which I would pity and
excuse if I cannot honour. With the instinct of the sick,
which at times indeed is marvellously successful but may
also be dangerous, they take this step. Manifestly they
are in a state of dismay and weakness. Avowedly they
require external support for a bewildered feeling or some

incantations to allay anxious dread and bad headache, or they seek an atmosphere in which weak organs, being less stimulated, would feel better, as many sick people must not seek the free mountain air but the exhalations of animals.

But the persons to whom I now refer, are neither one nor other, but, appear to me simply despicable, for they know not what they wish nor what they do. Is there any sense in what they say? Do the heroes of the Reformation impress any uncorrupted mind with godlessness and not with a truly Christian piety? Is Leo X. actually more pious than Luther, and Loyola's enthusiasm holier than Zinzendorf's? And where are we to assign the greatest productions of modern times in every department of science, if Protestantism is godlessness and hell? And in the same way that Protestantism is for them only irreligion, they love in the Roman church not what is in any way characteristic and essential, but only its corruption—a clear proof that they know not what they wish. Consider this purely historically, that the papacy is in no way the essence of the Catholic Church, but its corruption.[3]

What they are really in search of is idolatry. The Protestant Church, alas! has also to contend with idolatry, but in a less gorgeous, and therefore less seductive form. And because it is not pronounced and colossal enough here, they seek it beyond the Alps. For what is an idol, if not what can be made, touched, and broken with hands, and which yet, in its perishableness and fragility, is foolishly and perversely set up to represent the Eternal, not merely in its own place, and according to its indwelling power and beauty, but as if a temporal thing could be the Eternal, as if the Eternal could be handled and magically weighed and measured at pleasure. The highest they seek is this superstition in church and priesthood, sacrament, absolution, and salvation. But they will accomplish nothing thereby, for it is a perverse state of things and will show itself in them through increased perversity. Leaving the common sphere of culture, they will rush into a vain and fruitless activity, and the portion of art that God has lent them will turn to foolishness. This, if you will, is a prophecy, the fufilment of which lies near enough to be expected.

And now one more prophecy of a different sort, and may you, as I hope, also see its fulfilment. It refers to the second point I have just touched upon, the persistence of the opposition of the two parties. Unquestionably many in the Romish Church have rid themselves of her corruptions. Now it might happen that outwardly also this should take place, if not everywhere, and in all things, yet in a large measure. Seducers might then come, threatening the strong, and flattering the weak, persuading the Protestants that, as this corruption is held by many to be the sole ground of separation, they should return to the one, indivisible, original church. Even that is a foolish and perverse project. It may attract and terrify many, but it will not succeed, for the abolition of this opposition at present would be the destruction of Christianity. I might challenge the mightiest of the earth to attempt it. For him everything is a game, and I would allow all power and guile. Yet I prophesy he would fail and be put to shame, for Germany still exists, and its invisible power is not weakened. Once more it would take up its calling with unsuspected power and would be worthy of its ancient heroes and its renowned descent. It was chiefly appointed to develope this phenomenon, and, to maintain it, it would rise again with giant force.[4]

Here you have a sign if you require it, and when this miracle comes to pass you will perhaps believe in the living power of religion and of Christianity. But blessed are they by whom it comes to pass, who do not see and yet believe.

NOTES TO THE EPILOGUE

(1) Page 268.—This deliverance will now appear less strange than it did at first. At that time, looking from one side, it was easy to believe that both churches would unite in unbelief, in indifferentism ; from the other, that they would soon be two forms of superstition, only outwardly and accidentally different. Lately, however, many events have not only quickened the consciousness that the opposition still actually exists, but have made it very clear what holds the two sections apart. We cannot deny that the chief seat of the opposition is in Germany. In England, indeed, it is strong enough, but it is more political, in France again it plays a very subordinate part. It becomes us Germans above all to comprehend it both historically and speculatively. This happens, alas ! too seldom. We have fallen sadly into impassioned ways. If anyone among us would speak of the matter impartially, he will certainly be suspected by his brethren as a crypto-catholic, and he would be exposed to many importunate and flattering advances from the Romanists. Praiseworthy exceptions, when truly thorough-going moderation is acknowledged, are very rare. Leaving quite aside, therefore, the present state of things, I will indicate, in few words, wherein this opposition, regarded from the point of view of its historical development, seems to me still to exist. There is in both churches an evident disposition to be exclusive, and as far as possible to ignore each other. Of this the almost inconceivable ignorance of one another's doctrine and usages gives sufficient proof. This disposition is natural enough in the mass of men, for each section finds religious stimulus and nourishment enough in its own narrow circle, and the other section, though but little may be wanting to it, appears, if not as impure as members of alien religions to the Jews, at least utterly strange. This tendency rules in quiet times. It is only interrupted in the mass of men by outbreaks of passion, when one section gains some decisive advantage in political matters or, in a large number of single cases in private

life. As the educated, however, in whom a historical consciousness should dwell, ought not to share this lazy exclusiveness, neither should they share this hurtful passionateness. Between both churches there should be a living influence, even though it should not be direct. Quiet contemplation should stir up a keen rivalry in whatever in the other section is acknowledged to be good. The contrast in the character of both churches involves at least that one is receptive of the imperfections that the other more suppresses. May the Catholics be edified by seeing that the more prominently the religious tendency appears among us, the more any return to any kind of barbarity is hindered. And if they would not deceive themselves as though there were no difference in this respect between us, let them see how far they can advance in the demand for individual freedom. And we should, as passionlessly as possible, observe the secure position which in all outward matters the Catholic Church knows how to secure by strong organization. Let us then try how far we can attain to unity and coherence, yet it must be done in our own spirit and not by setting the spiritual order over against the laity in a way quite opposed to this spirit. Such healthy influences appear, and the results are seen from time to time. But the lazy exclusiveness of the mass checks them and all passionate moments interrupt them. It may therefore be long before the purpose of the disagreement is attained. Till then, we cannot say that the variance has reached its climax and has begun to diminish. When that comes to pass, there will be a common duty to exercise a vitalizing influence on the Greek Church. As it is almost quite defunct, both churches will need for a long time to employ all their powers and all their remedies. But, until they have succeeded in waking the dead, they cannot have fulfilled the destiny of their division.

(2) Page 268.—How seldom anyone in lands belonging entirely to one church, without interested views or artful suasion, but by a true inward impulse, is driven to the other church is apparent. In regions where the two sects commingle, how calmly we educate the children of parents of one faith in the paternal religion, and it does not in the least occur to us that they may have an inward destination for the other. As the different national character of Christian peoples was not without influence on the course the Reformation took, should it not be thought that this spiritual attitude is a matter of inheritance or birth? And is not this confirmed by the fact that when the adherents of another faith come over to Christianity, we do not consider the Christian sense pure and steadfast till after two generations. For children of mixed marriages, therefore, the natural rule would

not be for the sons to follow the father and the daughter the mother, but for each to follow the parent with whom there is more inherited resemblance. On the other side, however, it is not to be denied that the original relation of the two churches is not favourable to the hypothesis of a strictly innate inclination. It would rather lead us to expect a self-determination for one or other form, according to personal character. From this view the natural principle for mixed marriages and the principle that without extraneous interference would have effect, would be for the children to follow the more strongly religious parent. Under the special influence of this parent, the religious element would be most strongly developed, and then the child's own choice could be calmly and hopefully waited for. Were there no foreign motives, no influences that are almost violence, and were this natural course generally followed, change in the prime of life would be rarer. After a faith has been apprehended with love, and has for a long time guided the life, this step is always the result and the cause of confusion. It would be only taken by individuals who are in other respects exceptions, as it were capricious sallies of nature, or by persons who, from perverse guidance, have been made to see very clearly the imperfection and narrowness of the accepted faith, and are thereby driven to the opposite faith—a thing not rare at present in both churches.

(3) Page 269.—Only a few will require a defence of this position, that the Catholic Church, not merely in the old sense, but in the sense we understand when we contrast it with the Evangelical Church, might shake off the papal authority and return from the monarchical to the aristocratic form of the episcopal system, without removing the difference between the churches, or, in any marked degree, facilitating their union. Nor does it need much proof that the papal authority, whether considered in its rise or in its prevailing tendency, has striven for aims almost always false and beyond the church's sphere. It is noteworthy, however, that almost all who fall away from our church become strong papists. It is hardly possible to avoid the conclusion that they have not apprehended the true character of the Catholic Church, and are only destined to display their religious incapacity in two different forms.

(4) Page 270.—It would be bad if the very conclusion of a work could cause a smile that might efface any earlier good impressions. Yet this may do it in two respects. First, there is the dread that Bonaparte could have some design against Protestantism, for did he not afterwards threaten to go over with a large part of France to Protestantism,

and, quite recently, were not the Protestants in the south of France persecuted as his most attached followers? Then, again, I almost always speak as if all Germany were Protestant, and now many are hoping that sooner or later it will be once more altogether or almost Catholic. In respect of the former possibility, what I said expressed too accurately our feelings in the years of ignominy that I should not let it stand as I then wrote it. So much had been taken from us that we might well fear that all was threatened. Undeniably Napoleon acted in a quite different way in Protestant and in Catholic Germany, and it could not remain hidden from him that our religious sentiment and our political were intimately connected. On the other point let everyone take heed not to laugh too soon. However firmly he holds his hope, I hold mine as firmly. Further progress of a Papistical Catholicism in Germany on many grounds necessarily involves a return to every kind of barbarity. As the freedom of the Evangelical Church will remain the surest support of every noble endeavour, it cannot lie in the ways of Providence to weaken it and, at its expense, to allow Catholicism to prevail.

In the first chapter there are many changes, but for the most part merely of single words and phrases. The complimentary passage on us proud Islanders is even stronger in its original form. 'Religion can only be for us a dead letter, a sacred article in the constitution without any reality, for we are only occupied with fierce defence of national orthodoxy and the maintenance of superstitious attachment to ancient usages, while our pursuit of knowledge is limited to a miserable empiricism.'

P. 16, last par., has lost something of the irony of the Romanticist. "We have systems from all schools, yea, even from schools that are mere habitations and nurseries of the dead letter. The spirit is neither to be confined in academies nor to be poured out into a row of ready heads. It evaporates usually between the first mouth and the first ear."

On p. 17, foot, beginning "In isolation," a somewhat mighty figure has been weakened, doubtless as too youthfully daring. He is speaking of the work of the true heroes of religion. "Only single noble thoughts flash through their soul, kindled with celestial fire. The magic thunder of an enchanting speech accompanied the high phenomenon, and announced to adoring mortals that the Deity had spoken. An atom impregnated with heavenly power, fell into their soul, and there assimilated all, and gradually expanded till it burst like a divine fate in a world whose atmosphere offers too little resistance, and produced in its last moments one of those heavenly meteors, one of those significant signs of the time, of the origin of which none was ignorant, and with awe of which all mortals were filled. You must seek this heavenly spark which is produced when a holy soul is stirred by the Universe, and you must attend to it in the incomprehensible moment of its formation."

The earlier portion of the Second Chapter (pp. 26–66), has been materially altered, a large part of it having been entirely re-cast. The opening passage is little altered, the parallel drawn between the sociality of states and the combining of the mental activities is only verbally different, but it is used to explain that he frequently returns to more childlike times, not from depreciation of the present but in order to discover religion more by itself.

' Ultimately, metaphysics, morals and religion have the same object, the Universe. This has led to confusion. Yet your instinct and opinions are against making religion one with metaphysics, for you do not admit that it can tread with the same firm step, or with morals, for there are foully immoral parts in its history. It must, therefore, deal with the same matter in a different way. " What does your metaphysics do, or, if you will not have that antiquated, too historical name, your transcendental philosophy ? It classifies the Universe, gives the grounds for what exists, deduces the necessity of the actual, and spins from itself the reality and the laws of the world." Religion, however, has nothing to do with grounds and deductions and first causes. " And what does your ethics do ? It develops from the nature of man and his relation to the Universe a system of duties, it commands and prohibits actions with absolute authority. But religion cannot venture to use the Universe for the deduction of duties, or to contain a code of laws." The common idea of religion is that it is a mixture of fragments of metaphysics and ethics, but it is time this idea was quite annihilated. " The theorists in religion who seek to know the nature of the Universe and of a Highest Being whose work it is, are metaphysicians, but discreet enough not to despise a little morals ; the practical persons, to whom the will of God is the chief matter, are moralists, but a little in the metaphysical style. They import the idea of the good into metaphysics as the natural law of a Being without limits and without wants, and they import the idea of an Original Being from metaphysics into morals that the great work should not be anonymous, but that such a glorious code might be prefaced by a picture of the law-giver." Were this mixture anything more than a selection for beginners, and had a principle of union of its own, religion must be the highest in philosophy, and metaphysics and ethics only sub-divisions. All these are found together even in the sacred books, unavoidably and also of high design. But religion is like the diamond in the clay, enclosed not to remain hidden, but to be all the more surely found. It is simply a device for subtle winning of the hearer, but it has overstepped the mark when the shell conceals the kernel. " I have been put out by your common idea, it is taken out of the way I trust. Interrupt me now no more."

" Religion neither seeks like metaphysics to determine and explain the nature of the Universe, nor like morals to advance and perfect the Universe by the power of freedom and the divine will of man. It is neither thinking nor acting, but intuition and feeling. It will regard the Universe as it is. It is reverent attention and submission, in childlike passivity, to be stirred and filled by the Universe's immediate influences." To metaphysics, man is the centre of all, the condition of all existence ; to religion, he is, like every other finite thing, but a manifestation of the Universe. Morals proceeds from the consciousness of freedom and seeks to expand the realm of freedom to infinity ; religion regards man as needing to be what he is, whether he will or not. Religion, morals and metaphysics are equals, different but complementary. "To have speculation and practice without religion is mad presumption, audacious hostility to the gods, the unholy sense of Prometheus, who faintheartedly stole what he might have asked for in safety. Man has but stolen the feeling of his infinity and likeness to God, and as unjust goods he cannot prosper with it, for he must also be conscious of his limits."

"Practice is art, speculation is science, religion is sense and taste for the Infinite." Without religion, practice cannot get beyond venturesome or traditional forms, and speculation is only a stiff and lean skeleton. "Practice opposes man to the Universe, not having received him as a part of it from the hand of religion. It has, in consequence, a miserable uniformity, knows only one ideal and forgets to cultivate man himself. The feeling for infinite and living nature is wanting, whereof the symbol is variety and individuality." And why has speculation so long given delusions for a system and words for thoughts? From want of religion. "All beginning must be from intuition of the Universe, and if the desire to have intuition of the Infinite is wanting, there is no touchstone and there is need of none, to know whether anything has been rightly thought. Modern Idealism is in need of religion, p. 40.

On intuition of the Universe my whole Speech hinges. It is the highest formula of religion, determining its nature and fixing its boundaries. "All intuition proceeds from the influence of the thing perceived on the person perceiving. The former acts originally and independently, and the latter receives, combines and apprehends in accordance with its nature." Without mechanical or chemical affection of the organs, there is no perception. "What is perceived is not the nature of things, but their action upon us, and what is known or believed of this nature is beyond the range of intuition. The Universe is in unbroken activity, and reveals itself to us at every moment. Every form, every creature, every occurrence is an action of the Universe upon us, and religion is just the acceptance of each separate thing as a part of the Whole, of each limited thing as an exhibition of the Infinite. What would go further and penetrate deeper into the nature and substance of the Whole, is no more religion, and if it will nevertheless be taken for religion, it invariably sinks into vain mythology." Then follows, almost unchanged, the passage on p. 49, about what in the ancient world was religion, and what was mythology.

Intuition is always single and distinct. Union and arrangement into a whole are not the business of sense but of abstract thinking. For religion, each intuition and feeling is unconnected and independent, immediate and true by itself. As the Universe can be viewed from an infinite number of points of view, there can be no system. There can no more be a system of intuitions than of the stars. The only system among them is the primitive endeavour to group them in definite but wretched and inappropriate figures. You may sketch the wain on the blue scroll of the worlds, but your neighbour is free to enclose them in quite other outlines. "This infinite chaos, where each point is a world, is the best and highest emblem of religion." At each different point of the material world you see a new arrangement that leaves no trace of your arbitrary figures, and there are new objects within your ken. No horizon could embrace all, and there could be no eye which nothing could escape. In religion, from each different point of view you will see new intuitions and different groupings of the old. The infinity of speculation is in the endless variety of action and passion between the same limited matter and the mind; the infinity of morals is the impossibility of inward completeness; but religion is not only infinite in these respects, it is infinite on every side, in matter and in form and in way of perception.

The passage (pp. 54–56) follows little altered.

"But to complete the general sketch of religion, recollect that each intuition, from its very nature, is linked to a feeling. Your organs mediate the connection between the object and yourselves. The influence of the object that reveals its existence to you, must stimulate them in various ways, and produce a change in your inner consciousness. Frequently it is hardly perceived. In other circumstances it becomes so violent that you forget both the object and yourselves." Yet, even then, you will not ascribe the activity of your spirit that has been set in motion, to the influence of external objects. " Thus also in religion the same operation of the Universe, whereby it reveals itself in the finite, brings it also into a new relation to your mind and to your state." With the intuition you must necessarily have many feelings. The intuition does not, indeed, as in perception, preponderate so much over the feeling, but the eternal world may, like the sun, dazzle the eyes, casting its image and its splendour long after on all objects.

The kind of intuition of the Universe determines the type of your religion, the strength of feeling, its degree. The sounder the sense, the more clearly and definitely will each impression be apprehended ; the more ardent the thirst, the more persistent the impulse to be always and everywhere impressed by the Universe, the more easy, perfect and dominant will the impressions be. The feelings of religion should possess us and we should give them expression, but if they urge us to action, we are in another sphere. If you will still consider it religion, however good the action, it is only superstition. All actions must be moral, religion accompanying as a sacred music, "all should be done with religion, nothing from it." And even though you do not admit that all actions are moral, the same is true of those you exclude. The moralist, the politician, the artist must all act with calmness and discretion, not a possible thing if man is impelled to action by the violent feelings of religion. Religion, without any other impulse to activity, rather tends to inactive contemplation. To act on the Whole by feeling direct from the Whole, would be like acting towards a man according to the immediate impression he makes upon us. Morals condemns it because it gives room for alien motives, and religion because it makes man cease to be what gives him religious value—a part of the Whole acting by its own free power. Action proceeding from its own proper source with the soul full of religion, is the aim of the pious. Action from religion is the impulsion of bad spirits not good. The legion of angels with which the Father provided the Son were around Him not in Him.

The next matter to understand is intuitions and feelings. For clear consciousness, reflection and utterance they must be considered apart, but the finest spirit of religion is thereby lost. In our original consciousness there are two activities, one controlling and working outwards, and another subservient, sketching and copying. Straightway in the simplest matter the elements divide, one set combines into an image of the object and the other penetrating to the centre of our being, dashes itself upon our original impulses and developes a fleeting feeling. In the same way no creation of the religious sense can escape this fate of division. Yet intuition without feeling is nothing, and feeling without intuition is nothing. There is a mysterious moment in every sense perception, before intuition and feeling divide, when sense and object mingle and are one. " It is fleeting and indescribable, but I wish you could seize it and recognize it again in the higher, the divine religious activity of the spirit."

This moment is a kiss, an embrace, pp. 43, 44. Without it religion is but a spinning of formulas, pp. 47, 48.

The divine life is like a tender plant, the flowers of which are fertilized in the bud. The holy intuitions and feelings that you can dry and preserve are but the calixes and corollas that soon open and soon fall. But out of them I would now wind a sacred wreath.

First I conduct you to Nature as the outer court. The first intuition of the world and its Spirit is neither from fear of material forces nor from joy at physical beauty. Both had their place in preparing rude peoples, and may yet through art have a higher influence, but these influences naturally diminish with civilization, (p. 64) one god being made to conquer another, and the beauties of the globe being seen to be for universal matter pure delusion. " At a higher stage, perhaps, we shall see that to which here we must submit, ruling universally in all the vault of heaven, and a sacred awe will fill us at the unity and universality of material forces, and we may some time discover with astonishment in this delusion the same Spirit that quickens the Whole."

After p. 66 the alterations are less extensive.

On p. 93 the section on the idea of God has been re-cast, and some think entirely changed.

'For me the Deity is only one kind of religious intuition, of which any others there may be, are independent. I do not accept the position, ' No God, no religion.'

The idea of God may be very different. To most men God is merely the genius of humanity, man being the prototype. To this God mankind is everything, and His disposition and nature are determined by what man takes to be His doings and dealings. But to me mankind is not everything, but an infinitely small part, a fleeting form of the Universe. There may be many beings above humanity, but every race and individual is subordinated to the Universe. Can God in this sense then be anything for me but one type of intuition ?

Let us proceed to the highest idea, a Highest Being, a Spirit of the Universe who rules with freedom and understanding. On this idea also religion is not dependent. To have religion is to have an intuition of the Universe, and while this idea of God suits every intuition, a religion without God might still be better than another with God.

The stages of religion depend on the sense, the idea of God on the direction of the imagination. " If your imagination attach itself to the consciousness of freedom so that it cannot think of what originally operates on it, except as a free being, you will personify the Spirit of the Universe and have a God. If it attach itself to understanding, so that you always clearly perceive that freedom has only meaning in the individual and for individuals, then you have a World and no God. You will not I trust consider it blasphemy that the belief in God should depend on the direction of the imagination. You will know that imagination is the highest and most original activity in man, and that all besides is only reflection upon it." Your imagination creates the world, and you could have no God without the world. " The knowledge of the source of this necessity will not make anyone less certain, nor enable him to escape the almost absolute necessity to have this idea of God. Only as operative can God be in religion, and no one has denied the divine life and action of the Universe. With the God of existence and command religion has nothing to do."

In the Third Speech, p. 120, " Everyone misses in himself, etc.," was, till the third edition, " Seeing I myself miss not a little in myself."

On p. 138 another interesting personal reference has been toned down. " Were it not impious to wish to be more than one is, I would wish that I could see as clearly how the sense for art by itself passes into religion, how despite the rest into which through each separate enjoyment the spirit sinks, it yet feels itself urged to that progress which might lead to the Universe. Why are those who have gone this way, such silent natures ? I do not know this sense, it is my most marked limitation, it is the defect in my nature that I feel most deeply. But I treat it with esteem. I do not presume to see, but I believe. The possibility of the matter stands clear before my eyes, only it must remain a secret for me." Again, p. 139, By the sense for art the " divine Plato raised the holiest mysticism on the summit of divineness and humanness. Let me do homage to the goddess to me unknown, that she cherished him and his religion so carefully and disinterestedly."

In the Fourth Speech there are no changes of any consequence.

In the Fifth Speech, the first clause, " Man in closest fellowship with the Highest," was, " Man in the intuition of the Universe." That is the key-note of the changes. Intuition of the Universe gives place to relation to God. Thus p. 217, " The whole of all religions is nothing but the sum of all relations of man to God," replaces a passage that derives the need of an endless mass of religious forms from the number, variety, and independence of intuitions of the Infinite.

Later the additions are more striking than the changes. On p. 224, when he asks whether it is necessary to belong to an existing religion, he replies " By no means," without any " Provisionally " or any modification as in the paragraph at the top of p. 225. Further additions are, on p. 246 foot, " and that for man under the power of the finite, and particular, and too ready to imagine the divine itself in this form, salvation is only to be found in the redemption "; p. 248, after " Yet He never maintained He was the only mediator," " the only one in whom His idea actualized itself. All who attach themselves to Him and form His Church should also be mediators with Him and through Him "; further on, on the same page, the reason given why the person who sets out from the same point as Christ is a Christian, " It will naturally follow that they will acknowledge Him," and p. 249 the last clause in the second paragraph about the first-fruits of the Spirit having special holiness and worth. Page 251, first paragraph. " I at least can only believe," was " I at least fear."

INDEX